Evelyn Jacks'

ESSENTIAL TAX FACTS

*Simple tips for preparing your taxes
so you can build wealth*

2012 EDITION

KNOWLEDGE BUREAU
NEWSBOOKS

WINNIPEG, MANITOBA, CANADA

ISBN No. 978-1-897526-77-4

Printed and bound in Canada

Second Printing – 2011

Canadian Cataloguing in Publication Data

Jacks, Evelyn 1955-

Evelyn Jacks' Essential tax facts: Simple tips for preparing your taxes so you can build wealth – 2012 ed.

Includes Index

1. Income tax – Canada – Popular works. 2. Tax planning – Canada – Popular works. I. Title. II. Title: Essential tax facts

HJ4661.J212 2006   343.7105'2   C2006-904910-6

Published by:
Knowledge Bureau, Inc.
187 St. Mary's Road, Winnipeg, Manitoba R2H 1J2
204-953-4769 Email: reception@knowledgebureau.com

Research and Editorial Assistance: Walter Harder and Associates
Cover and Page Design: Sharon Jones

CONTENTS

INTRODUCTION

Understanding how to save money on your taxes is critical in today's volatile economic environment. That environment has been called treacherous by those in the know,[1] and it has left average people feeling uncertain about their financial affairs. Understanding how to maximize the benefits available under the tax system, however, is one positive and proactive way to play defensively and take more control of your financial future.

Do you pay more tax than your siblings or neighbors, despite earning similar income levels? It's possible that you do. Many taxpayers leave thousands, if not hundreds of thousands, of overpaid tax dollars on the table over their lifetimes, because they don't use their rights and entitlements under our personal taxation system. If you suspect you are one of them, you can fix that immediately.

This book will help do so you in two ways: it will show you how to file a more accurate tax return. But it will also help you find new money with which to increase your net worth over your lifetime. Your personal net worth represents your financial stability: your assets less your liabilities—what you own less what you owe to others.

The goal is to accumulate assets as tax efficiently as possible, pay down debt, and then grow and preserve what's left, so you will have purchasing power when you need it in the future. If you continue to do that well in retirement, you will maximize your financial legacy by passing down your wealth to your heirs, as intact as possible from tax and inflation erosion.

---

[1] September 27, 2011 Speech by Vice Deputy Governor Tiff Macklem, Bank of Canada, speaking on risk management.

Taxes and inflation, however, are formidable financial foes. Understanding how to defeat them is an important mission in securing your family's financial health in the current environment. Here's why:

Taxes strike three times: they blast away at your income as you earn it, in the form of required periodic remittances, like withholding taxes or quarterly instalments. You may also take a hit when you score an increase in your net income. That is, you may find your income is subject to a higher marginal tax rate, and some of the monthly government benefits you might qualify for, like the Old Age Security or the Canada Child Tax Benefit could be "clawed back", too. Finally, you'll face the taxman again, when he's poised to take a chunk out of your future savings— pensions and accrued gains in taxable assets.

If you can understand that taxes will erode both your income and investment performance, it makes sense that tax efficiency increases it. When you take advantage of your legal rights to plan your affairs within the framework of the law to pay the least taxes legally possible, you can increase your cash flow, protect your savings and build a financial fortress for your future financial security. This book will help you do that, showing you how to stay clear of marginal tax rate spikes, and manage those punitive clawback zones.

Your second financial foe, inflation, robs your money of its purchasing power over time. It is also the taxman's greatest partner, even when inflation rates are low. For example, when tax brackets, income ceilings for social benefits or personal amounts are not fully indexed to inflation, your money is exposed to a stealth hidden tax. Or, when you delay making your annual Registered Retirement Savings Plan (RRSP) contributions, inflation will erode away the value of the unused contribution room you are entitled to.

By learning how to hold on to more of every dollar you earn and closely monitor your family's net income, you can create new money for savings, as you tap into as many tax benefits as possible. That's a great hedge against the risks you face in the financial marketplace. In uncertain economic times, investing with tax efficiency is your most important weapon in bolstering your family's wealth.

In short, by filing a more accurate tax return and making more tax-astute investment decisions, you can add points to your financial scoreboard, stop worrying about things that are beyond your control, and start enjoying the good fortune you are building instead.

Yours in tax savings,
EVELYN JACKS

PART I
What's New in Tax?

The first step in building tax efficient wealth is to learn how to file your personal tax return—the most significant financial transaction of the year for most Canadians. Whether you actually prepare the return yourself, or have someone do it for you, filing it comes with some important responsibilities: the onus of proof is on you that the numbers are correct, for example. Failure to file the return and pay your taxes on time can also result in expensive penalties, and in severe cases, jail. You'll want to avoid this, of course: it's not the ideal way to build wealth.

What makes the tax filing process difficult are the two moving targets you must address each year: your personal affairs are constantly changing, and so are the rules behind filing your return accurately and to your family's best benefit. But it's the link between the two that can make you wealthier; that is, when you understand how tax changes apply to the changes in your life events, you can put new money from tax savings to work for you.

That's why it's good to take a purposeful dive into the tax news of the day at the start of every tax filing season. This will help you to build a cumulative and powerful tax knowledge over time, ask better questions of your tax and financial advisors, and discover new tax provisions; some of them potentially lucrative.

Good news? You don't need to be a tax expert to get started. Start by understanding the *basic elements of the federal T1 General Return*. All the lines you'll need to know about are addressed here, including income, deductions and non-refundable tax credits you may qualify for. For a sample of the 4-page T1 General and Schedule 1, go to www.knowledgebureau.com/ETF. You may wish to print it and have a close look as we discuss recent tax news, below.

CHAPTER 1

WHAT ARE THE BASIC ELEMENTS OF A TAX RETURN?

A tax return can be filed on paper, on the internet, or in some cases, over the phone. Regardless how you choose to file, there are six Basic Elements on the T1 General tax return you'll need to be familiar with:

- Taxpayer Identification on Page 1
- Total Income (Line 150)
- Net Income (Line 236)
- Taxable Income (Line 260) and
- Non-Refundable Tax Credits (Schedule 1)
- Calculation of Taxes Payable and Refund or Balance Due on Schedule 1 and on Page 4 of the T1 return.

To better understand your tax filing rights, it's also important to know some basic tax facts, which will be highlighted for you with the *Essential Tax Facts* features:

ESSENTIAL TAX FACT | There are many different definitions of "income" on the tax return: three of them appear on the list above, and there are others, like "earned income" for RRSP purposes, or "earned income" for the purposes of claiming child care expenses. These terms and their significance will be explained throughout this book.

Non-Refundable Tax Credits: Creating "Tax-Free Zones." Everyone in Canada qualifies for the Basic Personal Amount (BPA). These days that means you can earn almost $900 every month tax-free. The BPA is a non-refundable tax credit.

ESSENTIAL TAX FACT | Non-refundable tax credits are "tax preferences" provided to give recognition to the economic consequences of unique family circumstances.

There are many other non-refundable tax credits on the federal tax return, all of which increase your Tax-Free Zone, and reduce taxes payable. This means that these credits do not help those who do not pay tax—and you can't save them up and use them next year either.

Certain non-refundable tax credits can also be claimed for your dependants. These are often based on the dependant's net—not gross—income. Drawing from the list of basic elements, that means, Line 236 of the return. These credits will be reduced or "clawed back" if income levels rise over certain threshold amounts.

Review Schedule 1 of your T1 General Return for a complete listing of non-refundable tax credits available for your use. Try to identify those that your household will benefit from. They may seem familiar to you. That's because your employer will generally ask you to complete a TD1 Tax Credit form every year, to determine how much tax will be withheld from your income.

ESSENTIAL TAX FACT | To maximize your credits, keep an eye on net income on Line 236. This is one of the most important lines on the tax return because of its impact on the size of your refundable and non-refundable tax credits.

A focus on reducing net income should also influence the order in which you make your investments. For example, you can reduce your net income by making an RRSP contribution if you are eligible.

Net income is also reduced by claiming child care or moving expenses or carrying charges like your safety deposit box or tax deductible interest payments on certain loans taken for investment purposes. Even deducting your union dues will make a difference.

Taken together, when you know your family's "tax-free zones" you'll be able to better plan family income and the level of tax you'll pay on it over time. This will give your family unit more economic power, and help you build and retain more family wealth.

Refundable tax credits. In addition to the above, both the federal and provincial governments provide refundable tax credits to Canadian tax filers. Your eligibility for these credits depends on your family net income level, *not whether or not you pay taxes.*

Note that the actual amount of certain credits is not obvious; they are not on the return at all because CRA does the calculations for you. But knowing the numbers is important, so you can identify the opportunity, maximize the amounts owing to you, and plan to save the money if you can for important goals, like an education, for example. Tax software can help you identify the exact amount of refundable tax credits you are entitled to.

> **ESSENTIAL TAX FACT** | You can have zero income and pay zero taxes but still receive refundable tax credits—simply by filing a tax return. That's a tax bonus just for you!

Because many refundable tax credits are based on "family" rather than "individual" net income, you need to file tax returns together with your spouse or common-law partner and add together the combined net incomes for these purposes.

There are three important refundable tax credits from the Federal Government; in some cases, provincial governments may also provide similar income supports.

1. **Working Income Tax Benefit.** The Working Income Tax Benefit (WITB) is designed to offset, in part, the high effective marginal tax rates that low income earners experience when their income increases due to the clawback of income support programs, such as social assistance. By filing a tax return, lower earners can receive a supplement to these costs.

    To receive it, you must complete Schedule 6 on your return, be at least age 19 or have a child, and earn a minimum amount of net income. If your net income is under certain clawback thresholds, you'll receive a maximum credit of $944 in most provinces if you are single; $1,714 if you have a family. An additional supplement is available to disabled taxpayers.

> **ESSENTIAL TAX FACT** | The WITB is a refundable credit that is calculated as 25% of earned income in excess of $3,000 on the federal tax return, based on the total of employment and business income (ignoring losses).

    The WITB may be claimed by either spouse (or common-law partner) but only one spouse may make a claim for the family. Families may request a pre-payment of up to one-half of their expected WITB. These payments will be issued quarterly in April, July, October and January.

    This credit differs from the federal calculations in some provinces. (The earned income figure is also $3,000 in most provinces; $4,750 in BC,

$2,760 in Alberta and $6,000 in Nunavut, not including Universal Child Care Benefits and certain capital gains from stock options).

2. **GST Credit.** The GST Credit and Canada Child Tax Benefit are based on a July to June "benefit year" based on net income. You are eligible to receive the GST credit if you are at least 19 and a resident of Canada at the time the payment is due. So, you'll want to file a tax return if you will be 19 by April 30, 2012 to start receiving it after your 19th birthday, as it is paid quarterly. A GST credit can also be claimed for your child, but specifically not for a foster child.

3. **The Canada Child Tax Benefit.** This lucrative tax benefit is paid monthly, to parents with certain net income levels. Application for this credit generally happens upon the birth of a child and it also initiates another benefit: the Universal Child Care Benefit (UCCB). This latter benefit is not based on your income; rather it is universally received by all parents with children under the age of 6. Many provinces supplement the Child Tax Benefit for their residents. These supplements are included with the cheque received from the Federal government.

ESSENTIAL TAX FACT | **There is something new for payments received after June 2011:** In the case of separated families, each parent who lives with the child can receive 50% of any GST Credit, Child Tax Benefits and Universal Child Care Benefits.

Your Notice of Assessment. One document you must remember to keep track of after filing your return is your Notice of Assessment or Reassessment from the Canada Revenue Agency (CRA). This notice explains how your return was assessed, what your RRSP and TFSA contribution room is, and many other important pieces of information you or your tax advisors will want to use to recover all of your tax filing rights.

ESSENTIAL TAX FACT | The date on your Notice of Assessment or Reassessment is used to determine when your further appeal rights expire. File this form with your tax records.

CRA will now allow you to receive your Notice of Assessment either by mail or email. The word "mailed" has been changed to "sent" in numerous sections of the *Income Tax Act* to accommodate this change. This brings up an interesting issue around privacy.

The content of the notices will not be included in email messages but will instead be posted to the taxpayer's secure electronic account and the email message will indicate to the taxpayer that the notice has been posted. The existing "My Account" and "My Business Account" features on the CRA website will be used for you to access the Notice.

Because timing is so important to preserve your opportunities for appeal, in case you ever need to dispute an assessment of your taxes, your electronic notices will be presumed to have been sent and received on the date that the email message is sent to the *email address most recently received from the taxpayer*. Therefore, the onus is on you to check your email and notify CRA if you want email directed to another address. Taxpayers also have the right to revoke authorization for electronic transmission of notices regarding their accounts.

Understanding the basic element of a tax return, your entitlements to refundable tax credits, which may or may not appear on the return itself, and the importance of the Notice of Assessment in planning to take advantage of future tax savings opportunities are the basic elements of a tax return all Canadians need to know to start their journey towards a tax efficient financial future.

CHAPTER 2

WHAT ARE THE MOST RECENT TAX CHANGES?

Take a moment now to skim through this list of recent tax changes, which are provided to you according to the various tax filing profiles families find themselves in. Don't worry if you don't understand all the terms; we will be discussing them throughout the book.

At the time of writing the most recent federal budget changes were announced on March 22, 2011, and then re-introduced on June 6, after the federal election. Some of those changes will also affect your 2012 tax return.

> **ESSENTIAL TAX FACT** | Many tax provisions are transferable between family members. That's why it pays to prepare tax returns for each individual first, starting with the lowest earner, working your way up to the highest. Review this list of recent changes from that point of view.

Tax calculation changes

Changes to federal tax brackets and rates. Federal taxes are calculated on Schedule 1, based on the tax bracket your taxable income falls into; then a series of personal amounts will be used to reduce your taxes payable. Please take a moment to check these out below:

2011 Brackets	2011 Rates	2010 Brackets	2010 Rates
Up to $10,527	0	Up to $10,382	0
$10,528 to $41,544	15%	$10,383 to $40,970	15%
$41,545 to $83,088	22%	$40,971 to $81,941	22%
$83,089 to $128,800	26%	$81,942 to $127,021	26%
Over $128,800	29%	Over $127,021	29%

Note, that each province also has its own brackets and rates. These are calculated on the applicable provincial tax forms, based on your province of residence as of December 31.

Changes for claiming dependants

— New! The Children's Arts Tax Credit. Beginning in 2011, parents may claim a new non-refundable tax credit for up to $500 cost for enrolling children under age 16 in an eligible program of artistic, cultural, recreational or developmental activities. For disabled children (i.e. those eligible for the disability tax credit), an additional credit of $500 is available if more than $100 is paid for eligible expenses. This credit mirrors the Children's Fitness Tax Credit except that it applies to non-fitness programs. The dollar to the parent is 15% of the claim or a maximum of $75 per child ($150 if the child is disabled). Both credits may be claimed if children attend both sporting and other activities.

Eligible programs. A significant amount of eligible activities that are ongoing in nature is required. An eligible program will be either a weekly program lasting a minimum of eight consecutive weeks; or in the case of children's camps, a program lasting a minimum of five consecutive days. If all other requirements are met, the full cost of a child's membership in an organization (including a club, association or similar organization) will be eligible for the credit if more than 50 per cent of the activities offered to children by the organization include a significant amount of eligible activities. Programs that are part of school curriculums will not be eligible.

Eligible activities. An eligible activity is a supervised activity suitable for children that

- contributes to the development of creative skills, including a child's ability to improve dexterity or co-ordination, or acquire and apply knowledge in an artistic or cultural activity such as the literary, visual or performing arts, music, media, languages, customs and heritage.
- provides a focus on wilderness and the natural environment;

- helps children develop and use intellectual skills; or provides enrichment or tutoring in academic subjects.
- includes structured interaction to help children develop interpersonal skills.

An eligible activity will also include similar activities that have been adapted to accommodate the needs and abilities of a child who is eligible for the Disability Tax Credit. Like the Children's Fitness Tax Credit, this credit may be shared between eligible taxpayers (e.g. spouses) so long as the total claimed does not exceed the claim allowable for an individual.

Tax changes for students

Three tax changes apply to students this year:

- **Tuition Tax Credit – Examination fees.** The Tuition Tax Credit now includes fees paid to an educational institution, professional association, provincial ministry or other similar institution to take an examination that is required to obtain a professional status recognized by federal or provincial statute, or to be licensed or certified in order to practice a profession or trade in Canada as well as ancillary fees and charges. This includes the cost of examination materials used during the examination and certain pre-requisite study materials. Entrance examinations to begin study in a field will not be eligible.
- **Education Tax Measures – Study abroad.** The required study period to claim the Tuition and Education amount as well as to qualify for Education Assistance Payments (EAPs)* for students studying abroad will be reduced from 13 consecutive weeks to 3 consecutive weeks for students enrolled at a university in a full-time course. This change will be effective for courses taken in 2011 and subsequent years and EAPs made after 2010.
- **RESPs – Asset sharing among siblings.** Tax-free transfers between individual Registered Retirement Savings Plans (RESPs) for the benefit of siblings will now be allowed without triggering the repayment of Canada Education Savings Grants (CESGs) so long as the beneficiary of the recipient plan is less than 21 years old at the time of the transfer. This change applies to asset transfers after 2010.

Additional tax credits. Following is a summary of non-refundable and refundable tax credits that have been either changed or increased due to indexing.

---

*Payments out of a Registered Education Savings Plan (RESP)

Summary of federal personal amounts for 2008 – 2011

Personal Amounts		2008	2009	2010	2011
Basic Personal Amount	Maximum Claim[1]	$ 9,600	$ 10,320	$ 10,382	$ 10,527
Age Amount	Maximum Claim[1]	$ 5,276	$ 6,408	$ 6,446	$ 6,537
	Reduced by net income over[1]	$ 31,524	$ 32,312	$ 32,506	$ 32,961
Spouse or Common-Law Partner Amount	Maximum Claim[1]	$ 9,600	$ 10,320	$ 10,382	$ 10,527
	Reduced by net income over	$ 0	$ 0	$ 0	$ 0
Eligible Child under 18		$ 2,038	$ 2,089	$ 2,101	$ 2,131
Amount for Eligible Dependants	Maximum Claim[1]	$ 9,600	$ 10,320	$ 10,382	$ 10,527
	Reduced by net income over	$ 0	$ 0	$ 0	$ 0
Amount for Infirm Dependants	Maximum Claim[1]	$ 4,095	$ 4,198	$ 4,223	$ 4,282
	Reduced by net income over[1]	$ 5,811	$ 5,956	$ 5,992	$ 6,076
Pension Income Amt.	Maximum Claim	$ 2,000	$ 2,000	$ 2,000	$ 2,000
Adoption Expenses	Maximum Claim[1]	$ 10,643	$ 10,909	$ 10,975	$ 11,128
Caregiver Amount	Maximum Claim[1]	$ 4,095	$ 4,198	$ 4,223	$ 4,282
	Reduced by net income over[1]	$ 13,986	$ 14,336	$ 14,422	$ 14,624
Disability Amount	Basic Amount[1]	$ 7,021	$ 7,196	$ 7,239	$ 7,341
	Supplementary Amount[1]	$ 4,095	$ 4,198	$ 4,223	$ 4,282
	Base Child Care Amount[1]	$ 2,399	$ 2,459	$ 2,473	$ 2,508
Tuition and Education Amounts +Textbook Tax Credit	Minimum Tuition	$ 100	$ 100	$ 100	$ 100
	Full-time Education Amt. (per month)	$ 400 + 65	$ 400 + 65	$ 400 + 65	$ 400 + 65
	Part-time Education Amt. (per month)	$ 120 + 20	$ 120 + 20	$ 120 + 20	$ 120 + 20
Medical Expenses	3% limitation[1]	$ 1,962	$ 2,011	$ 2,024	$ 2,052
	Maximum claim for other dependants	$ 10,000	$ 10,000	$ 10,000	N/A
Refundable Medical Expense Credit	Maximum[1]	$ 1,041	$ 1,067	$ 1,074	$ 1,089
	Base Family Income[1]	$ 23,057	$ 23,633	$ 23,775	$ 24,108
Canada Employment Amount	Maximum[1]	$ 1,019	$ 1,044	$ 1,051	$ 1,065

Personal Amounts		2008	2009	2010	2011
Children's Fitness Amount	Maximum	$ 500	$ 500	$ 500	$ 500
Home Renovation Exp.	Maximum	N/A	$ 9,000	N/A	N/A
Home Buyers' Amount	Maximum	N/A	$ 5,000	$ 5,000	$ 5,000
Children's Arts Amount	Maximum	N/A	N/A	N/A	$ 500

¹ These amounts are indexed

As your net income rises, the value of your non-refundable tax credits may be subject to a reduction or "clawback". The clawback zones are described below:

Non refundable tax credit clawback zones for 2010 and 2011

Credit	2011 Reduction Begins	2011 Credit Eliminated	2010 Reduction Begins	2010 Credit Eliminated
OAS	$ 67,668	$110,123	$ 66,733	$108,214
EI	$ 55,250	Varies with EI amount	$ 54,000	Varies with EI amount
Age Amount	$ 32,961	$ 76,541	$ 32,506	$ 75,478
Spouse or Common-Law Partner Amount	$ 0	$ 10,527	$ 0	$ 10,382
Amount for Eligible Dependants	$ 0	$ 10,527	$ 0	$ 10,382
Amount for Infirm Dependants	$ 6,076	$ 10,358	$ 5,992	$ 10,215
Caregiver Amount	$ 14,624	$ 18,906	$ 14,422	$ 18,645

New for 2012! Family Caregiver Tax Credit. Beginning in 2012, the claim for the following amounts will be increased by $2,000 where a taxpayer's dependant is physically or mentally infirm. This should be taken into account when you complete your TD1 Tax Credit Return with your employer at the start of the year:

- **Spouse or Common-Law Partner Amount** ($10,780 becomes $12,780)
- **Child Amount** ($2,182 becomes $4,182) Where the dependant is under age 18, they will be considered infirm only if they are likely to be, for a long and continuous period of indefinite duration, dependent on others for significantly more assistance in attending to the dependant's personal needs and care when compared generally to persons of the same age.
- **Amount for Eligible Dependants** ($10,780 becomes $12,780)
- **Caregiver Amount** ($4,385 becomes $6,385, maximum income increases by $2,000 as well)

- **Infirm Dependant Adult Amount** ($4,385 becomes $6,385, maximum income increases by $2,000 as well). The income ceiling used for the phase-out of the infirm dependant amount will also match the spouse or common-law partner phase-out amount beginning in 2012.

Changes to refundable tax credits

Goods and Services Tax Credit. Benefits and income thresholds:

GST Credit	July 2010 to June 2011	July 2011 to June 2012
Adult maximum	$250	$253
Child maximum	$131	$133
Single Supplement	$131	$133
Phase-in threshold for the single supplement	$8,096	$8,209
Family net income at which credit begins to phase out	$32,506	$32,961

Canada Child Tax Benefit. Benefits and income thresholds also increase for 2009/2010 payments under this provision, as shown below.

The Canada Child Tax Benefit	July 2010 to June 2011	July 2011 to June 2012
Base benefit	$ 1,348	$ 1,367
Additional benefit for third child	$ 94	$ 95
Family net income at which base benefit begins to phase out	$40,970	$41,544
First child	$ 2,088	$ 2,118
Second child	$ 1,848	$ 1,873
Third child	$ 1,758	$ 1,782
Family income at which NCB begins to phase out	$22,855	$24,183
Family net income at which NCB supplement phase-out ends	$40,970	$41,544

Splitting child benefits. Effective for payments received after June 2011, each parent who lives with the child can receive 50% of any Canada Child Tax Benefit (CCTB), Universal Child Care Benefit (UCCB) and GST Credit. Each parent will want to invest these benefits in the name of the child to build up a great education fund, but also to avoid tax on resulting investment earnings.

Changes in marital status. Since June 30, 2011, CRA requires notification from recipients of the CCTB at the end of the month following the month in which a marital status change occurs. This was already the rule for recipients of the GST/HST credit and notification has to be made only once.

Changes for employees

A new T4 slip. Most employees won't notice any changes to their T4 slips this year. However, volunteer firefighters who receive "exempt income", explained below, will find the exempt amount reported on their slips.

New! Volunteer firefighters tax credit. A new non-refundable tax credit is available for eligible volunteer firefighters. The credit is (15% of) $3,000 starting in 2011. To be eligible, a volunteer firefighter must perform at least 200 hours of volunteer firefighting in the tax year that consist primarily of

- responding to and being on call for firefighting and related emergency calls,
- attending meetings held by the fire department, and
- participating in required training related to the prevention or suppression of fires.

If the firefighter provides services other than on a volunteer basis, they will not be eligible for this credit regardless of the number of volunteer hours performed. To claim this credit, certification confirming the number of volunteer hours will be required for the chief or delegated official of the fire department, and volunteer firefighters who claim this credit will not be eligible to exclude honoraria from income (currently, volunteer firefighters can exempt up to $1,000 of honoraria received for volunteer work).

Stock option benefit rules. The federal government has announced it will examine the appropriate use of employee profit sharing plans. The goal of these plans is to allow the employee to invest in the employer's company in order to get better results. However, the government has expressed concern that business owners are using EPSPs to transfer profits to family members and thereby avoid taxation.

Registered Pension Plan (RPP) contribution maximums. For money purchase plans, the annual contribution limit for 2011 was $22,970 and is indexed each year. For defined benefit plans, the maximum pension benefit per year of service is ⅑ the money purchase limit. Thus, for 2011, the maximum benefit was $2,552.22 per year of service.

Don't forget, you may be able to make past service contributions as well. Those about to receive a pink slip and a severance package should consider maximizing their RRSP contribution. In some cases, legal fees for challenging the amount of severance offered will be deductible too.

EI premiums and benefit clawbacks. EI premium rates increased to 1.78% for 2011. The maximum contribution for the employee is $780.36. As employers contribute 140% of what the employee contributes, the maximum contribution for the employer increased to $1,092.50.

EI benefits repayments. The net income for purposes of a clawback of EI benefits earned during the year is set at $55,250 for 2011. If you received regular EI benefits in 2011 and had net income in excess of $55,250 you'll be required to repay 30% of your EI benefits if you've received regular EI benefits at any time in the previous ten years.

Changes for pensioners and pre-retirees

Old Age Security. Retirees and pre-retirees should be concerned with income level in any given taxation year to stay on the right side of "clawbacks" of the Old Age Security.

Old Age Security Payments

Monthly	1st Quarter	2nd Quarter	3rd Quarter	4th Quarter	Year Total
2011	$524.23	$526.85	$533.70	$537.97	$6,368.25

For 2011, the clawback of the Old Age Security begins at $67,668 and OAS will be fully clawed back when income reaches approximately $110,123. That is, if you received OAS benefits in 2011 and your individual net income exceeds $67,668, you'll have to repay a portion of your OAS benefits when you file your tax return.

Guaranteed Income Supplement. For low-income seniors (and their spouses if over 60) the Guaranteed Income Supplement tops up income to minimum income levels, depending on the individual's family circumstance. Beginning July 2011, seniors who little or no income other than the Old Age Security pension and the Guaranteed Income Supplement will receive an additional income top-up of $600 per year for singles (with outside income of $2,000 or less) and $840 for couples (with outside income of $4,000 or less).

CPP Benefits. The Canada Pension Plan (CPP) is a mandatory contributory retirement plan that provides an indexed retirement pension, generally beginning at age 65. It can also provide disability or survivor benefits to spouse and children if the contributor dies. How much the individual receives as a retirement pension benefit depends first on contributions made to the plan each year during the taxpayer's lifetime, up to maximum annual contributory earnings from employ-ment or self-employment ($50,100 for 2012). If you earn less than the annual maximum or have an extended period of low earnings, your pension entitlement may be reduced. To receive any benefits, there is a minimum contributory period of 3 years. The maximum benefits payable in 2011 are:

Type of benefit	Maximum amount
Retirement (at age 65)	$ 960.00
Disability	$ 1,153.37
Survivor – younger than 65	$ 529.09
Survivor – 65 and older	$ 576.00
Children of disabled contributors	$ 218.50
Children of deceased contributors	$ 218.50
Death (maximum one-time payment)	$ 2,500.00
Survivor/retirement (retirement at 65)	$ 960.00
Survivor/disability	$ 1,153.37

Starting in 2012 significant changes will take effect regarding benefit levels and premiums payable by those taking their CPP benefit early. These will be discussed later in the book.

Changes for investors and shareholders

Investors must focus on putting the right pools of money into the right hands so that resulting income is taxed in the future, at the lowest marginal rates. This year, there are several newsworthy items of concern to investors:

RRSP contribution maximums. You may contribute to your RRSP throughout the year and within the first 60 days of the new year in order to make a deduction to offset taxes payable. Maximum contributions are calculated as 18% of earned income to a maximum dollar contribution limit. **For 2011, the maximum contribution is $22,970, which is arrived at when earned income in 2010 is $127,611.** The contribution deadline is March 1.

Loss in RRSP/RRIF values on final return. When unmatured balances remain in an RRSP or RRIF of a deceased person and those balances have decreased in value in the period following death, a deduction can be claimed on the final return of the deceased for that reduction in value when the payment is actually made.

New RRSP anti-avoidance rules. Taxpayers who take exploit the RRSP or RRIF to obtain an unintended tax advantage will now have to pay a 100% tax in cases where investments are transferred into or out of a registered account at an increased value, and a 50% tax when prohibited investments are made (this could happen in cases where the shareholder owns 10% or more of a corporation) plus a 100% tax on income earned in such investments. This change should be discussed with a qualified tax and financial advisor.

The Registered Disability Savings Plan (RDSP). A new registered saving plan introduced late in 2008, was designed to accumulate capital and tax deferred income for the benefit of a disabled person in retirement. When an RDSP is opened, starting in 2011, the Canada Disability Savings Grant (CDSG) and Bond (CDSB) entitlements that are earned from the government when contributions are made to the RDSP, will be calculated for the 10 years prior to the opening date (but after 2008) based on the beneficiary's family income in those years. Two additional changes have been made:

- **RRSP rollovers.** Also, as of March 5, 2010, RRSP balances remaining at death can be used to make tax-free rollovers into the RDSP of a surviving child or grandchild. Such rollovers are limited to the recipient's RDSP contribution room and will not generate a Canada Disability Savings Grant (CDSG). Upon transfer, the recipient may claim a deduction for the lesser of the amount included in income and the amount transferred.

- **Specified Disability Savings Plans (SDSP).** Where a beneficiary of an RDSP has a shortened life expectancy (less than five years), a repayment of grants and bonds will not be required if a Disability Assistance Payment up to a specified limit is made to the beneficiary. In this case, the plan holder must file the prescribed form along with a certifying letter from a medical doctor with the RDSP issuer.

New prescribed interest rates. All taxpayers should keep an eye on the prescribed interest rates charged in their dealings with the CRA. The prescribed interest rate, which is used for the purposes outlined below, is set quarterly using a formula based on Treasury Bill rates. Given how relatively expensive the prescribed interest rates for delinquent taxes have been (you will note that 4% is added onto the Treasury Bill rate), it may make sense to pay off the tax man first before mortgages, or other debt.

On the flip side, with the historically low interest rates for inter-spousal loans shown in the last row of the table below, this may be a good time to look at setting up a loan between partners to transfer assets legitimately from a higher earner to a lower one.

QUARTER in 2011	1	2	3	4
Prescribed interest rate on overdue taxes	5%	5%	5%	5%
Prescribed interest rate on overdue CPP/EI premiums	5%	5%	5%	5%
Prescribed interest rate on tax overpayments	3%	3%	3%	3%
Prescribed rate use to compute taxable benefits, low or no-interest loans and shareholder loans	1%	1%	1%	1%

Donation of flow-through shares. When flow-through shares are donated to a registered charity, the inclusion rate for such capital gains is zero, providing a significant advantage to donors who receive a charitable donation receipt for the full fair market value of the donated shares, but have no capital gains tax to pay. Budget 2011 put an end to that advantage.

While the donation of flow-through shares to charity will still be allowed, the elimination of tax on the capital gain will be limited to the amount that exceeds the original cost of the flow-through share, rather than the entire amount. This change would be in effect for flow-through shares acquired through an agreement entered into on or after March 22, 2011.

IPP contributions. Individual Pension Plans can be established for business owners who are employees of a corporation that he or she controls. The 2011 budget made several changes which will affect retirement plans for individuals with these plans:

- Annual minimum withdrawal amounts will be required from IPPs once a plan member is 72. These amounts will be based on current RRIF rules.
- Contributions to an IPP related to past years of employment will have to come from RRSP or RPP assets or by reducing RRSP contribution room, before deductible contributions can be made.
- These provisions will apply to IPP past service contributions made after March 22, 2011.

Tax on split income. As of March 22, 2011, certain capital gains realized by or included in the income of a minor as a result of the disposition of shares of family-owned company to other family members will be treated as dividends, subject to a special prohibitive tax on split income. These transactions should therefore be considered in advance with the help of a tax professional.

Keep up with the news. It's important to keep up with tax changes throughout the year, as the Finance Department and CRA change both tax law and administrative procedures. You can do so by subscribing to a free weekly electronic newsletter from The Knowledge Bureau (see www.knowledgebureau.com).

Part II

Understand the Basics

CHAPTER 3

WHO NEEDS TO FILE A TAX RETURN AND WHY?

You may have heard the controversy last summer concerning American citizens, who are required to report to tax authorities, no matter where in the world they reside. This caused a great deal of hardship for millions of U.S. citizens living in countries throughout the world as they grappled with meeting their tax filing obligations as well as large penalties for their failure to file required forms.

The obligation to file a Canadian tax return, by contrast, is not determined by citizenship, but on residency. Your Canadian residency is also what entitles you to the lucrative tax deductions and refundable or non-refundable tax credits we summarized for you in the previous chapter.

In today's global economies, several grey areas can emerge, surrounding an individual's residency. Determining who needs to file a return in Canada, therefore can result in a case-by-case basis analysis of tax filing status, especially for those who leave Canada temporarily. There are various definitions of residency, for Canadian tax filing purposes, therefore, and understanding them is important, especially if you have family members working abroad.

ESSENTIAL TAX FACT | Canadian residents must report "world income" in Canadian funds on their Canadian tax return.

Individual residency. An individual is considered to be a resident of Canada for federal tax filing purposes if they have residential ties to Canada. These taxpayers must report their world income but are often eligible to claim a credit for any taxes paid to a foreign jurisdiction. Except for the province of Quebec, which requires the filing of a separate provincial return, provincial tax calculations are included in the federal tax return through additional schedules.

> **ESSENTIAL TAX FACT** | Provincial taxes for the whole year are based on your province of residence on December 31. Moves to more highly taxed provinces should therefore be planned for the start of a tax year.

Deemed residency. Some taxpayers are considered to be factual residents of Canada for the full year even if they have no established residential ties. These taxpayers file a tax return as a normal resident. This includes individuals who:

- Visit Canada for 183 days or more in the year
- Work overseas as a member of the Canadian Armed Forces
- Work as a minister, high commissioner, ambassador, officer or servant of Canada
- Perform services in a foreign country under a program of the Canadian International Development Agency
- Are a member of the Canadian Armed Forces school staff or
- Are a spouse or dependent child of one of the above

However you might also become a deemed non-resident if your ties to another country are so substantial that you are considered to be a resident there. In that case, you would file a tax return as a resident there.

Immigration into Canada. Those who enter the country permanently or leave and sever all ties are considered to be "part year residents", which requires the filing of a Canadian tax return for the period of residency.

In the year of entry or departure it's possible to be both a Canadian resident and a "part-year non-resident" for filing purposes. Accordingly, in those years, personal amounts would be prorated for the number of days of residency, and in the case of emigrants, some refundable tax credits would be denied on the final return, discussed below.

There are special tax filing rules for the year you immigrate to Canada. For example, you will value assets as of the date of entry, so that you can avoid paying capital gains taxes on any value accrual that occurred before you became a Canadian resident. You will also qualify for refundable tax credits if you can establish residency here by December 31 of the tax year.

It is therefore wise to receive professional advice on the tax consequences of both entry to or departure from Canada well in advance of your move. This can help you plan for a tax-advantaged fair market valuation date and meet all compliance requirements.

Non-residency. An individual is considered to be a non-resident of Canada if residential ties to Canada have not been established, or have been severed. These individuals may still be required to file a return in Canada if they earned income from employment or self-employment here, or have disposed of certain Taxable Canadian Property—that is property that is situated in Canada, upon which the Canadian government has reserved taxation rights.

Otherwise, they may elect to file a return if they have certain types of passive income sources like pensions or investments. These types of income will have taxes withheld at source when they are sent to non-residents. As a non-resident, you may be able to recover some or all of that withholding tax by filing an elective Canadian return.

> **ESSENTIAL TAX FACT** | "Departure taxes" must be calculated if you give up your Canadian residency.

It's important to plan ahead to leave Canada permanently. Those who sever ties permanently must first deal with a tax reckoning—a departure tax will apply to most taxable assets, based on valuation as at the date of departure. If such fair market valuation results in a capital gain, you'll need to square off with the tax department (cash or the posting of security is required).

Not all properties are subject to the departure tax. Specifically excluded properties include:

- pensions and similar rights including registered retirement savings plans, registered retirement income funds, and deferred profit-sharing plans
- rights to certain benefits under employee profit sharing plans, employee benefit plans, employee trusts, and salary deferral arrangements
- in the case of those who have been resident in Canada for 5 years or less, certain qualifying property that was owned at the time the person became a resident, or was inherited since the taxpayer last became a resident of Canada
- employee stock options subject to Canadian tax
- interests in life insurance policies in Canada (other than segregated fund policies)

Those who return to Canada may unwind the departure tax.

Summary: Tax Filing Requirements

Status	Rules to Note	Federal Return	Province of Residence
Canadian Resident	Actual, factual or deemed residents report world income in Canadian funds.	Yes	Yes, as at December 31
Immigrant— Part Year Resident	Fair Market Value of assets are calculated upon entry. Report world income while resident in Canada.	Yes	Yes, as at December 31
Emigrant— Part Year Resident	Departure taxes must be calculated. Report world income while resident in Canada.	Yes	Yes, as of departure date
Deemed Non-Resident	By virtue of your residential ties you are considered resident of another country; file as below.	If electing to file.	No
Non-Resident	For some income sources a filing election is possible to recover withholding tax.	If electing to file.	No

Now that you know who needs to file a tax return, it's important to understand why. Let's start with the potentially bad news:

ESSENTIAL TAX FACT | Tax evasion is a crime... with very expensive consequences.

Avoiding tax evasion. Tax evasion is the act of making false or deceptive statements in a return, certificate, statement or answer filed or made to the CRA in order to willfully evade or attempt to evade paying tax. Also, you can be guilty of this crime when you participate in destroying, altering, mutilating, or otherwise disposing of the records or books of account.

If convicted of tax evasion, besides paying the taxes, you are liable for a fine of not less than 50% and not more than double the amount of the tax that was sought to be evaded, or imprisonment for a term not exceeding 2 years.

In addition, CRA's gross negligence penalty will usually also apply to the false statement or omission of information. This amounts to 50% of tax properly payable. And of course, late filing penalties and interest could also be added if you did not file on time. We'll discuss penalties in more detail in Chapter 5 below.

It's always best to avoid evading taxes for obvious reasons, and the vast majority of Canadians do!

Filing to tap into your legal rights. There are far more reasons why most people will *want* to file a tax return. They want to tap into their legal rights to arrange their affairs within the framework of the law to pay the least taxes legally possible and to receive benefits from the numerous tax preferences and credits that are available.

You have learned in previous chapters that even those who have no income should file a tax return to tap into lucrative federal and provincial refundable tax credits that can increase their cash flow. In addition, however, millions of taxpayers file their returns every year to recover taxes that have been over-remitted through their workplace or through quarterly instalments, in the case of investors, retirees, or proprietors who are responsible for their own periodic tax remittances.

While Canadians love their tax refunds, you will learn that the object is to pay only the correct amount of tax, and no more. That way, you keep control of more of your money, investing it into the right "buckets" to work for you for emergencies, for lifestyle wants, and to create income for your future. Therefore from a wealth management point of view, arranging your affairs to receive your refund all year long, through reduced tax withholdings on your pay, will make you richer.

Your tax advisor can help you with the required forms; your financial advisors can help you with the required tax efficient investment opportunities.

CHAPTER 4

WHAT DOCUMENTS
DO YOU NEED?

The first step in maximizing your opportunities to find new money and build new wealth through the tax system is to get organized for your annual tax filing routine. This involves not only pulling together the receipts and slips from the current tax filing year, for each family member, but also requires that you keep track of certain "carry forward information" that is used to file tax returns to your family's best benefit.

A checklist to help you get better at this task—no matter how disorganized you may be—is provided below:

Carry forward information. Attach copy of previously filed forms or tax documents:
- Copies of the Notices of Assessment or Reassessment from prior three years
- Copies of Schedule 1: unused non-refundable tax credits of prior years:
  - Tuition, education and textbook amounts carried forward (prior Schedule 11)
  - Unused student loan interest carried forward
  - Unused medical expenses carried forward
  - Unused charitable donations carried forward
- Unapplied minimum taxes paid in previous years (Form T691 Minimum Taxes)
- Schedule 3: Capital gains and losses reported in prior years
- Schedule 7: RRSP contribution room; Home Buyer's Plan or Lifelong Learning Plan
- Business and rental income statements from prior years
- Capital Cost Allowance records: Asset acquisition, disposition and depreciation
- GST remittances of prior years

- Undeducted RRSP contributions and unused RRSP contribution room
- Unused Tax-Free Savings Account room
- Undeducted past service contributions to a Registered Pension Plan (RPP)
- T1A Forms: Undeducted capital losses or non-capital losses of prior years
- Undeducted business investment losses of prior years
- Any supporting documents to business and investment statements
- T1-M: Unused moving expenses of prior years
- Repayments of social benefits: OAS, Workers' Compensation, EI, government-funded plans
- Undeducted limited partnership losses of prior years
- Record of instalment tax payments
- Unused Labour-Sponsored Funds or Investment Tax Credits
- Capital gains elections made in 1994 – Copy of Form T664 from 1994 tax files
- Adjusted cost base information regarding assets held by the family

This information will not only provide an excellent start to filing a more complete and accurate tax return, but it will also help your advisors help you build, grow and preserve your net worth over time, with tax efficiency.

This year's documents. Gather the documents that relate to this year's filing:

- income slips (T4, T5, T3, etc.)
- business statements
- investment statements
- asset valuations
- rent, property taxes, home office, auto
- expenses for family events (children's activities, medical, charity, tuition, etc.)
- investing expenses (carrying charges)
- employment expenses

CHAPTER 5

WHAT DEADLINES MUST BE MET?

Most people dread the annual tax filing routine—it's a kind of triple negative. First, you have to spend a couple of Sundays gathering up your documentation for the whole family—that's really the hardest part, as we have seen. Then you have to actually do the return (or pay someone to do it for you). Finally, if you owe, you will have to write a cheque to CRA. Unpalatable!

However, these are not reasons to ignore your tax filing obligations. The alternative is even more costly: those who owe will face late filing penalties and interest.

ESSENTIAL TAX FACT | The tax filing deadline is midnight April 30 for most individuals. For the unincorporated small business owner (and their spouse) it is June 15… but if you owe, interest will accrue from May 1 onward. So it makes sense for everyone to file by April 30.

Remember, when you fail to file, you also set yourself up for the gross negligence or tax evasion penalties discussed earlier, on top of the interest and late filing penalties, described below:

1. **First failure to file a return on time.** 5% of unpaid taxes plus 1% per month up to a maximum of 12 months time from the filing due date.

2. **Subsequent failure to file on time within a 3-year period.** 10% of unpaid taxes plus 2% per month to a maximum of 20 months from filing due date.

Ouch! Perhaps you have heard this line before from a delinquent filer: "I don't have to file on time—I'm getting a refund anyways!" This can be complete folly! You will put yourself at risk for expensive late filing penalties if you're wrong about the refund and owe money instead.

> **ESSENTIAL TAX FACT** | Late filing penalties are costly, especially for repeat offenders.

If you are behind in filing your returns, you should also consider that in fact CRA could owe you money. Rather than giving the government an interest-free loan for the use of your money, file to receive your refund quickly for your own use instead. Know that you won't earn any interest on balances owed to you from CRA until 30 days after you file (or longer if you file before the deadline).

> **ESSENTIAL TAX FACT** | Interest and late filing penalties may be avoided in hardship cases—like illness, death of a family member or other factors beyond your control. Simply write a letter to your local CRA tax services office.

There is another reason to want to file on time every year… to receive refundable tax credits throughout the year from the federal and provincial governments. This is especially true for low income earners or those who are not taxable, like single mothers, widows/ers or students.

Finally, filing a tax return annually will help you invest with tax efficiency. You will be able to build up "contribution room" for the purpose of investing in an RRSP, for example, and you'll be able to carry forward capital losses, minimum taxes balances, and so on.

If you make false statements when you file your return, or if you purposely omit relevant information, you may be subject to gross negligence penalties. These amount to 50% of tax properly payable with a minimum penalty of $100.

These are just a few reasons why filing a tax return every year, and on time, can be one of the most significant financial transactions of the year.

CHAPTER 6

HOW IS YOUR INCOME TAXED?

There are often several different sources of cash that flows into a household budget every month, and each may be taxed differently. For tax purposes, your income sources break down into categories, including the following:

- **Active income:** The full amount of your employment income and benefits plus the full amount of self-employment, after expenses, is included in income.
- **Social benefits:** Employment insurance, Worker's Compensation, the Universal Child Care Benefit and certain provincial programs, including social assistance are all included in income. However, in the case of Worker's Comp and social assistance, the income is deducted again after the calculation of net income.
- **Pensions:** This category can include public pensions—the Old Ages Security (OAS) and Canada Pension Plan (CPP) and the Guaranteed Income Supplement (GIS). It can also include taxable foreign pension receipts, or private pension benefits from employer-sponsored Registered Pension Plans (RPPs), Registered Retirement Savings Plans (RRSPs), Registered Retirement Income Funds (RRIFs), and annuities. These amounts are added to income in full. However the GIS is deducted again after the calculation of net income.
- **Investments:** Passive income sources from investments in non-registered accounts must be reported on the tax return. These are also known as "income from property" in the *Income Tax Act*. Such income can include interest (reported in full), dividends (reported at advantageous rates), net rental income and royalties.
- **Capital dispositions:** A capital gain can occur when investors dispose of income-producing assets which have increased or decreased in value. This

can include stocks, bonds, mutual fund units, other securities, personal residences, rental properties, shares in small business corporations, farming or fishing enterprises, and other personal properties, like family art or other heirlooms. Only 50% of the capital gain is added to income. Capital losses will usually offset capital gains, depending on the classification of the asset disposed of.

- **Other taxable amounts:** This can include taxable alimony payments to a spouse, or income from a Registered Education Savings Plan, for example.

How much tax you'll pay on the next dollar of income you earn will depend on how your income sources are taxed. For example, the highest marginal tax rates will apply to ordinary income—that is, income from employment income, interest income, net business or rental income as well as income from public and private pension sources, such as RRSP or RRIF withdrawals. Dividends and capital gains are taxed at more attractive tax rates.

The trick is to build the cash flow you need in the most tax efficient manner to maximize your purchasing power. Usually, a diversity of income sources will help you "average down" the taxes you will pay on your income in total. In addition, when you have an opportunity to split income with family members, you may be able to save more tax dollars, by having each family member pay tax at lower tax rates. (However, certain "Attribution Rules" do need to be followed in that case; we will discuss these later.)

To build tax efficiency in your income mix, do an income analysis:

a. **What is the type of income are you receiving and what is the rate of tax on that income source?** Is this ordinary income, dividends from small business corporations, public or eligible dividends and/or capital gains income?

b. **How close is your income to the next tax bracket?** How much tax will the next dollar I earn attract? Will it be taxed at my current tax bracket, or jump to the next higher tax bracket and income.

c. **What can be done to stay clear of the next marginal tax bracket?** Should income be withdrawn over two tax years rather than all at once? Can certain deductions, like an RRSP contribution, keep your income in its current, lower tax bracket?

Then consider, how much income should I realize for tax purposes, from which source, and when? For example if your income is increased with the earning of dividends from shares in a publicly traded company, instead of from a withdrawal of ordinary taxable income from an RRSP, you'll save over 20% in the top marginal tax bracket.

By better understanding how your sources of income are taxed, you will be able to make better decisions about what income sources should be earned next.

ESSENTIAL TAX FACT | Small changes in the structuring of your income can create thousands of dollars in tax savings for your family... that increases the returns on your investments.

CHAPTER 7

WHAT INCOME SOURCES
ARE TAX EXEMPT?

ESSENTIAL TAX FACT | Certain income sources are tax exempt.

The best kind of income is tax-free income. The following income sources fall into that category. How many do you qualify for?

- **Return of capital:** These receipts represent a return of the original principal amount invested; therefore receipts are not considered taxable investment income until they exceed their original cost.

- **Refundable Tax Credits:** These are good sources of new cash flow, especially for families. They include the Child Tax Benefit or the Goods and Services Tax Credit.

- **Lottery winnings, gifts or inheritances:** These sources are tax-free.

- **Insurance proceeds:** Benefits from a life or certain wage loss and disability insurance policies are not taxable.

- **Income from Personal Injury Award property of a minor.** While the taxpayer was under 21 years of age, an award of damages or investment income or capital gains thereon received in respect of the taxpayer's physical or mental injury is tax exempt.

- **Income earned on First Nations reserves.** Employment income is considered to be personal property and will usually be exempt from income tax when:
  – at least 90% of the duties of an employment are performed on a reserve,
  – the employer is resident on a reserve and the employee lives on a reserve,
  – more than 50% of the duties of an employment are performed on a reserve and the employer is resident on a reserve, or the employee lives on a reserve, or

— the employer is resident on a reserve and the employer is an Indian band which has a reserve, a tribal council representing one or more Indian bands which have reserves, or an Indian organization controlled by one or more such bands or tribal councils.

When less than 90% of the duties of an employment are performed on a reserve and the employment income is not exempted by another guideline, the exemption must be prorated. The exemption will only apply to the portion of the income related to the duties performed on the reserve.

Note also that the receipt of EI benefits, retiring allowances, CPP (or QPP) payments, RPP benefits or wage loss replacement plan benefits will usually be exempt from income tax when received as a result of employment income that was exempt from tax.

- Canadian Service Pensions, War Veterans Allowance Act Allowances.
- Tax-free employee benefits.
- Proceeds from accident, disability, sickness or income maintenance plans where the taxpayer has made all the (non-deductible) premiums.
- Refundable provincial or federal tax credits.
- Payments for Volunteer Emergency Services—up to $1000 (unless the Volunteer Firefighter Tax Credit is claimed).
- Social Assistance payments for foster care.
- Scholarships and bursaries for students eligible to claim the Tuition, Education, and Textbook Amount.
- MLA and Municipal Officers Expense Allowances.
- Some or all of income of Canadian Forces Personnel and Police on High-Risk International Missions.
- Service pensions from other countries on account of disability or death arising out of war service received from a foreign country that was an ally of Canada at the time of the war service.
- Capital gains on publicly traded securities donated to a registered charity or private foundation.
- **Tax-free withdrawals from a TFSA:** These amounts can be used for any purpose and easily reinvested into investments that provide further tax efficiency.

Your monthly cash flow will increase for spending and savings purposes when you earn tax exempt income sources. Ask your tax and financial advisors how you can create more tax-free and tax-efficient income.

CHAPTER 8

WHAT IS YOUR TAX BRACKET?

In Canada, we have a progressive tax system, which means that those who have a higher taxable income during the year generally pay taxes at a higher rate. However, we have learned that the size of your tax bill can be affected by your income source as well. Tax rates are affixed to various tax brackets by two different levels of government: federal and provincial. This causes complexity for tax filers.

Federal tax rates are applied uniformly to all Canadians' taxable income and tax brackets are indexed for inflation each year. Provincial tax rates are applied to the same definition of taxable income (except in Quebec), but tax brackets and rates are different and are not indexed for inflation in all provinces.

> **ESSENTIAL TAX FACT** | You need to know your effective and marginal tax rates.

In planning to pay the least amount of taxes possible, it is important to understand what your effective and marginal tax rates are. **The effective tax rate is the average rate of tax paid on all income.** You can find it easily by taking the taxes paid on Line 435 and dividing this number by your total income on line 150. For example:

Line 435 Total Payable	$11,331*
Line 150 Total Income	$56,393
Effective Tax Rate	($11,331 / $56,393) = 20%

*Your results will vary depending on your province of residence and income mix.

Your effective tax rate takes "progressivity" into account: that is, tax rates will rise with your income level.

The marginal tax rate is the rate of tax paid on the next dollar earned. Remember, as income increases, taxes paid are proportionately greater and benefits of tax credits can be clawed back. For example:

Current income:	$56,393
Receipt of employment bonus:	$ 1,000
Taxes payable	$11,642
Taxes payable before bonus	$ 11,331
Difference	$ 311
Marginal Tax Rate	31%

So, depending on your province of residence, you'll pay about $311 more on $1,000 of employment income for rate of 31%. This is what it costs you to earn the next like dollar.

Or, taken another way, this is how much you would save if you put that $1,000 into an RRSP. It's significant—your return on the RRSP investment is a double-digit one, from a tax point of view alone... 31%!

Also because you know that different types of income may be subject to different marginal tax rates, as illustrated in the chart below, you'll want to plan how you earn your income carefully.

Federal and Provincial Marginal Tax Rates (BC) for 2011

	Taxable Income	Ordinary Income	Capital Gains	Small Bus. Corp. Dividends	Eligible Dividends
BC	Up to $10,527	0%	0%	0%	0%
	$10,528 to $11,088	15%	7.5%	2.08%	-2.03%
	$11,089 to $36,146	20.06%	10.03%	4.16%	-9.43%
	$36,147 to $41,544	22.70%	11.35%	7.46%	-5.70%
	$41,545 to $72,294	29.70%	14.85%	16.21%	4.17%
	$72,295 to $83,001	32.50%	16.25%	19.71%	8.11%
	$83,002 to $83,088	34.29%	17.15%	21.95%	10.64%
	$83,089 to $100,787	38.29%	19.15%	26.95%	16.28%
	$100,788 to $128,800	40.70%	20.35%	29.96%	19.68%
	Over $128,800	43.70%	21.85%	33.71%	23.91%

CHAPTER 9

HOW TO RECOVER REFUNDS
FROM PAST MISTAKES

ESSENTIAL TAX FACT | You can adjust prior filed returns to correct errors and omissions.

It may be too good to be true… if you learn something new in reading this book and find that you have missed lucrative tax provisions on prior tax returns, you may be able to recover tax gold by adjusting those prior filed returns. To do so, you'll want to keep your Notice of Assessment or Reassessment, which you'll receive with your refund cheque or balance due notice after filing your return, in a safe place.

The *Income Tax Act* contains a definition of a "normal reassessment period", which is often referred to as the "statute of limitations" since it limits CRA's ability to reassess any tax year to the period that ends three years after the mailing of the original Notice of Assessment or Reassessment for the tax year, except in the case of fraud, in which case, there is no time limit. You can avoid gross negligence or tax evasion penalties by voluntarily complying with the law to correct errors or omissions.

Taxpayers, however, can request adjustments to prior filed returns within ten years after the end of the taxation year being adjusted. This is a great way to recover "gold" from prior years. Many taxpayers miss claiming all the deductions and credits they are entitled to.

Here's how to adjust your return:
- If you think you missed claiming something on a prior filed return, call your tax practitioner to make an adjustment or do it yourself using form T1-ADJ, available on the CRA's website.

- Have supporting documentation available in case of audit.
- Never file a second tax return.

Most common filing errors
- Taxable benefits double reported
- Missed GST rebate on union dues
- Missed premium deduction on wage loss replacement benefits received
- Failure to report tips
- Failure to report taxable foreign pension
- Pension from Germany not reported; deduction taken, credit not taken
- Missed self-reporting interest on mortgage held privately
- Missed claiming brokerage fees
- Incorrect adjusted cost base due to missed capital gains election
- Lost RRSP receipt
- Child care expenses claims by high income earner
- Moving expenses—missed real estate commissions
- Missed safety deposit box fees
- Missed home office claim
- Business loss remained unused
- Prior year capital losses not recorded
- Spousal amount—gross rather than net income used
- Amount for eligible dependants—file when marital status changes
- Caregiver amount—missed claiming for infirm parent
- Disability amount—missed claim for sick child
- Tuition, education and textbook credits—missed transfer to parents
- Amounts transferred from spouse—missed transfer of age credit
- Medical expenses—missed multiple expenses
- Donations—claim on return of one spouse
- Instalment payment reduction request missed

CHAPTER 10

TAX PLANNING:
WHY THE TFSA IS SO IMPORTANT

You have already learned a lot about planning to file a more timely and accurate tax return and how to structure your taxable income sources to be more tax efficient. From a planning point of view, there is one more thing you need to know about your tax filing "basics": a cornerstone of every tax plan is the inclusion of a Tax-Free Savings Account in the taxpayer's investment portfolio.

Taxpayers over the age of 17 may contribute up to $5,000 each year (indexed each year to the nearest $500) to such an account, or their relatives and supporting individuals may make contributions for them. The TFSA is exempt from the normal "Attribution Rules" which require higher earners who transfer or loan money to their spouses to report earnings on the transferor's return.

This investment is so important because, given its full accumulation period (age 18 to date of death), every resident of Canada has the opportunity to become a millionaire, even with low returns, by simply investing $5,000 each year (indexed by formula).

For example, being very conservative, if you deposit $5,000 each year, indexed by 2%, for 50 years in a TFSA that earns only 4% interest on those deposits, the balance after the last deposit will be over $1,103,000.

> **ESSENTIAL TAX FACT** | Investors may take the money out of their TFSA for whatever purpose they wish and then put the money back into the TFSA to grow more.

However, there are penalties for "re-contributing" at the wrong time. You have to wait until the required contribution room is created: January 1 of the next year. There are three parts to this "Contribution Room," which must be considered however:

1. New Contribution Room created at January 1 of each new year. ($5,000 per year plus indexing, when applicable)

2. "Re-Contribution" Room based on prior year withdrawals. This "re-contribution room" is created at January 1 each year.

3. Carry forwards of the contribution and "re-contribution" room created above if left unfunded.

Neither withdrawals nor earnings can be included in income for any income-tested benefits, such as the Canada Child Tax Benefit or Goods and Services Tax (GST) Credit. Investors at lower income levels can therefore save and earn on a tax exempt basis while continuing to benefit from income redistribution provisions.

Following are some additional facts about TFSAs you may find helpful as you consider adding this investment to the portfolio of each adult in the family:

- **TFSA eligible investments.** The same eligible investments as allowed within an RRSP will apply to the TFSA. A special rule prohibits a TFSA from making an investment in any entity with which the account holder does not deal at arm's length.

- **TFSA excluded investments.** Prescribed excluded property for these purposes includes any obligation secured by mortgage so that individuals cannot hold their own mortgage loan as an investment in their TFSA.

- **Interest deductibility.** Interest paid on money borrowed to invest in the TFSA is not deductible. It should be noted that rules are in place so that if the loan is not an arm's length arrangement or was made to allow another person (or partnership) to benefit from the tax-free status of the TFSA, the TFSA will be deemed to no longer be a TFSA.

- **Stop loss rules.** A capital loss is denied when assets are disposed to a TFSA.

- **Using TFSA as security.** A TFSA may be used as security for a loan or other indebtedness.

- **Departure tax.** The TFSA is not caught by the departure tax rules. In fact, a beneficiary under a TFSA who immigrates to or emigrates from Canada will not be treated as having disposed of their rights under a TFSA. No TSFA contribution room is earned for those years where a person is non-resident and any withdrawals while non-resident cannot be replaced. However, it will make sense to remove capital properties from the TFSA on a tax-free basis immediately prior to emigrating and then trigger the deemed disposition on departure to avoid taxation in the destination country.

- **Marriage breakdown.** Upon breakdown of a marriage or common-law partnership, the funds from one party's TFSA may be transferred tax-free to the other party's TFSA. This will have no effect on the contribution room of either of the parties.
- **Death of a TFSA holder.** Death of the TFSA holder, the funds within the account may be rolled over into their spouse's TFSA or they may be withdrawn tax-free. Any amounts earned within a TSFA after the death of the taxpayer are taxable to the estate.
- **Excess contributions.** When taxpayers make contributions over the allowed maximum, they are subject to a 1% per month penalty until the amounts are removed. However, if taxpayers are willing to pay the penalty tax in order to keep the money in the plan, hoping to reap an even higher tax-free return on the excess contribution, 100% of the gains will be subject to tax when deliberate overcontributions occur after October 16th, 2009.
- **TFSA eligible investments.** A special rule prohibits a TFSA from making an investment in any entity with which the account holder does not deal at arm's length, and for occurrences after October 16th, 2009, a 100% penalty tax on the income so earned will apply.
- **Swapping for tax-free gains.** When taxpayers swap investments from non-registered accounts for cash in the TFSA, and then swap them back out for a revised, higher price point, thereby leaving gains in the TFSA to be tax-free, 100% of the gains are subject to tax, after October 16th, 2009.

Part III

Bring in the Family

CHAPTER 11

WHY IS FAMILY FILING IMPORTANT— EVEN FOR SINGLES?

ESSENTIAL TAX FACT | Families make economic decisions as a unit; when you prepare taxes as a family unit, you'll get the best tax benefits.

Families that are successful in accumulating wealth over time strive to achieve the best tax filing results for the family unit over time. The focus is on reducing taxes on income earned by each family member; and then preserving the asset pools that are accumulating in the family unit. Fortunately using the rules of the tax system can help.

That's because it's possible for families to transfer various tax credits, split and shift income from higher to lower taxed individuals to get better overall results. How to structure a "tax-efficient family income" is therefore important; so is the transfer of assets into the right hands throughout life cycles and at the end of life, too.

Who is a family member for tax filing purposes? It would seem to be a simple question, but not always in an age of blended family units. Here's what you need to know:

- A *spouse*, for tax purposes, is someone to whom you are legally married.
- A *common-law partner*, for tax purposes, is someone who is not your spouse but is:
  - a person of the same or opposite sex with whom you lived in a relationship throughout a continuous* 12-month period, or

– someone who, at the end of the tax year, was the actual or adoptive parent of your child.

* Note that separations of less than 90 days do not affect the 12-month period.

For income tax purposes, all rules that apply to a spouse apply equally to a common-law partner.

You will claim a spouse or common-law partner on your tax return under the Spousal Amount if net income levels are low enough; you will also qualify to transfer certain other provisions, described below. In addition, you will have to combine net income levels for the purposes of claiming refundable tax credits. The family unit will also be allowed one tax exempt family residence, as well.

Dependants. Taxpayers who support minors or adult dependants, or both, may reap additional tax benefits. A dependant is generally defined as:

- a child of the taxpayer,
- the taxpayer's parent or grandparent or
- a person related to the taxpayer who is under 18 years of age or if over 18, wholly dependent on the taxpayer because of mental or physical infirmity.

These qualifications need not be met throughout the year but must be met at some time during the year. The supporting individual may claim medical expenses for these dependants as well as provisions for providing care in the case of incapacity. In some cases transfers of tuition, education and textbook amounts available to students may also be made, if the student is not taxable.

File family tax returns together. Begin your quest maximize your family tax filing opportunities by doing all family tax returns at the same time, starting with the lowest income earner and working your way up to the highest, to ensure that income is taxed at the lowest possible rates and the family can maximize eligibility for available tax credits. Consider the following tax provisions, which impact the tax returns filed by individuals in the family:

TAX ELEMENT	PROVISION	CAN BE CLAIMED BY
Income	Canada Pension Plan Benefits	After age 60, split CPP income by making an equal assignment of benefits to each spouse.
	Taxable Dividends	Dividends can be transferred to high earning spouse* if by doing so a Spousal Amount is created or increased.
	Eligible Pension Income	Up to 50% can be transferred to the other spouse by election each year.
Deductions	Safety Deposit Box	Either spouse may claim if it holds household investment documents.
Non-Refundable Tax Credits on Schedule 1	Basic Personal Amount	Not transferable.
	Age Amount, Pension Income Amount, Disability Amount, Tuition, Education and Textbook Amounts, Amount for Dependent Minors	These five amounts are transferrable to the higher earner if lower earner is not taxable. In the case of the Disability Amount and Tuition, Education and Textbook Amounts transfers from dependants other than spouse may also be made.
	Claims for Spouse or Equivalent to Spouse	They are claimed by the supporting individual with higher taxable income in general.
	Claims for Infirm Adults, Caregiver, Donations, Adoption Expenses	Can be claimed by either spouse or shared between them.
	Medical Expenses	Usually claimed by spouse with lower net income for best benefit (if that spouse is taxable); can include medical expenses for other dependant adults.
	Canada Employment Amount	Not transferable.
	Public Transit Amount	Can be claimed by either spouse or shared between them.
	Children's Fitness and Arts	Can be claimed by either spouse or shared between them.
	New Home Buyers' Amount	Can be claimed by either spouse.

*Throughout this book, spouse references include common-law partner.

ESSENTIAL TAX FACT | When everyone in the family keeps individual net income levels low by maximizing available tax deductions, the family unit as a whole will benefit by qualifying for higher refundable and non-refundable tax credits.

Keep these transfer provisions in mind when you plan tax and investment activities throughout the year and account for them at tax time. You will be in a position to ask better questions about the tax and investment planning decisions you would like to make; for example:

- How are tuition, education and textbook credits transferred from our children?
- How can we increase the Child Tax Benefits we receive?
- Will an RRSP help? Who should contribute?
- Should we pay down the mortgage first, then invest in the RRSP?
- How should we invest the Child Tax Benefits received? In whose account?
- How can we split income between family members to reduce taxes?
- What should we do with our family's tax refunds?
- Who should own a TFSA?
- Is an RESP a good idea for our family?
- Should we borrow money to invest? If so who should do this?
- Should we consider buying life insurance and how should we fund this?

ESSENTIAL TAX FACT | Even singles should look into their family tax filing rights.

Singles may, for example, be able to claim an Amount for Eligible Dependant, which is an "equivalent to spouse amount" if they are supporting a child or dependent adult in their domestic establishment. Singles may also be supporting a disabled person by making a contribution to a Registered Disability Savings Plan (RDSP), contributing to a child's Registered Education Savings Plan (RESP) or supporting their community with charitable donations. These provisions require some tax planning, too.

CHAPTER 12

HOW CAN WE RECEIVE MORE REFUNDABLE TAX CREDITS?

By now you should know that the filing of a tax return serves several financial purposes for Canadian residents:

1. To reconcile and recover overpaid taxes withhold through employment or pension source deductions or as a result of overpaid tax instalments.

2. To redistribute income to low and middle income earners with special family circumstances. This is done through the delivery of refundable federal tax credits like the Canada Child Tax Benefit, Goods and Service Tax Credit and the Working Income Tax Benefit, or in some provinces through provincial refundable tax credits. Families with children under age 6 may also be in receipt of Universal Child Care Benefits (UCCB), regardless of income.

3. To transfer taxable assets from one taxpayer to another.

ESSENTIAL TAX FACT | Even those with little or no taxable income should file a return to receive lucrative refundable tax credits.

Refundable tax credits can be increased by reducing family net income; that's the combined amount from line 236 of the tax return of each spouse. You may wish to check back at the income ceilings at which those credits are clawed back in Chapter 2, to refresh your memory.

Family net income can be reduced in a number of ways, including the splitting of income sources with other dependants, but one of the most popular ways, is to make a contribution to an RRSP. This can still be done within 60 days after the end of the tax year, thereby making it possible to create higher refundable tax credits in the current "benefit year" which runs from July 1 to June 30, as the CRA determines the level of the credits based on the immediately prior tax year.

When you miss this important opportunity to reduce family net income, you are subject to very high marginal tax rates because of the clawback of your refundable tax credits—which can be as high as 33.3%. If it's too late for this year, be sure to get a handle on those clawback zones for next year and plan to contribute to an RRSP or make more of the other deductions the reduce net income on the tax return:

Deductions that Reduce Net Income

- Contributions to employer-sponsored Registered Pension Plans (RPPs)
- Contributions to RRSPs
- Elected split pension amount
- Union and professional dues
- Universal child care benefit repayments
- Child care expenses
- Disability supports deduction
- Business Investment Losses
- Moving expenses
- Spousal support payments
- Carrying charges and interest expenses
- Deductions for the CPP contributions on self-employment income
- Exploration and development expenses
- Clergy residence deductions
- Other deductions like certain legal fees or social benefit repayments
- Clawbacks of Employment Insurance and Old Age Security benefits

> **ESSENTIAL TAX FACT** | A "taxable income" is the figure upon which federal and provincial taxes are calculated. However, a low "net income" is your goal if you want to increase the refundable and non-refundable tax credits your family will be entitled to.

CHAPTER 13

WHAT NON-REFUNDABLE TAX CREDITS APPLY TO US?

While refundable tax credits are automatically calculated by government and sent directly to Canadian homes, or electronically into your bank accounts when you file family tax returns, non-refundable tax credits must be proactively chosen on your tax return. These credits will reduce your taxes payable, so are really not of benefit to you unless you have taxable income.

You should be familiar with many of them because, if you are an employee, your employer will require you to indicate which ones you qualify for so that he or she can reduce your tax withholdings to reflect the costs of caring for family members. These credits also include amounts to account for special expenditures like public transit costs, amounts paid for children's arts or fitness activities, medical expenses and charitable donations.

These credits are totaled on Schedule 1 and then multiplied by the lowest tax rate, which is the real dollar value in reducing taxes payable.

To begin understanding these credits better, so that you can claim more of them if you qualify, know that every Canadian resident qualifies for the Basic Personal Amount, which is indexed for inflation each year on the federal tax return. The provinces extend tax reductions through personal amounts as well, but here the two tax system part ways, with several provinces embellishing on the tax credits, or deciding on their own whether or not to index them for inflation.

One of the hallmarks of family income splitting is to ensure that everyone in the family makes enough taxable income to use up their Basic Personal Amount each year. You have learned that this amount is not transferable, nor may it be carried forward to a future tax year if you don't need it this year. Therefore, using up this "tax-free zone" is an important way for each member of the family to earn tax-free income.

Let's review now, some of the more common non-refundable tax credits claimed by supporting individuals for their family members, all of which increase tax-free zones:

Amount for spouse or common-law partner. The definition of who is your spouse has been previously defined as someone to whom you are legally married or if not, a person of the same or opposite sex with whom you lived in a relationship throughout a continuous 12-month period, or someone who, at the end of the tax year, was the actual or adoptive parent of your child. It has been noted that separations of less than 90 days do not affect the 12-month period.

The net income for the whole year for this person with whom you live in a conjugal relationship is taken into account in making the claim.

> **ESSENTIAL TAX FACT** | A non-refundable tax credit of over $2,000 is available for each child under 18 at the end of the year who is the child of the taxpayer or his/her spouse or common-law partner.

Amount for eligible children under 18. Look for this credit on Schedule 1. The full amount of this credit can be claimed for the entire year including the year of birth, death or adoption, even if these life events happened right at the end of the year. Also know that:

- Either parent may claim the credit.
- Unused credits can be transferred between spouses and common-law partners.
- Where parents are estranged, the credit can be claimed only by the parent who would be eligible to claim the "eligible dependant credit" if that child were the parent's only child.
- Unused credits cannot be carried forward.

An equivalent-to-spouse or amount for "eligible" dependant is possible if you were single, separated, divorced, or widowed and supporting a dependant if these rules are followed:

- only one person can claim the amount for an eligible dependant in respect of the same dependant,
- no one may claim the amount for an eligible dependant if someone else is claiming the amount for spouse or common-law partner for that dependant,

- only one claim may be made for the amount for an eligible dependant for the same home,
- where more than one taxpayer qualifies to make the claim, the taxpayers must agree who will make the claim or no one will be allowed to,
- if a claim for the amount for an eligible dependant is made in respect of a dependant, no one may claim the "Amount for Infirm Dependants" or the "Caregiver Amount" in respect of the same dependant.

Amount for infirm dependant adults. If you support a dependant who is:

- at least 18 years of age, and
- dependent on you because of mental or physical infirmity,

you may claim certain tax credits in respect of that dependant. To qualify, the dependant must be:

- the child or grandchild of you or your spouse or common-law partner, or
- the parent, grandparent, brother, sister, uncle, aunt, niece or nephew of you or your spouse or common-law partner and resident in Canada at any time in the year.

> **ESSENTIAL TAX FACT** | The terms "infirm" or "infirmity" as indicated in CRA's Interpretation Bulletin IT-513, means "lacking muscle or mental strength or vitality".

These definitions will help you co-ordinate tax filing requirements for the whole family—spouse or common-law partner, minor and adult dependants.

Other important non-refundable tax credits that may be claimed by family units are all shown on Schedule 1 of the T1 general return and in the information in Part 1 of this book. Please review them carefully; they will be discussed in more detail later in the book.

CHAPTER 14

WHAT IS FAMILY INCOME SPLITTING?

ESSENTIAL TAX FACT | If you gift or transfer money or assets to your spouse or minor children, any income earned on the transferred asset is usually "attributed back" to you (transferor) and added to your income.

Canadians are taxed as individuals, not as economic units or households. Because of the advantages of income splitting under our progressive tax system with its graduated tax rates—that is, the more you earn the higher your rate of tax—we are generally prohibited from obtaining a tax advantage by splitting income with family members. The details are set out in the Income Tax Act and known as the Attribution Rules. Specifically, here is what you need to know:

- **Transfers and loans to spouse or common-law partner.** If you transfer or loan property either directly or indirectly, by means of a trust or any other means to a spouse or common-law partner for that person's benefit, any resulting income or loss or capital gain or loss from that property is taxable to you.

- **Transfers and loans to minors.** Where property is transferred or loaned either directly or indirectly to a person who is under 18 and who does not deal with you at arm's length or who is your niece or nephew, the income or loss resulting from such property is reported by you until the transferee attains 18 years of age. Capital gains or losses do not, however, attribute back to you.

These rules thwart an otherwise perfect investment opportunity: the transfer of assets from the higher earner to the lower earners in the family to take advantage of income splitting so that tax on income is paid at lower tax brackets, leading to lower overall family taxes payable.

However, where there are rules, there are exceptions, which is true of the Attribution Rules as well. But, let's cover off the tax filing basics on income splitting first:

ESSENTIAL TAX FACTS | Asset Transfers to the Spouse:
- Assets transferred to a spouse will result in the income and capital gains resulting from investment of those assets being taxed in the transferor's hands.
- Where a spouse guarantees the repayment of a loan to a spouse, made for investment purposes, attribution will apply to any income earned from the loaned funds.

ESSENTIAL TAX FACTS | Asset Transfers to a Minor Child:
- Income resulting from assets transferred to a minor child will trigger attribution of rental, dividend or interest income, but not capital gains.

Exceptions to the Attribution Rules:
- **Tax-Free Savings Accounts.** If you make contributions to a Tax-Free Savings Account for your spouse or adult children they will earn income on those deposits with no income tax payable, either by them or by you, so long as the contribution is a true gift and not a scheme to allow you to earn that income on a tax-free basis. These earnings will have no effect on your ability to claim the Spousal Amount.
- **Spousal RRSPs.** Attribution does not apply to contributions made to a spousal RRSP, unless there is a withdrawal within three years. This is discussed in greater detail in the next chapter.
- **Wages paid to spouse and children.** Where a spouse or children receive a wage from the family business, the attribution rules won't apply if the wage is reasonable, and is included in the recipient's income.
- **Interest income from Child Tax Benefit (CTB) or Universal Child Care Benefit (UCCB) payments.** If CTB or UCCB payments are invested in the name of a child, the income will not be subject to attribution. In other words, interest, dividends and other investment income may be reported in the hands of the child. Be sure this account remains untainted by birthday money and other gifts.

ESSENTIAL TAX FACT | The Attribution Rules will apply to joint accounts held by parents and minor children as well as spouses.

- **Joint accounts.** T5 Slips are issued by banks in the names of the account holders to report earnings on investments including interest and dividends. This does not mean that the income on those slips is taxable to those whose names are on the slips. Instead, report income on the return of the individuals who contributed the funds to the account in the proportion that the funds were supplied. For example, if only one spouse in a family works and is the source of all of the deposits, then all of the interest earned on the account is taxable to that person, no matter whose name is on the account.

- **Property transfers to a spouse.** A special rule applies when property is transferred to a spouse. Normally, such property transfers at tax cost, so that no gain or loss arises. This is true even if the spouse pays fair value for the property. The property will not transfer at tax cost, but at fair market value, provided the transferor files an election to have this happen with the tax return for the year of transfer. Unless this election is made, the attribution rules will apply to the property, even if the spouse has paid fair value consideration.

- **Transfers for fair market consideration.** The Attribution Rules will not apply to any income, gain or loss from transferred property if, at the time of transfer, consideration was paid for the equivalent of fair market value for the transferred property by the transferee. The person acquiring the property must use his or her own capital to pay for it.

- **Transfers for indebtedness.** The Attribution Rules on investment income will not apply if the lower income spouse borrowed capital from the higher earner, and the parties signed a bona fide loan that bore an interest rate which is at least the lesser of:
  - the "prescribed" interest rates in effect at the time the indebtedness was incurred and
  - the rate that would have been charged by a commercial lender.

ESSENTIAL TAX FACT | The prescribed interest rate used in establishing bona fide inter-spousal loans is set quarterly by the CRA. It is based on average yields of 90-day Treasury Bills for the first month of the preceding quarter.

- **Payment of interest on inter-spousal loans.** Interest must actually be paid on the indebtedness incurred by the spouse, under a formal loan agreement described above, by January 30 of each year, following the tax year, or attribution will apply to income earned with the loaned funds.

- **When spouses live apart.** If spouses are living separate and apart due to relationship breakdown, they can jointly elect to have Attribution Rules not apply to the period in which they were living apart. The Attribution Rules do not apply after a divorce is finalized.
- **Assignment of Canada Pension Plan Benefits.** It is possible to apply to split CPP benefits between spouses, thereby minimizing tax on that income source in some cases.
- **Pension income splitting.** The election to split pension income between spouses does not involve the actual transfer of funds from one spouse to another but an election to have the split pension taxed as if it were the other spouse's income. As such, the attribution rules do not apply. (However, if funds are actually transferred from one spouse to the other, the attribution rules will apply to any income earned on the transferred funds).
- **Investments in spouse's business.** Investments in the spouse's or common-law partner's business venture are not subject to Attribution Rules as the resulting income is business income rather than income from property.
- **Second generation earnings.** Where the income earned on property transferred to the spouse must be reported by the transferor, any secondary income earned on investing the earnings is taxed in the hands of the transferee.
- **Spousal dividend transfers.** One spouse may report dividends received from taxable Canadian corporations received by the other spouse if by doing so a Spousal Amount is created or increased.
- **Inheritances.** Attribution does not apply to inheritances.
- **Assets transferred to an adult child (over 18).** This will, in general, not be subject to attribution. However, when income splitting is the main reason for the loan to an adult child, the income will be attributed back to the transferor. An exception again occurs when a bona fide loan is drawn up with interest payable as described above, by January 30 of the year following the end of the calendar year.
- **The kiddie tax.** The Attribution Rules will not apply when an amount is included in the calculation of Tax on Split Income on Line 424 on Schedule 1 of the tax return. This special tax is assessed on income earned by minor children from their parents' or other relatives' ventures. Specifically, dividends or shareholder benefits earned either directly or through a trust or partnership, from a corporation controlled by someone related to the child, are extracted from the normal tax calculations and reported on Form T1206 so that tax on this income can be calculated at the highest marginal rates, thereby eliminating any tax benefits of such an arrangement. Beginning in 2011, capital gains on the sale of shares in the business are also subject to the kiddie tax.

- Additional Attribution Avoidance Strategies:
  - Have the higher income spouse pay household and personal expenses, and the lower income spouse acquire investment assets with income earned in his or her own right.
  - Reinvest spouse's income tax refunds and refundable tax credits.
  - Contribute to an RESP for your child. Accumulate education savings on a tax-deferred basis, as discussed later.

CHAPTER 15

TAX PLANNING: WHY THE RRSP IS SO IMPORTANT

For the vast majority of working taxpayers and their families, the most powerful, tax efficient investment is the RRSP. It plays many roles in building family wealth, as we will explain below. But let's begin by comparing it to our tax sheltered investments.

From an income perspective, it's tough to beat the advantages of the Tax-Free Savings Account (TFSA), because all your earnings will remain tax-free, while the money is in the account and after when you withdraw your earnings, too. However, the savings you invest in that plan is money upon which someone in the family has likely already paid taxes. Also, your annual investment is limited to a maximum of $5000, and some indexing, depending on future inflation rates.

Investments in Registered Education Savings Plan (RESP) and the Registered Disability Savings Plan (RDSP) are also important tax shelters. In the case of the RESP and the RDSP, the government adds grants and bonds to sweeten the investment. Free money is always a good thing and so that's an important advantage to be considered, too. Again, funding for these plans comes from tax-paid savings, and there are contribution maximums to consider.

None of these three plans will help you decrease your family's tax burden today, however, nor will they help you maximize social benefits. That's where the RRSP can really pull rank. If you want to accumulate savings, grow your money exponentially, and maximize all the family tax filing benefits available to you, it pays to invest in an RRSP, because it reduces both net and taxable income, as further explained below.

To participate, you do need to be age-eligible (under age 72—or have a spouse under 72) and have the required "unused contribution room." This room can only be created by filing a tax return, and the taxpayer must earn the requisite "earned income" sources; most commonly, income from employment, and self employment, in the previous tax year. The actual contribution is limited to 18% of earned income to an annual dollar maximum.

There are four main benefits to the family in making an RRSP contribution:

- **Decreased taxes for each individual.** A tax deduction is created for the RRSP contribution made to the plan, up to your available contribution room. That deduction will reduce the taxpayer's net income. It can be carried forward to a future year, too, if income is too low for tax benefits this year. That's a powerful coup in cases where incomes fluctuate (seasonal employment/self-employment, commission sales, bonus, severance receipts). However because this contribution is not indexed to inflation, it pays to use it sooner rather than later.

- **Increased social benefits and preserved monthly income.** The reduction in net income will ultimately trickle down to reduce taxes payable. Where applicable, the reduction in a taxpayer's net income will also increase social benefits received from federal and provincial refundable tax credits or the Old Age Security, by decreasing clawbacks. Retirees and others on fixed income sources will want to plan to receive all the credits and benefits they possibly can and an RRSP can help. Those on Employment Insurance may be subject to clawbacks of that income source too in some cases. Again an RRSP can help preserve that income.

- **Tax deferred income growth.** The income earned on the principal invested loses its identity within the plan, in that the whole amount—principal and earnings—will be taxed as income on withdrawal. It's important to plan for that early—with the first dollar invested—to withdraw the money over a longer period of time and average down tax rate exposure. However, while in the plan, the earnings are not taxable, providing for a tax deferral and an opportunity for more rapid growth than if the funds were held outside this registered account.

- **Tax leveraging.** The tax savings generated by the RRSP contribution will be in the double-digit zones, depending on the taxpayer's marginal tax rates and these large and immediate tax savings can be leveraged into other tax efficient investments. Deposits to a TFSA make the most sense first, as they can accumulate tax-free forever—and there is no upper age barrier. This means seniors who are age ineligible for RRSP purpose, can shelter at least some savings in the TFSA.

- **Debt management.** In other cases, advisors and clients will want to review paying off debt that results in high, non-deductible interest

- **More retirement savings—but home buyers and students benefit too.** By making another RRSP contribution, which leads to a bigger tax refund and more new capital for investment purposes, taxpayers can continue to build wealth for the future in retirement. However, in other cases, the RRSP can be used to supplement home ownership and education on a tax-free basis, by allowing tax-free withdrawals under the Home Buyer's Plan and the Lifelong Learning Plan. That makes it a versatile and important investment for taxpayers of all ages.

RRSP room is very valuable. A taxpayer's contribution room is decreased by any RRSP contributions deducted in the year. If the contribution room earned is not used in the year, the unused RRSP contribution room may be accumulated and carried forward for use in the future.

> **ESSENTIAL TAX FACT** | Unused RRSP contribution room can be an important bonus in reducing net income for retirees who are no longer age-eligible for RRSP contributions if they have a spouse who is under age 72.

There is no lower age limit for contributing to an RRSP; however, the RRSP must be collapsed by the end of the year in which the taxpayer turns 71. Therefore, in addition to the requirement for contribution room, in order to be eligible to contribute to his own RRSP, a taxpayer must be under 71 years of age. However, it's still possible to fund a spousal RRSP, if your spouse is younger and you have RRSP room.

Remember, careful planning is required when you withdraw funds from the RRSP account so that you avoid unusual spikes to marginal tax rates (and an incrementally higher erosion of the capital invested) or a clawback of Old Age Security or other benefits. Talk about income splitting between spouses along the way to avoid this, and therefore a discussion on whether the money should go into a spousal RRSP is most important, together with the optimal age to start making those withdrawals.

In the meantime, don't miss out on claiming increased tax refunds as a result of your RRSP contribution.

> **ESSENTIAL TAX FACT** | Put more money in your family's saving funds all year long by reducing your withholding taxes as a result of your RRSP contributions. Ask your tax advisor about filing Form T1213 to do so.

CHAPTER 16

EDUCATION PLANNING:
WHY THE RESP IS SO IMPORTANT

A Registered Education Savings Plan (RESP) is a tax-assisted savings plan set up for the purposes of funding a beneficiary's future education costs. It also serves as a way to split income earned in the plan with the beneficiary, who will be taxed at a lower rate than the contributor, as a general rule, when earnings are withdrawn.

A contributor can invest up to $50,000 per beneficiary as a lifetime maximum. Annual contribution limits in place prior to 2007 are no longer in effect however, government contributions are maximized if contributions are spread over time rather than in one lump sum.

The following rules apply to RESPs:
- The plan must terminate after 35 years (unless the beneficiary is disabled).
- Minor siblings can substitute as plan beneficiaries if the intended beneficiary does not become a qualifying recipient.

Transfers may be made between RESPs with no income tax consequences. In fact, tax-free transfers between individual Registered Retirement Savings Plans (RESPs) for the benefit of siblings will now be allowed without triggering the repayment of Canada Education Savings Grants (CESGs) so long as the beneficiary of the recipient plan is less than 21 years old at the time of the transfer. This change applies to asset transfers after 2010.

ESSENTIAL TAX FACT | The Canada Education Savings Grant and Bonds sweeten the tax advantages under the RESP.

There are several tax advantages to an RESP investment. The subscriber, who contributes money into the plan, does not receive a tax deduction at the time of investment. However, income earned within the plan on the contributions is tax-deferred until the beneficiary student qualifies to receive education assistance from the plan by starting to attend post-secondary school, either on a part-time or on a full-time basis.

The **Canada Education Savings Grant** provides additional funds for education. This grant is added to the RESP each year by the Department of Human Resources and Skills Development. The grant is received on a tax-free basis by the plan. Started in 1998, it provides for a federal grant of 20% of the first $2,500 contributed to an RESP for children under the age of 18. The lifetime maximum CESG is $7,200.

To receive the money, the beneficiary of the RESP must have a Social Insurance Number. The CESG room of up to $500 a year (20% of $2,500) can be maximized each year including the year the child turns 17. Unused CESG contribution room can be carried forward until the child turns 18, however, the grant may not exceed $1,000 a year. This means that the catch-up of the grants is limited to two years at a time so it's better to make contributions each year rather than in a lump sum.

An additional CESG is available if the family net income is low enough. For families with net income below $41,544, an additional grant is 20% of the first $500 deposited (maximum $100 addiitonal grant). For families with net incomes between $41,544 and $83,088, the additional grant is 10% of the first $500 deposited (maximum $50 additional grant).

ESSENTIAL TAX FACT | A Canada Learning Bond increases RESP savings for lower income families.

The Canada Learning Bond. The first time a child becomes eligible to receive benefits under the National Child Benefit, which is part of the Child Tax Benefit calculations, an initial Canada Learning Bond entitlement of $500 is available. This will generally happen under one of two circumstances:
- the year of birth or
- a subsequent year if the family net income is too high in the year of birth.

The entitlement is $100 in each subsequent year that the family qualifies for the NCB until the year the child turns 15. Once 16, the CLB is no longer allocated to the child.

In order to turn the entitlement into real money, the Canada Learning Bond must be transferred into a Registered Education Saving Plan (RESP) for the benefit of the child. This can be done at any time before the child turns 21. If the CLB is not transferred to an RESP by the time the child turns 21, the entitlement will be lost.

The Canada Learning Bond transfers to an RESP do not otherwise affect the limits of contributions to the RESP and CLB amounts are not eligible for the Canada Education Savings Grant. No interest is paid on unclaimed Canada Learning Bonds so it is important that the CLB be transferred to an RESP as quickly as possible so that the amount can begin to earn income within the plan.

In the year the child is born, if the parents are eligible for the National Child Benefit Supplement, the parents should:
- obtain a social insurance number for the child (required for an RESP)
- open an RESP account with the new child as beneficiary*
- apply to have the Canada Learning Bond amount transferred to the new RESP.

* An extra $25 will be paid with the first $500 bond to help cover the cost of opening an RESP.

Education Assistance Payments. When a student is ready to go to post-secondary school full time, payments can be made out of an RESP. These are called Education Assistance Payments (EAPs). The amounts represent earnings in the plan and are taxable to the student on Line 130 of the return. The actual contributions may be either returned to the subscriber or paid to the student with no income tax consequences. The CESG will form part of the EAPs.

For full-time studies, the maximum EAP is $5,000 until the student has completed 13 consecutive weeks in a qualifying education program at a post-secondary educational institution. Once the 13 weeks have been completed, there is no limit to the amount that may be withdrawn from the plan.

For part-time students, who spend a minimum of 12 hours a month on course-work, the maximum EAP is $2,500 per 13-week semester. Beneficiaries under an RESP are allowed to receive EAPs for up to six months after ceasing enrolment in a qualifying educational program. However, if, for a period of 12 months, the student does not enroll in a qualifying education program, the 13-week period and the $5,000 limitation will be imposed again.

ESSENTIAL TAX FACT | Beginning in 2011, the 13-week period for full-time students is reduced to 3 weeks for students studying outside Canada.

If amounts are withdrawn from the RESP for purposes other than EAP payments, the lesser of the undistributed CESG amounts and 20% of the amount withdrawn will be returned to the Department of Human Resources by the RESP. Should the beneficiary be required to repay any CESG amounts received as Educational Assistance Payments, a deduction for the amount repaid may be taken.

Accumulated Income Payments. If the student does not attend post-secondary school by the time s/he reaches the age of 31, and there are no qualifying substitute beneficiaries, the contributions can go back to the original subscriber. If this happens, the income earned in the plan over the years will become taxable to the subscriber, and the income is subject to a special penalty tax of 20% in addition to the regular taxes payable. Such income inclusions are called "Accumulated Income Payments" or AIPs. Form T1172 must be completed to compute this tax.

As an alternative, if the subscriber has unused RRSP contribution room, AIPs can be transferred into the subscriber's RRSP, up to a lifetime maximum of $50,000. If amounts are transferred to an RRSP, Form T1171 may be used to reduce or eliminate tax withheld on the AIP.

You may want to consider using a Tax-Free Savings Account as an adjunct to an RESP for accumulating funds for your adult child's education. Although the TFSA does not have the added incentives of the CESG or CESB, it does offer flexibility that is not available in the RESP. There are no time limits on the contributions, no age limits on the beneficiaries, and no limits to the amount that can be withdrawn in any given year, and the withdrawals will not have to be reported in income—whether the beneficiary becomes a student or not.

ESSENTIAL TAX FACT | It takes a village to raise a family. The RESP and its related CESGs and CESBs provide a tax sheltered opportunity for family members to help the young with education, an investment which will result, statistically, in higher individual earnings and wealth accumulation.

Part IV
Tax Efficient Employment

CHAPTER 17

HOW IS INCOME FROM EMPLOYMENT TAXED?

"I've got just a simple tax return—garbage in, garbage out." Tax practitioners usually smile at this comment by employees with one T4 slip. In fact, it's employment income on line 101 of the tax return, that links to more line of deductions and credits than any other on the tax return. Employment tax status is anything but simple, unless you want to keep overpaying your taxes.

> **ESSENTIAL TAX FACT** | Employees are restricted in the types of deductions they can claim, but many tax advantages from bonuses, tax-free and taxable perks, health care, education, retirement savings, severance packages and even death benefits can be included in your compensation.

By investing in yourself, your company, and the tax benefits available to employees under the tax system, you'll kick start your own wealth creation, by leveraging the lower-taxed corporate dollars available to build compensation with. But you need to know some tax basics first. CRA defines an employer-employee relationship as follows:

> "A verbal or written agreement in which an employee agrees to work on a full-time or part-time basis for a specified or indeterminate period of time, in return for salary or wages. The employer has the right to decide where, when and how the work will be done. In this type of relationship a contract of service exists."

The employer has several obligations to you to meet in this relationship. An employer is required by law to make statutory deductions from your gross pay for contributions to the Canada Pension Plan (CPP), Employment Insurance (EI) and Income Taxes (IT).

These are usually remitted once a month, although very small businesses have the option to remit each quarter. Minors need not contribute to the Canada Pension Plan; nor do those over 70 (except in Quebec) or those who are in receipt of CPP benefits. This last rule for CPP recipients is changing in 2012—see Part 5 for details.

Everyone who is employed must contribute to EI; that is, there is no age limit. Employees who earn $2,000 or less from employment will have their premiums refunded when they file their tax returns.

Know your T4 slip. Your employer must prepare a T4 slip for each employee and issue it to the employee by the end of February each year, for use in filing the income tax return. One copy is remitted to CRA at this time as well. But that T4 slip can contain much more information that's required to file an accurate tax return:

- Commission income against which employment expenses can be claimed
- Deductible union or professional dues
- Deductible contributions to company pension plans
- Creditable charitable donations
- Creditable medical premiums to private health care plans
- Perks that can be offset with tax deductions like the Northern Residents Deductions, auto expenses, carrying charges for low-interest investment loan benefits, Securities Options Deductions, Home Relocation Loan Deductions, RRSP contributions and rollovers, deductions for Worker's Compensation Benefits received, and so on.
- Volunteer firefighters will see a new box for 2011 showing their exempt income from firefighting. This amount will limit access to the new Volunteer Firefighter's Tax Credit.

These notations on your T4 slip will lead you to specific deductions or credits on your tax return, so you should find out more about them, or remind your tax practitioner to explain them to you.

> **ESSENTIAL TAX FACT** | If you didn't get your T4 slip or after attempting to secure it, find you can't because your employer is insolvent or gone, you must estimate your income and source deductions in filing your return. Include a note describing why you had to do this.

Minimizing your tax withholding. You may be familiar with the TD1 *Personal Tax Credit Return*. It's a form you'll complete every time you start a new job, to let your employer know how much income tax to withhold from your pay. It is based on non-refundable tax credits you are entitled to, like your basic personal amount, spousal amount, amount for dependent children, caregiver amounts, tuition and education amounts, and special deductions like the deduction for Northern Residents. The purpose of the form is for you to direct your employer to recognize the increased tax deductions and credits you are entitled to and to take these into account when computing how much tax to withhold from your pay.

> **ESSENTIAL TAX FACT** | Proper completion of the TD1 *Personal Tax Credit Return* and its sister, Form T1213 *Request to Reduce Tax Deductions at Source*, will help you pay the right amount of tax all year long.

This form, however, won't take into account other tax deductible expenditures you may have; for example RRSP contributions, deductible spousal support, significant interest costs, rental losses, child care, commission sales or other expenses of employment, medical expenses or large charitable donations. If you're eligible for any of these deductions or credits, file Form T1213 *Request to Reduce Tax Deductions at Source* so that your employer can further reduce withholding taxes and increase your take-home pay.

Grab these forms off the internet, from your human resource department, or ask your tax or financial advisors to help you. Then use legal tax provisions to accumulate more wealth.

Begin by adjusting source deductions for income taxes on each payroll period to take into account the deductible portion of employee contributions to Registered Pension Plans (RPPs) and Registered Retirement Savings Plans (RRSPs).

> **ESSENTIAL TAX FACT** | Reduce your withholding taxes whenever possible. Less tax will be taken from your earnings—a wise move— especially if you prefer to use your hard earned wages to pay off non-deductible credit card debt, your mortgage, or invest in a TFSA or RRSP.

CHAPTER 18

WHAT BENEFITS SHOULD YOU NEGOTIATE FOR?

ESSENTIAL TAX FACT | Many employees fail to accumulate wealth because they allow for too much tax to be taken at source; another reason is they don't diversify their income sources.

We have shown you how to take control of more of the first employment dollars you earn—your gross income. If you want to become wealthy, it's important to reframe your thinking around your master-servant relationship with your employer. You can earn equity as well as employment income, with proper tax planning. Again, there are just a few basics you'll need to know in negotiating a better employment contract.

Remember that when you are employed the taxman benefits every two weeks, by taking a share of your labor right off the top. When you have the opportunity to invest in stocks, bonds and other securities including shares in your employer's company, the taxman must wait for his share. In fact, done well, he may have to wait decades to benefit from the accrued growth in value of these income-producing assets.

There are several sources of employment income within a master-servant relationship:

- Income from salary or wages, which is taxable in the year received
- Director's fees (these are subject to CPP but not EI premiums)
- Employee Benefit Plans like a self-funded leave of absence

- The value of benefits or perks, including your car, vacations, education, uniforms, meals, memberships to fitness clubs, and so on. Some of these benefits are taxable, some are not.

Employment income is always reported on the cash basis—when received. You will also report your employment income on a calendar year basis—January to December—in every case. Sometimes, an opportunity for salary or income deferral to a following year may be available.

Salary deferral arrangements. Under a salary deferral arrangement, receipt of salary or wages is postponed into the future; generally the next tax year. However, here's a trap: the deferred amount is generally included in income in the current year or year of contribution—which means that no tax deferral is actually allowed.

Sabbaticals. In addition, however, it is possible to defer salary or wages for a self-funded leave or sabbatical. The employee who saves in this way will not be subject to tax in the year the leave is earned as long as salary is deferred for no more than 6 years and no more than ⅓ of the salary is deferred. The leave of absence must start no later than the 7th year and must be for a period of at least six months. The employee must then return to work for at least the same amount of time as the leave. The amounts are taxable in the year withdrawn.

Employee benefit plans. You should also be aware that there are numerous types of employee benefit plans available. Often the employee will not be taxed when contributions are made to these types of plans but benefits received from them are generally taxable when received.

Tax-deferred plans include registered pension plans, group sickness or accident plans, supplementary employment plans, deferred profit sharing plans, wage loss replacement plans, and certain employee trusts.

Therefore, while employment income is usually taxable as received, a few special tax preferences exist to help the employee defer some compensation into the future. Tap into this wherever you can. But start with a good, long term contract and a substantial perk package.

Negotiate the perk package. In turbulent times, when employment situations change, there is also opportunity. Your next employer may be open to negotiating for both cash and perks of value to you and your family.

ESSENTIAL TAX FACT | Besides your salary or wage, which is reported on Line 101 of the tax return—from Box 14 of the T4 slip—it is possible to earn taxable or tax-free benefits in your employment package.

Taxable benefits. Taxable benefits that may be available to you include the following:

- Board and lodging
- Rent-free and low-rent housing
- Travel benefits for the employee and his/her family
- Personal use of an employer-provided vehicle
- The value of holidays, prizes, and other awards
- Frequent flyer program points used for personal use if earned on business trips, where employer controls the points
- Premiums under provincial hospital plans
- Interest-free or low-interest loans
- The cost of relocation benefits, for example, reimbursement for losses suffered on sale of an old residence, but only one half the amounts over $15,000 must be added to income.

Taxable benefits are considered to be part of your remuneration and are already included in income in Box 14 of the T4 slip when you file your tax return in the spring, so there is no need to add them to income again when you prepare a return. This is a common tax filing error.

You should also know that certain taxable benefits qualify for deductions on the tax return. These include:

- **Housing, board and lodging.** The taxable benefit will include a cleric's housing allowance, rent-free or low-rent apartments provided to care-takers or subsidized meals or travel in a prescribed zone or for medical travel. Board and lodging provided at a remote or special worksite can be received tax-free, however. Offsetting deductions may be included for clerics and those who qualify for the northern residents' deduction.

> **ESSENTIAL TAX FACT** | Employees who use their company car less than 50% for business should discuss the reduction of standby charges with their payroll department.

- **Personal use of employer's auto.** An automobile "standby charge" taxable benefit recognizes the personal use component of an employer-provided vehicle. It is calculated at 2 per cent per month of the original cost of the vehicle where the employer owns the vehicle, or two-thirds of the lease payment for leased vehicles. However, for car sales persons the benefit is 1½%.
- **Operating costs.** Amounts paid for the operation of the employer's vehicle will also be taxable as a benefit, unless they are reimbursed by the employee within 45 days after the end of the tax year. The benefit is determined as a

flat per kilometre rate, regardless of how or how much the employer paid for the expenses. This rate is announced every year in December. Alternatively, the benefit can be assessed at one half the normal stand-by charge.

- **Reduction in standby charges.** It is possible that the employee may offset this benefit with a claim for Employment Expenses using Form T777 *Employment Expenses* or through a reduction in standby charges if personal driving is less than 20,000 kilometres per year and the car is used more than 50% of the time for employment.

- **Interest-free loans and low interest loans.** A deduction for the benefit enjoyed from an employer-provided loan will be allowed if you use the loan for investment purposes. This might result, for example, if you borrowed to invest in company shares. This is a great way to participate in the growth in equity of the company, which you are investing so much of your personal effort into.

- **Employee home relocation loan deduction.** A deduction may be possible on Line 248 for amount paid to the employee when home relocation is required by the employer. When your employer provides you with a low-interest home relocation loan, the difference between the prescribed rate at the time the loan was made and the loan rate is a taxable benefit. If the loan is outstanding after five years, the current prescribed rate is substituted. In each of the first five years of the loan, you are entitled to a deduction for the taxable benefit on the first $25,000 of that loan.

- **Security options deductions.** A deduction may be possible on Line 249 for those who have generated a taxable benefit from employee stock option purchases and disposals. There have been recent changes to the rules for those who participate in these lucrative plans. For options exercised before March 4, 2010, the taxable benefit could be postponed until the optioned securities were disposed of. For options exercised after March 4, 2010, the taxable benefit will be included in income in the year that the option is exercised and the employee will be eligible for a security options deduction equal to one-half of the taxable benefit in that same year.

- **Other taxable benefits**, including amounts included in income for health or educational benefits received may qualify for non-refundable credits on the personal tax return—such as medical expenses or tuition, education and textbook amounts.

- **Cost of tools.** Where your employer makes payments to offset the cost of tools required to perform your work, the amount of the payment must be included in income. However, an offsetting deduction may be allowed for the cost of tools for a trades-person or an apprentice.

ESSENTIAL TAX FACT | Employment Commissions included in income may be offset by Employment Expenses on Line 229 and the GST/HST Rebate on Line 457 under certain conditions.

We will discuss this subject in more detail later in this part of the book.

Tax-free benefits. It's possible to earn tax-free benefits, too. This can be a very lucrative way to improve your lifestyle, your income-earning capacity and your personal net worth. For example, consider the following:

ESSENTIAL TAX FACT | Employer-paid education costs may be received tax-free.

Employer-paid educational costs. You are not taxed when training is paid for by your employer for courses taken primarily for the benefit of the employer. However, a taxable benefit arises when the training is primarily for your personal benefit. Amounts included in your income for tuition will be eligible for the tuition tax credit if they would have been eligible had they been paid by you personally.

Financial counselling and income tax return preparation. Financial counselling services or income tax return preparation provided directly or indirectly by an employer normally produce a taxable benefit. However, financial counselling services in respect of your re-employment or retirement will not result in a taxable benefit. This is important during difficult financial times when employees are forced to accept an early retirement package or a layoff. Be sure to ask for these services.

ESSENTIAL TAX FACT | Frequent Flyer Points used personally by an employee may not be a taxable benefit.

Frequent Flyer Points. Up until 2009, CRA took the position that where you accumulate frequent flyer points while travelling on employer-paid business trips and used them to obtain air travel or other benefits for personal use by you or your family, the fair market value of such air travel or other benefits must be included in your income. For 2009 and subsequent years, the CRA no longer requires frequent flyer points earned why flying on business to be included in an employee's income, so long as:

- the points are not converted to cash
- the plan or arrangement is not indicative of an alternate form of remuneration, or
- the plan or arrangement is not for tax avoidance purposes.

Where an employer controls the points (e.g., a company credit card), the employer will continue to be required to report the fair market value of any benefits received by the employee as income on the employee's T4 slip when the points are redeemed.

> **ESSENTIAL TAX FACT** | An employee can receive any number of non-cash gifts from the employer, up to a value of $500 annually, tax-free. Gifts containing corporate logos may have no tax consequences.

Gifts under $500. A gift (either in cash or in kind) from your employer is an employment benefit. However non-cash gifts and non-cash awards to an arm's length employee, that is someone not related to the employer, regardless of the number of them, are non-taxable to the extent that the total aggregate value of all non-cash gifts and awards to that employee for the year is less than $500. The total value in excess of $500 annually will be taxable.

In addition, a separate non-cash long service/anniversary award may also qualify for non-taxable status to the extent its total value is $500 or less. The value in excess of $500 will be taxable. In order to qualify, the anniversary award cannot be for less than five years of service or for five years since the last long service award had been provided to the employee.

For the purposes of applying the $500 thresholds, the annual gifts and awards threshold and the long service/anniversary awards threshold are separate.

Items of an immaterial or nominal value, such as coffee, tea, T-shirts with employer logos, mugs, plaques, trophies, etc., will not be considered a taxable benefit to employees. There is no defined monetary threshold that determines an immaterial amount. Factors that may be taken into account include the value, frequency, and administrative practicability of accounting for nominal benefits.

Overtime meals and allowances. Beginning with tax year 2009 the CRA considers no taxable benefit to arise if:

- the value of the meal or meal allowance is reasonable (a value of up to $17 will generally be considered reasonable),
- the employee works two or more hours of overtime right before or right after his or her scheduled hours of work, and
- the overtime is infrequent and occasional in nature. Less than three times a week will generally be considered infrequent or occasional. This condition may also be met where the meal or allowance is provided three or more times per week on an occasional basis to meet workload demands such as major repairs or periodic financial reporting.

If overtime occurs on a frequent basis or becomes the norm, the CRA considers the overtime meal allowances to be a taxable benefit since they start taking on the characteristics of additional remuneration.

> **ESSENTIAL TAX FACT** | Taxable vacations include use of the employer's vacation property by you, your family or both.

Vacations. Where an employer pays for a vacation for you or your family, the cost is considered to be a taxable benefit. In such cases, the benefit is equal to the fair market value of the travel and accommodation less any amount you repay to your employer. The taxable benefit may be reduced if there is conclusive evidence to show that you were involved in business activities for your employer during the vacation.

In a situation where your presence is required for business purposes and this function is the main purpose of the trip, no benefit will be associated with the travelling expenses necessary to accomplish the business objectives of the trip if the expenditures are reasonable in relation to the business function.

Where a business trip is extended to provide for a paid holiday or vacation, you are considered to have received a taxable benefit equal to the costs borne by the employer with respect to that extension.

Note that if your spouse accompanies you on a business trip the payment or reimbursement by the employer of the spouse's travelling expenses is a taxable benefit unless the spouse was, in fact, engaged primarily in business activities on behalf of the employer during the trip.

> **ESSENTIAL TAX FACT** | Reimbursement of up to $15,000 of losses on the sale of your home may be tax-free, where the employer required the move.

Relocation costs. If your employer reimburses you for a loss suffered in selling the family home upon being required to move to another locality or upon retirement from employment in a remote area, only a portion of the reimbursement must be included in income as a taxable benefit.

Where the loss and reimbursement are both less than $15,000 no taxable benefit will accrue. Where the loss and reimbursement exceed $15,000 the benefit is one-half of the excess of the reimbursement over $15,000.

ESSENTIAL TAX FACT | The tax status of employer-paid parking has been the subject of court challenges.

Employer-paid parking. Parking costs paid by your employer will generally be included as a taxable benefit, calculated at fair market value. Parking is excluded from the value of a stand-by charge, or auto operating expense benefits, or benefits for disabled employees. However, recent court challenges have found in favour of the taxpayer in establishing a non-taxable status for parking, when it was found to be in the employer's favour to offer parking to employees.

Employer-paid health care premiums. The tax status of premiums paid and benefits received from employer-sponsored group and non-group health plans can be confusing, but is very important in the overall scheme of compensation to the employee. These plans can provide important peace of mind when expensive health care costs arise.

ESSENTIAL TAX FACT | Premiums paid by the employer under provincial hospitalization and medical care insurance plans are taxable; private plans are not.

Premiums will be taxable in two instances: where the employer pays or reimburses you for the employee portion of premiums to a provincial health care plan; or where the employer pays some or all of the premium under a non-group plan that is a wage loss replacement, sickness or accident insurance plan, a disability insurance plan, or an income maintenance insurance plan. However, payroll source deductions made for the payment of the premiums are considered to be payments made by you, not the employer.

If the wage loss replacement plan is a group plan, or if the health care plan is private, then the employer's portion of the premiums paid is not considered to be a taxable benefit.

ESSENTIAL TAX FACT | If you paid all of the premiums to a wage loss replacement plan, then periodic payments (or a lump sum paid in lieu of periodic payments) from the plan are tax-free and should not be reported on an information slip.

If the plan was funded, in whole or in part, by the employer, then the benefits received are taxable, but you are entitled to a deduction for the lesser of the amount received from the plan and all premiums that you have paid since 1968 and not previously deducted. The deduction should be claimed on Line 229 of the tax return.

Using the employer's capital pool. Employees should always strive to build capital—assets that can produce other sources of income or grow in value. One way to do so is to use your employer's money—at preferred low or no-interest rates. This however, will give rise to a taxable benefit.

For example, the employer may loan funds to you or your spouse. In either case, a taxable benefit would accrue to you, unless your spouse is also an employee of the same employer. The same rules will apply when you receive a loan from a third party, if the employer is involved in securing the loan for you.

On a no-interest loan, the amount of the benefit is equal to:

- the interest on the loan at CRA's currently prescribed rate (see Part I for details for the current tax year), plus
- any payments made by the employer, less
- amounts of interest paid back by you to the employer either during the year or within 30 days after the end of the year.

This benefit is included in your income and will be reported on your T4. Now is a good time to take advantage of these prescribed rates, as they have rarely been lower.

If the loan bears interest, there is no taxable benefit where the interest rate on the loan is equal to or greater than a commercial rate so long as you actually pay the interest. Special rules apply to housing loans and home relocation loans, discussed later.

Note: The rules above apply to shareholders as well as to employees. The difference between a shareholder loan and an employee loan is that the benefit accrues to the employee, even if the loan is to someone else. However, the benefit accrues to the debtor if the loan is a shareholder loan.

This is because of a special anti-avoidance rule that prevents a shareholder from indefinitely postponing the recognition of income from a corporation by taking continuous shareholder loans. Professional help should be sought to report these transactions.

ESSENTIAL TAX FACT | Where the employer-provided loan is forgiven or settled for an amount less than the amount outstanding, the forgiven amount must be included in your income.

Where the shareholder is also an employee, certain loans will be allowed the treatment given to any employee if it can be established that bona fide loan arrangements are made, the loan is repaid over a reasonable period of time and the loan is a direct result of the employer-employee relationship. This means that the company must make similar loans available to all employees.

ESSENTIAL TAX FACT | Employees may no longer defer up to $100,000 in stock option benefits after March 4, 2010.

Employee stock option plans. Employees may be presented with an opportunity to purchase shares in the employer's corporation at some future date, but at a price set at the time the option was granted. This is known as the exercise price.

ESSENTIAL TAX FACT | There are no tax consequences when an employee stock option is granted.

When you exercise these stock or security options a taxable benefit arises, equal to the difference between the market value of the shares purchased and the exercise price. When is this taxable? It depends on the type of corporation.

If the employer is a Canadian Controlled Private Corporation (CCPC), the taxable benefit is deemed to arise when you dispose of the shares. In the case of a public corporation, the taxable benefit arises when you exercise the option.

ESSENTIAL TAX FACT | When the security options taxable benefit is included in income, you will also be eligible for the Security Options Deduction which is equal to one-half of the taxable benefit.

It is wise to get some professional help before stock options are acquired or disposed of, as complicated new technical provisions must be observed. For example, if the shares acquired under such a stock option are donated to a registered charity or to a private foundation (after March 19, 2007), you may claim a deduction equal to the taxable benefit. In addition, be sure to get professional help if you previously deferred your stock option benefits; a provision no longer available after March 4, 2010.

CHAPTER 19

HOW TO DEDUCT EMPLOYMENT EXPENSES

The *Income Tax Act* is very specific about the expenses that may be claimed by employees. Unfortunately, for most employees, there is not much tax relief by way of deductions. Those who do qualify must file two forms:

- Form T777 *Statement of Employment Expenses* and
- Form T2200 *Declaration of Conditions of Employment*, which must be signed by the employer.

Anyone who receives a T4 slip and wishes to claim employment expenses must complete these forms. Other important forms are the following:

- GST370 *Employee and Partner GST/HST Rebate Application*

Employees who claim employment expenses on Line 229 and who are not in receipt of a reasonable auto allowance for those expenses or who clam union and professional dues on Line 212 may apply for a cash rebate of any GST or HST paid on these expenses on Line 457 of the tax return. Form GST 370 must be completed.

> **ESSENTIAL TAX FACT** | Members of a partnership that is a GST/HST registrant may also claim this rebate on the expenses that are deductible from their share of the partnership income.

Expenses eligible for the rebate include:

- office expenses
- travel expenses
- entertainment expenses

- meals and lodging (deductible portion only)
- motor vehicle expenses
- leasing costs
- parking cost
- miscellaneous supplies (e.g. street maps, stamps, pens, pencils, and paper clips), and
- capital cost allowance on motor vehicles, aircraft, and musical instruments acquired after 1990.

In the case of GST, the rebate is 5/105 of the expenses on which GST was paid. In the case of HST, the rebate rate varies according to the HST rate paid on the expenses.

ESSENTIAL TAX FACT | Taxpayers who have failed to claim the GST/HST Rebate in prior years may file adjustments to recover this credit for the prior four year period.

For employees, the portion of the GST/HST rebate that relates to current expenses must be reported as income on Line 104 in the year the rebate is received. Partners receiving the rebate should include the amount in their partnership income in the year it is received. The portion that relates to a capital asset (vehicle, musical instrument or airplane) must be used to reduce the Undepreciated Capital Cost of the class to which the asset belongs.

TL2 *Claim for Meals and Lodging Expenses*
Transport employees are eligible to claim the cost of meal and accommodation while on schedule trips of 24 hours or more. Claims for meals may be made using the detailed method, which requires receipts for each meal purchased, or using the simplified method. Under the simplified method, a maximum of three meals per day may be claimed at a rate of $17 per meal. Lodging expenses must be claimed based on actual amounts paid.

As a general rule, only 50% of meal expenses may be claimed but special rules apply to long-haul drivers. For more details, see Chapter 24.

T2222 *Northern Residents Deductions*
Individuals who resided in a prescribed northern or intermediate zone for a period of at least six consecutive months beginning or ending in a taxation year will qualify to claim a Northern Residents Deduction, and in some cases, a deduction for travel benefits provided by the employer or a member of the employee's household for travel expenses incurred in connection with any trips made to obtain medical services not available locally and up to two trips per year for other reasons, to the extent that the value of these benefits is included in employment income.

ESSENTIAL TAX FACT | For 2008 and subsequent years, both the basic residency amount and the additional residency amounts available are $8.25 per day. Form T2222 *Northern Residents Deductions* must be filed with the return.

Summary: Deductible Employment Expenses

- accounting and legal fees, not including income tax preparation
- advertising and promotion
- motor vehicle expenses including Capital Cost Allowance (CCA), interest or leasing costs and operating costs like gas, oil and maintenance
- travel expenses including rail, air, bus or other travel costs if away from the employer's home base at least 12 hours
- parking costs (but generally not at the place of employment)
- meals*, tips and hotel costs providing the excursion is for at least 12 hours and away from the taxpayer's metropolitan area.
- food, beverages and entertainment expenses*
- supplies used up directly in the work (stationery, maps, etc.)
- salaries paid to an assistant (including spouses or children if Fair Market Value is actually paid for work actually performed)
- office rent or certain home office expenses
- Employed artists are allowed to claim the cost of supplies used up in their employment to a maximum of 20% of net income or $1,000, as explained later.
- Long distance truck drivers may claim the cost of meals and lodging according to specific rules while en route; certain forestry employees may claim the cost of operating their power saws.
- Tradespersons may claim the cost of tools purchased if required by their employer for use in their employment (subject to claim maximums as described later).

* Note: Meals and tips are subject to a 50% restriction except for long-haul truck drivers whose deduction is higher, as described in a later chapter. Have on file a signed form T2200 *Declaration of Conditions of Employment.*

ESSENTIAL TAX FACT | Employees are entitled to the Canada Employment Credit to help offset their employment expenses.

There are certain non-refundable tax credits employees will be entitled to, however, to offset the costs of going to work: dry cleaning, travel, clothing for example. These are discussed in a later chapter on claiming non-refundable tax credits.

CHAPTER 20

DEDUCTIONS FOR AUTO EXPENSES

There is often confusion about the claiming of amounts received for the use of an auto at work. This can range from auto allowances to the use of a company vehicle, both of which may have tax consequences.

Auto allowances. When you receive an additional amount as an auto allowance from your employer, in addition to salary or wages, the amounts will generally be taxable, unless the amount is "reasonable".

> **ESSENTIAL TAX FACT** | To be considered reasonable, the allowances must be based solely on the number of kilometres driven. An allowance will be considered unreasonable (and therefore taxable) if you are paid a combined flat rate and per-kilometre rate allowance.

Reasonable tax-free travel allowances include:
- Travel allowances paid to members of the Canadian Forces,
- Reasonable allowances for travel expenses paid to a commission salesman,
- Reasonable allowances for travel expenses paid to a clergyman,
- Reasonable allowances for use of a motor vehicle paid to an employee for travel in the performance of the employee's duties,
- Reasonable allowances received by Members of Parliament.

An allowance is also deemed not to be reasonable, and is therefore taxable, if you are also reimbursed for actual expenditures (exception: your employer may reimburse for supplementary insurance charges, toll or ferry charges).

Amounts paid to part-time employees (such as visiting professors) may also qualify under these rules, as long as:

- the employer and employee are dealing at arm's length
- the employee had other employment or was self-employed and
- the duties of employment were performed more than 80 kilometres from the employee's residence and other employment/self-employment.

Reasonable amounts paid in advance (on a periodic basis) by your employer may also be excluded from income if:

- they are based on distance travelled (i.e. a cents per kilometre basis),
- the rate is reasonable,
- you are required to report distance travelled for business purposes, and
- there is a year-end reconciliation of distance travelled to amounts advanced and you are required to repay any excess amounts received.

A prescribed per kilometre rate is generally stated by CRA each year as the reasonable rate to use in calculating these amounts.

Where the allowance is not reasonable the whole amount of the allowance is included in computing your income and, if you qualify, an appropriate amount may be deducted for actual travel expenses. Note that special rules also exist for those employed at a remote worksite.

Claiming auto expenses. Auto expenses are one of the most common deductions for the employed and self-employed and also amongst the most audited. Therefore it is important to understand the rules surrounding "mixed use"; that is, what happens for tax purposes when a vehicle is driven for both employment and personal use.

> **ESSENTIAL TAX FACT** | Only parking costs can be claimed in full without proration.

Important: Personal use includes vehicle use by other family members, friends, etc. and travel to and from the place of business or employment.

> **ESSENTIAL TAX FACT** | If you use your vehicle for both personal and business/employment purposes, it is necessary to record distances driven for each purpose.

To make the claim on a tax return, actual expenses are first totalled, using the actual receipts and/or log of cash expenditures like car washes or parking meters.

Then the total amount expended and so supported is pro-rated by the portion of business/employment kilometres over the total kilometres driven in the year.

Beginning in 2010, the government allows taxpayers to keep a logbook for a sample period of time rather than for the full year. In order for the sample log book to be accepted:

- a full-year log must have been kept previously (2009 or later) to establish a base
- the sample log book must be for a continuous period of at least three months
- business usage during the sample period must not vary by more than 10% from the business usage in the full-year base log.

Automotive expenses can only be deducted if they are not reimbursed by your employer or business. If they are reimbursed, but the amount of the reimbursement is not reasonable, the reimbursement can be shown as income and the actual auto expenses otherwise deductible (as discussed above) can be deducted in computing net income.

To claim auto expenses, you must pay your own auto expenses and be required to use your vehicle in carrying out duties of employment. Form T2200 *Declaration of Conditions of Employment* must be signed by your employer. Also, you cannot claim auto expenses if you are in receipt of a non-taxable reasonable allowance from your employer.

ESSENTIAL TAX FACT | There are two types of auto expenses that can be claimed: fixed expenses and operating costs.

Operating expenses include:

- gas and oil, tires, maintenance and repairs, car washes, insurance, license fees,
- auto club memberships, parking (generally this is fully deductible and not subject to a proration for personal component)

Fixed expenses (and their maximum claimable amounts as at the time of writing) include:

- Capital Cost Allowance (subject to a maximum cost of $30,000 plus taxes)
- Leasing costs (subject to a maximum of $800 a month plus taxes)
- Interest costs (subject to a maximum of $300 a month)

The restrictions above on fixed expenses apply only to "Passenger Vehicles". "Motor Vehicles" are excluded; that is,

- autos acquired for less than $30,000 plus taxes or

- if over this amount, vehicle used more than 50% of the time to transport goods or equipment (in the case of a pick up truck) or 90% of the time in the case of a van, ambulances, taxis, clearly marked police and fire emergency-response vehicles, busses used in the business of transporting passengers, hearses and other vehicles used in the transport of passengers in the course of a funeral, a motor vehicle acquired to be sold, rented or leased, extended cab pick-up trucks used primarily for the transportation of goods, equipment or passengers in the course of earning or producing income at a work site at least 30 km. from any community having a population of at least 40,000.

Capital Cost Allowance (CCA). Specifically, when you own your vehicle, you can deduct a specified percentage of the undepreciated capital cost (UCC) of the asset each year, to account for wear and tear. The UCC is the cost of the vehicle less the CCA claims you made in prior years. For the purposes of claiming Capital Cost Allowance, passenger or luxury vehicles are scheduled in Class 10.1, and each vehicle has its own class. Only $30,000 (plus taxes) of the cost is added to the CCA pool. Motor vehicles are placed in Class 10, which features a "pooling" of capital costs.

In each Class 10 and Class 10.1, the undepreciated capital cost qualifies for a 30% CCA rate, and all other deductibility rules are similar, including a special half-year rule on acquisition. However, in addition to the restriction on the capital cost itself, there are several differences in tax results when the asset is disposed of.

What you need to know, before you buy or lease a vehicle, is that a "passenger" or luxury vehicle purchase will result in a restricted claim for CCA, interest or leasing costs and this tax result should be taken into account before you buy.

CHAPTER 21

DEDUCTIONS FOR
HOME WORKSPACES

Many employees and self-employed work out of their home and may make
legitimate claims for the cost of running a home workspace. What is important
is to prorate total costs to remove any personal use component by the following
fraction:

$$\frac{\text{Square footage of the home workspace}}{\text{Square footage of the entire living area}} \quad \text{X} \quad \begin{array}{c}\text{Total Eligible} \\ \text{Expenses}\end{array} \quad = \quad \begin{array}{c}\text{Deductible} \\ \text{Expenses}\end{array}$$

> **ESSENTIAL TAX FACT** | Non-deductible home office expenses may
> be carried forward and are treated as having been incurred in the
> next year.

Claims by employees. You may not claim home office expenses in excess of
income from employment for the tax year. In order to claim home office
expenses you must have a Form T2200 *Declaration of Conditions of Employment*
signed by your employer to certify that you are required to maintain the home
office and pay the expenses of operating it. Your claims for home office expenses
are made on Form T777 *Statement of Employment Expenses*.

Deductible expenditures claimed depend on whether you are employed, an
employed commission sales person or self-employed.

Employees. To qualify for home office expenses, the space must be

- the place where the individual principally (more than 50% of the time) performs the office or employment duties, or
- used exclusively to earn income from the office or employment and, on a regular and continuous basis, for meeting customers or others in the ordinary course of performing the office or employment duties.

Commission sales employees can claim:

- utilities, maintenance and repairs including light bulbs and cleaning supplies,
- rent, insurance, property taxes.

Employees who are not on commission may claim:

- utilities, maintenance and repairs including light bulbs and cleaning supplies,
- rent.

For the self-employed, deductible home workspace expenses include:

- utilities, maintenance and repairs including light bulbs and cleaning supplies,
- rent, insurance, property taxes, mortgage interest, and
- Capital Cost Allowance (CCA) (although this is not recommended as the exempt status of the principal residence is then lost on the portion of the home on which CCA is claimed).

CHAPTER 22

DEDUCTIONS FOR COMMISSION SALES EMPLOYEES

If you earn your living negotiating contracts for your employer or selling on commission you may claim employment expenses for travel and sales costs under these circumstances:

- you are required to pay your own expenses
- you regularly perform your duties away from the employer's place of business
- you do not receive a tax-free travel allowance.

Deductible travel expenses allowed include:

- automobile-related operating expenses like gas, oil, repairs and fixed costs like licenses, insurance, interest, leasing and Capital Cost Allowance. The latter three expenses are limited to certain annual maximums if a passenger or luxury vehicle is used. This is discussed in more detail later.
- the cost of air, bus, rail, taxi or other transportation which takes the employee outside the employer's metropolitan area.

ESSENTIAL TAX FACT | When travel expenses only are claimed, the amounts may exceed commissions earned and excess expenses may offset other income of the year.

Deductible sales expenses allowed include promotional expenses, entertainment expenses (subject to a 50% restriction), travel, auto and home office costs.

ESSENTIAL TAX FACT | Sales expenses may not exceed commissions earned in the calendar year except for interest and capital cost allowance on a motor vehicle.

Typical sales expenses include:
- Advertising
- Promotional items
- Gifts for client and prospective clients
- Entertainment of clients and prospective clients

Limitation on capital assets. Employees are not allowed to make a claim for capital expenditures with the exception of the purchase of vehicles, musical instruments or aircraft and a tradesperson's tools. Therefore it is more tax efficient to lease computers, cell phones or other equipment, or ask the employer to pay for these.

Home office expenses. This subject was covered in Chapter 21.

Commission salespeople: adjusting source deductions. More generous deductions are allowed to the commissioned sales employee, who must pay their own out-of-pocket expenses in negotiating contracts for their employers. Those who are not commissioned may deduct some out-of-pocket expenses, but only up to the amount of their earnings from employment; no carry over of deductions is allowed to the following year (with the exception of home workspace expenses). These special rules are discussed in separate chapters in this Part of the book.

ESSENTIAL TAX FACT | If you're a commission salesperson and you have deductible out of pocket expenses, you may reduce withholding taxes. Use Form TD1X *Statement of Commission Income and Expenses for Payroll Tax Deductions* to estimate your commission expenses for the year.

This form must be submitted to your employer no later than one month after you start with a new employer or one month after the end of the year if you stayed with the same employer.

CHAPTER 23

DEDUCTIONS FOR EMPLOYED ARTISTS

Employed artists and musicians fall into a separate classification for the purposes of claiming certain expenses specific to their field. The following activities are classified as artistic activities by CRA:

- Composing a dramatic, musical, or literary work;
- Performing as an actor, dancer, singer, or musician in a dramatic or musical work;
- Performing an artistic activity as a member of a professional artists' association that the Minister of Canadian Heritage has certified; or
- Creating a painting, print, etching, drawing, sculpture, or similar work of art.

Certain employed artists are allowed to claim the cost of supplies used up in their employment including:

- ballet shoes,
- body suits,
- art supplies,
- computer supplies,
- home office costs.

The maximum claim is the lesser of 20% of net income or $1,000. The deduction is only available, however, to artists who engage in the following activities:

- the creation, but not the reproduction, of pointing, prints, etchings, drawings, sculptures or similar works of art;
- the composition of a dramatic, musical or literary work;

- the performance of a dramatic or musical work as an actor, dancer, singer or musician; and
- any artistic endeavour with respect to which the taxpayer is a member of a professional artists' association, certified as such by the Minister of Communications.

Musicians. Musicians are restricted to the amount of their income when claiming their costs relating to their instruments, which can include

- maintenance,
- rental,
- insurance, and
- capital cost allowance claimed at a maximum rate of 20% in CCA Class 8.

When artists claim musician's expenses, however, those costs will be included for the purposes of the $1,000 or 20% of net income restriction. Note that these restrictions are on artists' expenses only, and do not include other employment expenses the artist may be entitled to claim, such as travel expenses.

Any amounts in excess of the limitation may be carried forward and applied against employment income in future years. The amounts are claimed on Form T777 *Statement of Employment Expenses*. To qualify, Form T2200 *Declaration of Conditions of Employment* is required to certify that the expenses were required to be paid by the employee and not reimbursed by the employer.

If an artist or musician's employment expenses include GST or HST, then the GST Rebate should be claimed on Form GST370 *Employee and Partner GST/HST Rebate Application*.

CHAPTER 24

DEDUCTIONS FOR TRADE APPRENTICES, TRUCKERS AND FORESTRY WORKERS

ESSENTIAL TAX FACT | Tradespersons may claim a deduction for the cost of new tools purchased for use in their job if they spend over $1,065 in a year.

A tradesperson who is required to purchase new tools for use in employment may deduct the cost in excess of $1,065 (for 2011). or their income as a tradesperson if less, to a maximum of $500. This claim, which is made on line 229 of the tax return, will only be accepted if the employer certifies (on Form T2200) that you are required to purchase your own tools for use in your job as a tradesperson. This deduction is in addition to the Canada Employment Credit.

Apprentice vehicle mechanics may claim expenses incurred in purchasing tools in excess of $1,565 (for 2011). If the apprentice does not take the maximum deduction in the tax year, the unused portion may be carried forward to apply against income earned in a future year.

If either a tradesperson or an apprentice vehicle mechanic subsequently sells the tool for which a deduction was claimed, it may be necessary to report the excess of the proceeds over the cost base of the tools (cost – deduction claimed) as other income on line 130.

Truckers. If an employee of an airline, rail company, trucking company or other such organization whose main business is the transport of goods or passengers must:

- regularly travel away from the municipality or metropolitan area where the home terminal is located, and

• use vehicles provided by the employer to transport goods or passengers,

then, a deduction may be claimed for meals and lodging while on the road.

> **ESSENTIAL TAX FACT** | Long distance truckers and other employees in the transport business may deduct certain unreimbursed board and lodging expenses.

It is possible to claim the cost of meals using one of two methods:
• the "simplified method": here unreceipted claims can be made for one meal every four hours from check-out time, up to a maximum of three meals per 24-hour period at a flat rate per meal. Currently, and since 2006, this is $17.00 per meal (maximum $51.00 per 24-hour period). For trips in the US, the amount is $17.00 US
• the "detailed method," whereby claims are made according to actual receipts submitted.

Note: When a transport employee who is normally required to travel out of town is on a scheduled run of ten hours or less they are expected to eat before and after work and therefore may only claim one meal per day. Special rules also apply for crews of workers who are provided cooking facilities. Under the "batching method", receipts are not required but the claim is limited to the equivalent of two meals per day (currently $34.00).

> **ESSENTIAL TAX FACT** | For most taxpayers, only one-half of the amount of meal costs is deductible, but the full cost of lodging while away from home is also deductible (with receipts).

If you claim deductible expenses, including the Claim for Meals and Lodging (which requires completion of Form TL2 and signature by the employer) you may receive a rebate of the GST/HST paid, discussed later. Rebates are added to income in the year received. You must support the claims with time and distance logs.

Special rules for long-haul drivers. Over the past few years, the portion of meal expenses that may be claimed by long-haul drivers has increased from 50% and reached 80% in 2011. The enhanced deduction is limited to an employee whose principal duty or an individual whose principal business is to drive a long-haul truck in transporting goods, and to employers who pay or reimburse such expenses. To qualify for the enhanced deduction:

- the long-haul truck must have a gross vehicle weight rating in excess of 11,788 kg,
- the driver must be away for at least 24 continuous hours from the employer's municipality or metropolitan area to which the employee reports (employed drivers) or the municipality where the driver resides (self-employed drivers);
- the trip must involve the transport of goods to or from a location at least 160 km from the location described above.

Forestry workers. Employees working in forestry operations who use a power saw to earn their employment income may deduct expenses for buying and using a power saw (including a chain saw or tree trimmer) if they were required to pay for them under their contract of employment and their employer does not reimburse them.

The net (of trade-in allowance) cost of a power saw may be deducted in the year it is purchased.

CHAPTER 25

CLAIMING MOVING EXPENSES

Lucrative moving deductions, like real estate commissions, removal and travel costs, can be claimed on Line 219 using Form T1-M *Moving Expenses Deduction*. To qualify, the taxpayer must earn salary, wages, or self-employment income at the new location. In addition, the taxpayer must stop working or operating a business at the old location, and establish a new home where the taxpayer and family will reside.

Students who move to attend post-secondary education may claim moving expenses against the taxable amount of scholarships and bursaries.

ESSENTIAL TAX FACT | To be eligible, the new home must be at least 40 km closer to the new work location than the old home.

The following income sources earned at the new location will not be considered "qualifying income" for the purposes of claiming moving expenses:
- investment income
- employment insurance benefits
- other income sources, except student awards.

The distance of the move is measured by the shortest normal route open to the travelling public. Generally the move must be within Canada although students may claim moving expenses to attend a school outside Canada if they are otherwise eligible.

Expenses for moves between two locations outside Canada may be possible if you are a deemed resident or factual resident of Canada and the move was from the place you ordinarily resided, to a new place where you will ordinarily reside.

Summary: Deductible moving expenses

File Form T1-M

- cost of selling the former residence, including real estate commissions, penalties for paying off a mortgage, legal fees, and advertising costs
- costs of keeping a vacant old residence (to a maximum of $5,000) while actively attempting to sell it, including mortgage interest, property taxes, insurance premiums and heat and power
- expenses of purchasing the new home (as long as the old home was owned), including transfer taxes and legal fees
- temporary living expenses (meals and lodging) for up to 15 days
- removal and storage costs including insurance for household effects and costs of moving a boat, trailer, or mobile home, transportation costs, costs of meals on route (100%—no 50% restriction), cost of cancelling an unexpired lease
- cost of revising legal documents to show the new address, replacing drivers licenses and auto permits, cost of utility connections and disconnections

The following expenses are not deductible:

- expenses to make the former property more saleable,
- losses on the sale of the former property,
- expenses incurred before the move (such as house hunting or job hunting),
- value of items that could not be moved,
- expenses to clean a rented residence,
- replacement costs for items not moved such as tool sheds, firewood, drapes, etc.,
- mail forwarding costs,
- expenses that are reimbursed.

ESSENTIAL TAX FACT | Travel expenses may be calculated using a rate per kilometre basis rather than claiming the actual amount spent. Meals can be claimed on a flat rate, too.

The simplified method does not require receipts to be kept for travel expenses, only a record of the distance traveled during the move. The rate is calculated based on the province in which the move began. Meals en route may also be charged at a flat rate per meal ($17.00 at the time of writing) with a maximum of three meals per day (total $51.00) per family member. The per-kilometre rate is generally revised each January so for ongoing current rates, visit the CRA web site at http://www.ccra-adrc.gc.ca/travelcosts.

> **ESSENTIAL TAX FACT** | If income at the new location does not sufficiently offset all moving expenses in the year of the move, expenses may be carried forward and applied against income at the new location in the following year.

Note: If you receive reimbursements for moving expenses you may only deduct expenses if the amount received as a reimbursement is included in income, or if the amounts claimed are reduced by the amount of the reimbursement.

> **ESSENTIAL TAX FACT** | The home relocation loan deduction is available for the first five years of the loan, and, if the loan is $25,000 or less, is equal to the taxable benefit charged the employee.

Employee home relocation deduction. When an employer relocates an employee to another area, the employer may offer the employee a low-interest or no-interest loan to assist with the costs of relocating. The difference between the interest charged on the loan and the interest calculated at the prescribed interest rate is a taxable benefit and included on the employee's T4 Slip. If you receive this benefit you may qualify for the Employee Home Relocation Loan Deduction claimed on Line 248.

If the term for repayment for the home relocation loan is more than five years, the balance owing at the end of five years (from the day the loan was made) is considered a new loan. The taxable benefit will be calculated as if the loan were made at that time. However, in this case, no home relocation loan deduction is available.

The rules for the calculation of benefits for a home relocation loan are similar as for any employer-provided loan. The difference is that for a home purchase loan and a home relocation loan the prescribed interest rate used for the calculation of the taxable benefit is the rate in effect at the time the loan is made.

CHAPTER 26

CLAIMING CHILD CARE EXPENSES

Child care is always an issue for working parents; and it is a contentious one when the child care provider does not provide the receipts required to make a claim for the child care expenses deduction. If the reason for not providing receipts is that the provider will not report the income, this is tax evasion, and a criminal offence. Assuming that the provider does provide receipts, the child care deduction can be lucrative. It is also important because it reduces net income, the figure upon which refundable tax credits such as the monthly Canada Child Tax Benefit and non-refundable tax credits will be based. Therefore, it's really unfair to hardworking parents when tax evasion prevails in these situations.

Calculate this lucrative deduction on Form T778 *Child Care Exenses Deduction for 2011* and claim it on Line 214 of the T1 Return, according to the checklist of rules, outlined below:

Eligible taxpayers. Costs must be paid to earn income from employment or self-employment or so that taxpayer may attend school either full or part time or carry on research under a grant.

Eligible dependants. Under the age of 16 (at any time during the year) or who are physically or mentally infirm (no age limit). This must be your child, or that of your spouse or common law partner or a child who was dependent on you or your spouse. Otherwise the child's net income must be less than Basic Personal Amount.

Eligible babysitters. Expenses must actually paid to a Canadian resident or paid to a non-resident for services outside Canada for a resident or deemed resident of

Canada. Babysitters may be related to you, but if they are, the sitter must be over age 17.

> **ESSENTIAL TAX FACT** | Payments made to a parent of the child or to a supporting person are not deductible; nor are payments to those who are claimed as a dependant by the taxpayer. However, payments to grandparents are allowed so long as the grandparent is not also a dependant of the taxpayer.

The cost of paying a non-related nanny, however, including all benefits paid under source deductions, is deductible; as are payments made to day nursery schools and centres, educational institutes and after-school activities providers, day camps and day sports schools where primary goal is to provide care, and boarding schools, overnight sports schools or camps.

As mentioned above, receipts are required and in the case of an individual, the Social Insurance Number must be provided.

Earned income definition. Includes salaries and wages, net profits from self-employment, training allowances, the taxable portion of scholarships, bursaries, fellowships and research grants (*note however that for 2006 and subsequent years most of these sources are tax exempt*), and disability pensions under CPP or QPP. This definition does not, however, include benefits received from the Universal Child Care Benefit, or Employment Insurance.

Students who are parents. Full time students are limited to: $100 for each child age 7 – 16 for which the disability amount cannot be claimed, plus $175 per child under 7 for which the disability amount cannot be claimed, plus $250 per disabled child times the number of **weeks** of full-time attendance.

Part time students are limited to: $100 for each child age 7 – 16 for which the disability amount cannot be claimed, plus $175 per child under 7 for which the disability amount cannot be claimed, plus $250 per disabled child times the number of **months** of part-time attendance.

High income earners. If you are the higher income spouse, you may only claim child care expenses during periods in which:

- The other supporting person was in full or part-time student
- The other supporting person was incapable of caring for the children because of mental or physical infirmity
- The other supporting person was confined to a prison or similar institution for at least two weeks

- You have separated from the other supporting person due to a breakdown in your relationship for a period of at least 90 days but have reconciled within the first 60 days after the taxation year

Maximum claim. Claim the least of:
- Eligible child care expenses paid to eligible child care providers, two-thirds of earned income and the following limits
  - $4,000 for each child aged 7 – 16 for which the disability amount cannot be claimed plus
  - $7,000 for each child under 7 for which the disability amount cannot be claimed plus
  - $10,000 for each disabled child

Note that the limit is for the family, not for an individual child. Thus, for example, if you had two children ages 9 and 14, your maximum claim is $8,000. If you paid $7,000 child care for the younger child and none for the older, your $8,000 limit allows you to claim the full $7,000 paid for the younger child.

Restrictions to Child Tax Benefit, disability amounts. If you are claiming the disability amount to a dependant who is under 18, your claim includes a supplement. Reduce this by any child care expenses in excess of a threshold ($2,508 for 2011).

Eligible expenditures. The following expenses may be claimed: baby sitting costs, day care costs, costs of a live-in nanny, lodging paid at boarding schools, day camps, day sports camps and overnight camps.

Ineligible expenditures. Medical or hospital care, clothing, transportation, tuition fees for a regular program or sports study program, or for recreational or leisure activities. Any child care expense that is reimbursed (example by the employer) cannot be claimed.

CHAPTER 27

CLAIMING NON-REFUNDABLE TAX CREDITS

Employees qualify for certain non-refundable tax credits on Schedule 1 of the return. For example, a credit for premiums paid into the CPP and Employment Insurance is possible. It's important not to overpay these amounts.

EI premiums are calculated at 1.78% of your employment income, regardless of your age. The maximum EI premium for 2011 is $780.36.

CPP contributions are calculated at 4.95% of your employment income if you are between ages 18 and 70. The maximum contribution for 2011 is $2,217.60. The first $3,500 of employment income is exempt from contribution. For taxpayers who are under age 18 or over age 70 (except in Quebec), no contribution is required.

For 2011, no contribution is required once you begin receiving CPP disability or retirement benefits. Beginning in 2012, those who continue to earn employment income after they begin receiving CPP retirement benefits will have to continue contributing until at least age 65 and may optionally contribute between age 65 and 70.

In the year that a taxpayer turns 18 or 70 (or dies or begins receiving CPP benefits), their contribution is prorated according to the number of months in the year in which they were eligible to contribute.

ESSENTIAL TAX FACT | The Canada Employment Credit increases each year due to inflation adjusting, but is set at $1,065 in 2011. It's a non-refundable credit available to all employees, effective for July 1, 2006, claimable on line 363 of Schedule 1.

Credit for public transit. A non-refundable tax credit is available for the cost of an eligible public transit pass purchased on or after July 1, 2006. It will be claimable by the individual or the individual's spouse or common-law partner in respect of eligible transit costs of the individual, the individual's spouse or common-law partner, and the individual's dependent children that are under 19 years of age at the end of the taxation year. The claim may be split between two taxpayers so long as the total amount claimed does not exceed the maximum allowed.

An eligible public transit pass includes:

- a document issued by or on behalf of a qualified Canadian transit organization that identifies the right of an individual to use public commuter transit services of that organization on an unlimited number of occasions and on any day during which the services are offered during an uninterrupted period of at least 28 days,
- an electronic payment card, provided the card provides at least 32 one-way trips in a period not exceeding 31 days, or
- a weekly transit pass covering a period of 5 to 7 days, so long as the taxpayer purchased at least four consecutive weekly passes.

CHAPTER 28

TAX PLANNING: MAXIMIZING YOUR COMPENSATION

We have discussed various ways to diversify income sources and average down taxes paid if you are an employee, utilizing taxable and tax-free benefits in your employment negotiations. There are a few other things you may wish to know, to round out your employment tax advantages.

Annualizing tax on bonuses. If you receive a bonus, the amount of income tax withheld could be substantial, especially if your payroll department treats the bonus as income in the current pay period. The CRA will allow your payroll department to use a "bonus tax method" to annualize tax on your bonus. Be sure to request that they use that method. You may be able to further reduce the amount of tax withheld from a bonus by having a portion of the bonus contributed directly to an RRSP.

Registered pension plans. A registered pension plan (RPP) is a private pension plan set up for employees, which has been registered with the Minister of National Revenue. The plan may be instituted by the employer or a trade union in cooperation with the employer.

> **ESSENTIAL TAX FACT** | The employer must make contributions to the plan, and that makes it very important to you as a way to leverage your employer/employee relationship. You will not be charged a taxable benefit on these contributions.

The plan may be structured as a defined benefit or a money purchase arrangement or a combination of the two. It is important as you negotiate a new employment contract to find out the details.

Under a money purchase plan the employer and employee contributions in each member's separate account accumulate investment earnings on a tax-deferred basis and the sum total determines the size of pension benefits that can be purchased at retirement. There is no promise that a certain level of retirement benefits will be provided and no uncertainty regarding the employer's financial obligation to the plan.

A defined benefit plan on the other hand, is a plan under which the ultimate retirement benefits promised are determined by formula. The employee's contributions are predetermined and the employer generally contributes whatever is required to ensure those promised retirement benefits materialize.

An employee may make contributions to an RPP:

- for the current year or
- for past service for years after 1990.

Current year employee contributions. These amounts are tax deductible and appear in Box 20 of your T4 slip. They are only deductible in the current tax year and may not be carried over to another taxation year.

> **ESSENTIAL TAX FACT** | Any past service contributions that are not deductible may be carried forward to a subsequent year and deducted with the same limitations.

Past service contributions for service before 1990. In addition, you may deduct, within limits, your contributions to an RPP in respect of service in years before 1990. Such amounts are included in Box 20, 74 and 75 of your T4 slip or Box 032 of a T4A slip. The deduction limitations are complicated, as shown below:

- Employee contributions for pre-1990 past service while not a contributor – You may deduct the least of:
  - contributions made in the year or a previous year in respect of such service less deductions previously claimed
  - $3,500
  - $3,500 per year of such service to which you made past service contributions minus deductions previously claimed in respect of those contributions and deductions claimed before 1987 for "additional voluntary contributions"
- Employee contributions for pre-1990 past service while a contributor – Deduct the lesser of:

- The amount of the contributions made in the year, or a previous year, less deductions previously claimed
- $3,500 minus the amount deducted in the year for
  - current service
  - post-1989 past service contributions and
  - pre-1990 past service contributions while not a contributor

Any amounts contributed but not deductible may be carried forward to a subsequent year and deducted with the same limitations.

> **ESSENTIAL TAX FACT** | When a taxpayer dies, the deduction of unclaimed past service contributions in the year of death may be made in full, without regard to the $3,500 per year limitations.

Your ability to claim undeducted past service contributions carried forward is not affected by changes in employment status. That is, you may retire or change companies and still be allowed to deduct past service pension plan contributions carried forward.

> **ESSENTIAL TAX FACT** | It is generally not possible to claim the cost of interest on money borrowed to contribute to a registered pension plan as a carrying charge.

Pension adjustments. This is a term you need to know. Employees who are members of a Registered Pension Plan will be assigned a Pension Adjustment for the year. This is reported in Box 52 of the T4 slip or Box 034 of the T4A slip and decreases your RRSP contribution limit for the year. You should also know that employees who contribute in respect of past service will also be assigned a "Past Service Pension Adjustment" (PSPA).

> **ESSENTIAL TAX FACT** | Pension adjustments are not considered to be income but limit the deduction available for RRSP contributions.

Note that benefits received from a registered pension plan are taxable. When paid out as a retirement pension, they qualify for the Pension Income credit. See Part V for more details on planning for retirement with the tax deferral plans you contribute through in your active employment years.

Planning for job termination and severances. All good things may one day come to an end. When it comes to the end of the road with your employer, consider these tax consequences of termination:

Plan a tax-free rollover of your termination or severance into an RRSP. The amount eligible for rollover to your (but not your spouse's) RRSP depends on when service was provided to the employer:

- For service after 1995, no amount of severance can be rolled over to an RRSP and therefore the full amount is exposed to income taxes.
- For service after 1988 and before 1996, a single limit of $2,000 per year of service can be rolled over.
- For service before 1989, it is possible to roll over $2,000 for each year of service plus $1,500 for each year in which none of your employer's contributions to a company pension plan vested in you.

You'll find the amount that is eligible for rollover in Box 026 of your T4A slip. The amount that can't be rolled over will be shown in Box 027.

Remember, the amount that can't be rolled over can be used to top up unused RRSP contribution room and take this deduction against the exposed income. Then, plan to make any taxable withdrawals from the RRSP as required while you hunt for new work. If the withdrawal occurs in a year in which income falls into a lower tax bracket, you'll see a net tax saving from this strategy.

Also, the possibility of taking severance over two taxation years should be explored to determine whether the tax brackets and rates at which the income will be taxed can be reduced, and whether eligibility for social benefits, like the Child Tax Benefit, can be created.

- **EI maximization.** Employment Insurance benefits you may receive throughout the year may be clawed back when you file your income tax return, if your net income for the tax year is $55,250 or higher and you've received regular EI benefits in the prior ten years. This can be avoided with astutely planned RRSP contributions.
- **CTB creation.** Many high income earners who find themselves unemployed often fail to plan for new eligibility for Child Tax Benefits, because they didn't qualify for them in the past. These refundable monthly payments are maximized at lower family net income levels, but partial benefits may be paid if income is higher, depending on the number of children in the home.
- **Medical expense deductibility.** Taxpayers often forget that group health benefits end with employment. Negotiate for continuation wherever possible.

Part V

Tax Efficient Retirements

CHAPTER 29

MAXIMIZING YOUR
TAX EFFICIENT RETIREMENT

ESSENTIAL TAX FACT | To maximize your economic power in retirement—no matter when you stop working—tax efficient retirement income planning begins with the first dollar you save. That makes retirement planning important for everyone. *Good news: it's never too late to start.*

Done well, the money you save throughout your lifetime will end up in the right "buckets", allowing you to split income with your spouse, and withdraw from different sources, all designed to average down the taxes you pay in retirement. This will give you more purchasing power against rising prices for your changing needs, like the cost of medical services, for example, travel or maintaining your home. It also adds points to your investment returns so you can minimize the risk you take in your portfolio.

Therefore, even if you have never paid attention to your taxes in the past, doing so in order to achieve peace of mind in retirement becomes a very important part of your financial success.

If you are an employee, when transitioning from work life to retirement make sure you have the knowledge to leave your structured financial environment, where your employer took care of things like tax remittances, RRSP or Registered Pension Plan (RPP) contributions, your health care plans and in some cases, your employer-provided vehicle, communications devices and investment loans, too. It's quite possible that your new life in retirement will be the first time you will take care of many of those financial decisions on your own.

For self-employed people, the thought of giving up control of their business interests, which have generated predictable income returns, can bring considerable financial stress, especially in volatile economic times. But these folks have a leg-up on their employed fellow taxpayers, because they already manage relationships with financial advisors and understand the importance of diversifying income sources, maximizing tax provisions and staying onside with CRA.

This is important, too, as a move from an active work life into an active retirement, brings a change in your relationship with the tax department. You will want to understand your new responsibilities to self-remit taxes on time, and benefit from new tax provisions available to reduce tax on your retirement income.

ESSENTIAL TAX FACT | Planning for a tax efficient retirement requires the management of both income structure and the continued growth and preservation of your capital accumulations.

Most people will experience three retirement income planning stages, from a tax efficiency point of view:
- Pre-retirement
- Phased-in retirement
- Full retirement

Three distinct age groups typically correspond to these phases:
- **Pre-age 60:** At the younger end you'll save for retirement, at the upper end; you may begin a phased-in retirement;
- **Age 60 to 64:** These are the "early retirement" years, before Old Age Security is received.
- **Age 65 and beyond:** Full retirement begins for the purposes of generating taxable income from the Old Age Security (age 65), Canada Pension Plan (it's mandatory at age 70) and the Registered Retirement Savings Plan (you must withdraw funds after age 71).

ESSENTIAL TAX FACT | To get ready for retirement, try to invest on a pre-tax basis, earn investment income on a tax exempt or tax deferred basis, and then withdraw retirement benefits at the lowest possible marginal tax rates to increase your purchasing power in retirement. A good relationship with tax and financial advisors can help.

How do you know if you are receiving the right advice? It is possible to be proactive about your future by ensuring you lead the decision-making process for your family. Leaders probe for the right solutions though preferably with a team of tax and financial advisors trained as specialists in the area of tax efficient retirement income planning.[1]

Six retirement planning parameters

1. **Retirement period.** What is your anticipated retirement period, based on your expected life, taking average retirement periods and family health histories into account?

2. **Income level.** What is the required income level for your vision for retirement? This requires budgeting and how to fund basic needs and lifestyle wants.

3. **Inter-spousal planning.** Does your retirement vision match your spouse's? If not, this needs to be discussed to make decisions about income levels and capital preservation.

4. **Risk management.** What expectations do you have for return on your investments in both the short and long term, and how much risk are you willing to take to achieve that?

5. **Savings.** How much additional capital can you expect to create by taking a tax efficient approach to the accumulation, growth, preservation and transition of your capital?

6. **Withdrawal strategy.** What is the precise amount of capital encroachment you are prepared to make to fund needs or wants, and what are the rules for withdrawal in changing economic circumstances?

Frameworks for achieving results. A Real Wealth Management™[2] (RWM) strategy provides a framework for strategic planning and joint decision-making with your advisors. (Advisors holding an MFA™ designation are trained in this discipline.) The following *Retirement Income Planning Guide*, a format we teach to undergraduates in the MFA program at the Knowledge Bureau, can help with the retirement income planning process:

---

[1] Look for someone with the MFA-Retirement Income Planning Specialist designation. For more information contact The Knowledge Bureau.

[2] RWM is a trademark of Knowledge Bureau, which teaches this methodoloy to tax and financial advisors and their clients in order to accumulate, grow, preserve and transition sustainable family wealth.

RETIREMENT INCOME PLANNING GUIDE
©Knowledge Bureau, Inc.

PART 1

Triggers	What are Your Financial Trigger Questions?	Stage Your Solutions
Life triggers	I want to retire in 3 to 5 years. What should I be thinking about?	Pre-age 60
	What do I need to do to retire today?	Age 60 to 64
	I wish to retire gradually. What's the most savvy way to do this?	Age 65 plus
Financial triggers	How should I save for my retirement: RRSP or TFSA? Something else?	Pre-retirement
	When should I begin to encroach upon my investments? Should I take CPP early at age 60? How much can I receive in benefits from my employer-sponsored plan?	Phased in retirement
	I have lost my job and will not be going back to work. What is the most tax efficient way for me to carry on?	Manage unexpected retirement
	I have enough money, I have achieved my goals and will retire.	Full retirement
Economic triggers	• Portfolio loss • Inflation • Interest Rates • Currency valuations • Fees for investment services • Debt management	

PART 2

Probe	Work with advisors	Document it
Who? What?	Planning for one retirement or two? **Important Data:** Family member details, cash flow details: assets, liabilities, tax filing profile	• Budget, income • Expenses • Net worth statement • Tax returns
Expectations	What would provide you with peace of mind? How much is enough?	• Expectations for income • Short term needs and wants: 1, 3 and 5 years from now • Long term: 10-20 years

PART 3: THE RETIREMENT INCOME PLANNING PROCESS

Sources	Data	Analysis
Analyze income and capital	List sources of income • Employment • Wage loss replacement • Employment insurance • Self employment • CPP, OAS benefits • Investment income • Capital gains and losses • Periodic pensions List sources of capital • RPPs, IPPs, RCAs • TFSAs, RRSPs, RRIFs • Non-registered pools • Non-financial assets	Tax status of income source: • Tax exempt • Taxable • Tax preferred • Tax deferred • Transfer to kids? Personal net worth: Are there deficiencies in any capital pool—registered, non-registered, other? Investment fees too high?
Income management	• How much from each source? • When? • From which source first? • Which taxpayer? • Debt managed?	• At what income level is next tax bracket? • Can income be split? • Clawbacks minimized?
Portfolio management	Accumulation of capital: • Which bucket? • Which bucket first? Withdrawal of capital: • Pre-tax? • Post-tax? • How to replenish? Preservation: • Can we improve rates of return, yields? • Are assets, income tax efficient? • Can we reduce risk exposure? • Should we insure against tax, health risk?	Asset allocation: • Have you maintained or reduced risk? • Are you protecting, growing or recreating capital? • Is the portfolio still in sync with risk profile? Product selection: • Tax exempt • Tax preferred • Tax deferred • Taxable

	The Action Plan	Benchmarks
Tomorrow	Income Plan: Layer in the income sources: Employment: Full or part time Public Pensions: CPP and OAS Private Pensions: RPP, RRSP, Other Investments: TFSA Interest-bearing Mutual funds Stocks, bonds Real estate Business interests Insurance Return of capital only Blend: income/capital	How does the income plan affect portfolio construction? • Capital encroachment? • Redundant income? • Risk and return? • Asset allocation • Taxes

To define some of the terms above and learn more about how to structure your retirement income plan with tax efficiency do read on.

> **ESSENTIAL TAX FACT** | A tax focus can help you withdraw only the right amount of pension income for cash flow purposes, and this will ensure that you don't over-encroach on other savings, especially when your investment returns are low.

CHAPTER 30

PUBLIC PENSIONS: THE OAS AND NEW CANADA PENSION PLAN

You have learned that retirement income planning involves staging both your savings and the withdrawal of your benefits throughout your lifetime. Age 65 is a particularly significant milestone in planning for retirement. There are three specific reasons:

1. Old Age Security begins.

2. New tax credits and income splitting opportunities become available.

3. Most Canadians start drawing pension benefits from the Canada Pension Plan, which is a based on contributions from employment or self-employment.

Cumulatively speaking, the OAS is lucrative. It could represent in excess of $250,000 of income in retirement for a couple, if each spouse lives 20 years. The OAS is also indexed to inflation. It's therefore very important to preserve this income source from tax erosion.

While it is a universal payment, which means every Canadian resident receives it; unfortunately, the OAS can be "clawed back" at higher individual net income levels, beginning at approximately $68,000, and this must be managed by planning your income from other sources carefully.

The Old Age Security is also taxable each year. For those age 65 and over, a non-refundable tax credit known as the Age Amount is available to offset some of that tax erosion, and is in addition to the Basic Personal Amount, found on Schedule 1 of the T1 return. Individual retirees will therefore be able to earn over $17,000 completely tax-free each year.

However, in the case of the Age Amount, again there is a clawback for every dollar earned above a net income threshold; this time approximately $33,000. These clawback zones are indexed each year; please refresh your memory by reviewing the numbers for this tax year in Chapter 2.

> **ESSENTIAL TAX FACT** | Managing the clawback of the Old Age Security Benefit and the offsetting Age Amount is an important cornerstone of retirement income planning.

Beyond this, tax efficient retirement income planning hinges on two things: what your tax bracket is, and at what marginal tax rate your income will be taxed above this. Therefore when making decisions about how much money to withdraw from your various capital pools (pension accumulations or your investments) consider three income thresholds carefully before you act:

- Income Levels up to the top of the Age Credit Clawback Zone
- Income levels up to the top of the OAS Clawback Zone
- Income levels up to the top of your Current Tax Bracket

Structuring income around these income thresholds should be discussed with your advisors whenever you make investment decisions that will affect your income in retirement.

The problems with dividends. Astute retirement income planners understand how various withdrawals are taxed and when they are realized for tax purposes. In fact, you need to ask what your marginal tax rate on the next dollar you withdraw from each income source will be. That marginal tax rate needs to include the impact of clawbacks.

Dividend income withdrawals from non-registered accounts, for example, artificially increase the net income upon which clawback zones for OAS, refundable and non-refundable tax credits are based on. Actual dividend income earned, is "grossed up" in value on the tax return, thereby increasing net income. Later this amount is offset by a corresponding dividend tax credit, used when tax on taxable income is computed. The end result is that dividends are taxed very efficiently when compared with interest income or other "ordinary income" sources, like pensions or employment income.

> **ESSENTIAL TAX FACT** | It is the "grossed-up" portion of dividends that artificially inflate net income, which may erode eligibility to social benefits like the OAS when clawback zones are reached.

Therefore, while dividend income is widely considered to be a very tax-efficient source of investment income, it can cause erosion of other sources, which is very expensive if you could, in fact, plan your affairs differently.

With this in mind, it is also important to acknowledge that there are three types of tax treatments for dividend income. The dividend income you receive from a public company is taxed in one manner, whereas the dividend income received from a privately owned business is taxed at slightly higher levels, depending on which province you live in. Finally, the dividend income you receive from foreign (e.g. U.S.) public companies is fully taxed as income in Canada. There is no gross-up or offsetting credit for dividends received from non-Canadian public companies.

Have your tax advisors work with your investment advisors to achieve the right dividend mix in planning retirement income withdrawals.

OAS and non-residents. Non-residents who receive OAS payments must submit an *Old Age Security Return of Income* (T4155) to determine whether a recovery tax for OAS clawback purposes is required. Age and years of residence in Canada determine eligibility. Those who live in Canada qualify for the OAS if they are 65 or older, living in Canada and are a Canadian citizen or a legal resident at the time your pension is approved. Also, those who lived in Canada for at least 10 years after reaching age 18 qualify.

When people living outside Canada want to receive the OAS, they also must be 65 or older, meet the citizenship/residency requirements described above and lastly, lived in Canada for at least 20 years after reaching age 18.

The New Canada Pension Plan

The Canada Pension Plan is a mandatory, contributory pension plan to which employees and employers must contribute, in return for a variety of benefits. It is more than a retirement savings plan, for example, in that provides some protection to contributors and their families against the loss of income due to retirement, disability and death. It features benefits for survivors and some indexing to inflation.

The Canada Pension Plan is governed by a separate Act (*Canada Pension Plan*) and is jointly administered by the Canada Revenue Agency and Social Development Canada. Benefits received under the Canada Pension Plan are reported on the recipient's T4A(P) *Statement of Canada Pension Plan Benefits* slip and must be reported on the recipient's tax return.

ESSENTIAL TAX FACT | CPP retirement benefits are not eligible for the $2000 Pension Income Amount. However, spouses may equalize the taxable CPP retirement benefits by assigning them equally for a better after-tax result.

Service Canada provides you with Canada Pension Plan Statement of Contributions which shows how much your pension entitlement is. Your Statement of Contributions shows your pension entitlement as of age 65, the date most people elect to retire. You should review this annually as part of your planning process.

The maximum retirement benefit receivable, in return for your lifetime contributions is based on 25% of the average maximum pensionable earnings over the prior five years. It's close to $1,000 a month. (The maximum monthly benefit for 2011, for example, was $960.)

When calculating your CPP retirement benefits, the number of working years less a portion of nil or low earnings due to work interruptions such as job loss is taken into account. Under the *Child Rearing Provision*, the years in which the contributor left the work force to raise children, will also be removed.

Survivor benefits: When one spouse dies, the surviving spouse may be eligible to receive a CPP survivor benefit if the deceased spouse had made contributions to CPP. If the surviving spouse was under age 35 at the time of death and there are no minor children, no survivor pension is paid until the surviving spouse reaches age 65. Otherwise, both the surviving spouse and minor children (or children up to age 25 who are attending post-secondary education) are likely eligible to receive a survivor benefit.

Note that once the surviving spouse begins to receive their CPP retirement benefit, the maximum benefit (retirement plus survivor benefits) is limited to the maximum monthly retirement benefit ($960 per month for 2011). For those who have earned the maximum pension through their own contributions, this effectively means that the survivor benefits may be lost, and this is an unpleasant surprise to those who have contributed their maximums to the CPP throughout their careers.

What's new with CPP planning? Important changes, which will affect decisions about contributing and receiving CPP benefits in retirement, begin in 2012, including:

- An increase in the number of low-earnings drop out years, used to calculate your benefits
- An elimination of the requirement to stop working before you can start receiving CPP early (that is before age 65).

- All CPP benefit recipients will be required to continue making CPP contributions if they go back to work in the "early retirement period" of 60-64.
- An election to continue to contribute to the CPP can be made if you work between age 65 and 70, thereby increasing your pension entitlements.
- Employer portion mandatory

Common questions pre-retirees have in relation to these changes include:
- When to begin to take benefits from the CPP—early or later?
- When to stop contributing to the CPP?
- What is the effect of these decisions on CPP benefits over your lifetime?
- What other income sources should I draw on if I delay benefits?

> **ESSENTIAL TAX FACT** | Expected longevity plays a role in assessing the cost-benefit ratio of contributing to the CPP, especially when deciding whether or not to draw your taxable retirement benefits early at age 60.

What are the tax implications? CPP benefits are fully taxable. There are also other tax implications to consider. For example, receiving a larger income from CPP may increase clawbacks of certain personal credits and/or Old Age Security benefits. Waiting to receive larger benefits from the CPP in the future, could also coincide with higher minimum payments from the Registered Retirement Income Fund (RRIF), causing a spike in marginal tax rates. However, do the math, because this may not be true in every case as RRIF value may be lower due to withdrawals that began earlier.

Also, tapping into other saving early, while you continue to pay into the CPP, may ultimately significantly reduce estate values, depending on the survivor benefits available to your spouse. So there are many things to consider in layering your retirement income properly.

Important CPP milestones: How much you will receive on a monthly basis will depend on how much you contribute, how long you contribute and when you apply to receive benefits. Most people will apply to receive benefits at age 65; however, some can elect to start receiving the benefits early at age 60. Others may elect not to receive the CPP until age 70. After this, the receipt of the CPP retirement benefit is mandatory. A life events approach to managing your CPP is therefore important, as outlined in the chart below:

CPP PLANNING MILESTONES

Milestone	Pre-Retirement	Early Retirement	Late Retirement	Mandatory Retirement
Age	18-59	60-64	65-70	71
Contributions	Required	Required	Optional	Not required
Regular Retirement Benefits	Maximum benefits available at 65; reduced at 60	Reduced; but PRB may increase	Increased	Benefits depend on when benefits began
Post-Retirement Benefits (PRB)	Regular benefits may be increased if working age 60-70	Mandatory contribution to PRB* (see below) may increase	Optional contribution to PRB**	Contributions must cease

*Employer/employee contributions mandatory
**Employers must contribute if employee chooses to contribute.

ESSENTIAL TAX FACT | A tax efficient approach to planning your entitlements to the CPP includes paying only the correct amount of premiums; claiming available non-refundable tax credits, deductions in the case of the self-employed and refunds of overpayments along the way. Then, minimize taxes by splitting benefits equally with your spouse and averaging in your benefits with other pension income sources.

CHAPTER 31

WITHDRAWING PRIVATE
PENSION BENEFITS

Imagine: you have spent much of your life accumulating money in your employer-sponsored pension plan (RPP) and your RRSP and now it is time to spend it! Believe it or not, that's a difficult concept for lifelong savers, who don't want to touch their precious accumulations. However, the purpose of your RPP and RRSP is to create a retirement pension, and if you do so over a longer period of time, you'll be able to average down tax erosion.

> **ESSENTIAL TAX FACT** | The withdrawals received from your registered savings accounts—RPPs, RRSPs, IPPs, DPSPs[1]—are taxable in the year received. Structured as a periodic pension, the amounts may qualify for a $2,000 federal pension income amount and pension income splitting with your spouse.

Let's discuss these in more depth now.

Registered Pension Plans (RPPs). Commuting your employer-sponsored pension plans to provide a periodic pension plan also requires planning, and depending on the type of plan you have contributed to, may involve some withdrawal restrictions.

Particularly important however, is a feature that allows those age 55 or older, to begin a "phased-in retirement" under a defined benefit pension plan, available since 2008.

---

[1] Individual Pension Plans, Deferred Profit Sharing Plans common to owner-managed business environments.

ESSENTIAL TAX FACT | Members of some RPPs may choose to work on a part time basis, drawing up to 60% of the benefits that have otherwise accrued and at the same time continue with contributions to an RPP.

It's a triple win for some. Those living with a spouse or common-law spouse may split periodic income from an RPP by election when the tax return is filed. This can be done at any age; providing an advantage over those with RRSP accumulations only, who must wait to age 65 to take advantage of pension income splitting, as you will learn later in this section.

No conditions are imposed on whether the employee works part- or full-time. However, this ability to draw a pension while continuing to accrue benefits will not be extended to designated plans (more commonly called "top-hat plans"), which are those that cover only one employee or a small group of highly compensated individuals. Check with your employer and tax advisor about your eligibility for this option.

Tax-free/direct transfers. When an employee changes employers, arrangements to move the accumulated amounts in the employee's pension plan are often made. The *Income Tax Act* provides details of the allowable tax-free rollovers of funds from one RPP to another or to the taxpayer's Registered Retirement Savings Plan (RRSP) or RRIF[2] or LIRA[3]. Such transfers must be made directly from one registered plan to the other without tax consequences.

Amounts that are received in the hands of the taxpayer as a lump sum will be considered to be taxable income, so it's best to avoid that and plan for periodic withdrawals instead to minimize marginal tax rate spikes.

ESSENTIAL TAX FACT | Given the income splitting opportunities under the RPP, for taxpayers under age 65, it is likely more advantageous to structure periodic pension benefits from an RPP rather than through the transfer to an RRSP or RRIF or LIF[4], where you must wait to age 65 to split income with your spouse. Discuss with your advisors in advance.

Individual Pension Plans (IPP): If you are running an incorporated business you may be in financial position to supplement your RRSP with an IPP, which is a defined benefit pension plan. The IPP offers both maximum tax relief and a maximum retirement pension. To qualify for an IPP, you must:

---

[2] RRIF – Registered Retirement Income Fund
[3] LIRA – Locked-in Retirement Account
[4] LIF – Life Income Fund

- Have employment income reported on a T4;
- Be an employee of an incorporated company; and
- Own at least 10% of the shares of the company or be paid at least 2.5 times the maximum CPP pensionable earnings (i.e. $120,750 for 2011).

There are significant advantages including the following:
- IPP contributions and expenses are fully tax-deductible to the business. If you borrow money or amortize the past service cost, you can deduct the interest charges.
- Employees may enjoy an annual maximum contribution that is higher than the maximum contribution for an RRSP.
- Pension benefits are protected from creditors under pension legislation.
- Extended contribution period: A company has 120 days after its year end to make an IPP contribution.
- Ownership of plan assets: At retirement, the IPP member owns any actuarial surplus. It may be used to upgrade pension benefits or the plan holder may pass it on to his or her spouse, heirs, or estate.
- Guaranteed lifetime income to IPP member and their spouses: This pension plan offers a predictable retirement income. An actuary determines the current annual cost of the future retirement income. Spouse pension benefits may be upgraded to 100% when the member retires or dies. The company is on the hook for this money.
- Additional benefits: Full consumer price indexing, early retirement pension with no reduction, and bridge benefits can be structured to fortify gaps left by other retirement income pools like the CPP or OAS.

ESSENTIAL TAX FACT | The 2011 budget made several changes which will affect retirement plans for individuals with these plans.

- Annual minimum withdrawal amounts will be required from IPPs once a plan member is 72. These amounts will be based on current RRIF rules.
- Contributions to an IPP related to past years of employment will have to come from RRSP or RPP assets or by reducing RRSP contribution room, before deductible contributions can be made. These provisions will apply to IPP past service contributions made after March 22, 2011.

Deferred Profit Sharing Plans (DPSPs). A deferred profit sharing plan (DPSP) provides for payments by an employer to a trustee, in trust, for the benefit of the employees or former employees, based on an employer's profits from the employer's business.

ESSENTIAL TAX FACT | Employees may not contribute to a DPSP so there is no deduction available to the employee when contributions are made. Employer's contributions are deductible to the employer however. Members of a DPSP will be subject to a pension adjustment which means that contributions to an RRSP will be limited as a result of membership in the DPSP.

Direct transfers to another DPSP, RPP or RRSP. When the employee leaves the employer, vested DPSP funds may be transferred to another DPSP, RPP or RRSP or RRIF. The transfer must be a direct transfer, using form T2151 *Direct Transfer of a Single Amount Under Subsection 147(19) or Section 147.3* to recognize the transfer. On death of the DPSP plan member, the funds in the DPSP may be transferred tax-free to the surviving spouse or common-law partner's RPP, RRSP, DPSP or RRIF. Use Form T2151 *Direct Transfer of a Single Amount Under Subsection 147(19) or Section 147.3* to recognize the transfer.

Amounts received by the taxpayer out of a DPSP are taxable. Such amounts will be eligible for the Pension Income Amount if received by a taxpayer who is over 64. The DPSP must pay all amounts vested in the plan to the beneficiary no later than the end of the year in which the beneficiary turns 71. However, the DPSP may provide for the conversion of the plan funds to an annuity.

The RRSP. Making a contribution to a deductible registered plan, like your RRSP, is a good thing if you want to reduce the taxes you pay along the way and claim more non-refundable credits like medical expenses. That's because net income, the figure upon which these amounts is calculated, is reduced by making an RRSP contribution. A lower net family income will also increase federal refundable tax credits like the Child Tax Benefit, the Working Income Tax Benefit, or the GST/HST Credits. It all means more cash for you throughout the year.

When it comes to tax advantages, investing within a registered account essentially enables some double-dipping: new dollars are created for investment purposes with your tax deduction, while tax on investment earnings is deferred into the future.

But there is one catch: you will be restricted in the amounts you can sock away in your RRSP; for example only "earned income" sources qualify, and a maximum contribution rate and dollar limit exist. In addition you have to be under 72 to contribute (or have a spouse who is under 72). Check your Notice of Assessment from the CRA for your Unused RRSP Contribution Room. If you have no available RRSP contribution room, be sure to contribute to a TFSA.

Understanding Contribution Room. The RRSP is an essential tool in building up your savings for retirement. So just how much can you contribute? RRSP contribution room is the lesser of:

- 18% of earned income from the prior tax year minus any net "Pension Adjustments" (PAs) for the current year, and
- the maximum RRSP "contribution limit" for the current year minus any net Pension Adjustments for the current year.

Let's define some of those terms. The "Pension Adjustment" is a measure of benefits accruing to you as a member of another tax-deferred plan at work, such as an RPP (Registered Pension Plan) or DPSP (Deferred Profit Sharing Plan).

The RRSP "contribution limit" is 18% of earned income to a dollar maximum of $22,450 for 2011.

ESSENTIAL TAX FACT | If you don't make the full allowable contribution to your RRSP, the unused RRSP contribution room carries forward for use in the future.

Figuring out how much you can contribute begins with looking for your Unused Contribution Room on your Notice of Assessment or Reassessment from the CRA.

The RRSP deduction is recorded on Schedule 7 and from there on Line 208 of the tax return. This deduction can include:
- RRSP contributions made in prior years and not deducted or refunded
- RRSP contributions made in the tax year
- RRSP contributions made in the first 60 days after the end of the tax year.

Age eligibility. Note that there is no lower age limit for contributing to an RRSP. As long as CRA has the unused RRSP contribution room recorded, even a young adult can make a contribution. But, RRSPs must be collapsed by the end of the year in which you turn 71.

ESSENTIAL TAX FACT | Besides the requirement for unused RRSP contribution room, a taxpayer must be under 72 years of age to contribute to an RRSP... unless there is a younger spouse.

Spousal RRSPs. You may contribute to your own RRSPs based on available RRSP contribution room, and may also contribute some or all of the amounts to a spousal RRSP. This may provide for income splitting advantages on retirement and can help an age-ineligible taxpayer prolong the ability to use an RRSP deduction. Spousal RRSPs are not subject to the Attribution Rules; that is, you can contribute to a spousal RRSP and have the resulting income taxed in the spouse's hands…but there is a catch. Withdrawals from a spousal RRSP will be taxed in the contributor's hands if the money is withdrawn within 3 years of the last contribution to any spousal plan.

ESSENTIAL TAX FACT | If you are "age ineligible" you may still contribute to a spousal RRSP, based on your RRSP contribution room, if your spouse is under 72 years old.

John, for example, has been making contributions every year to equalize pension accumulations. If his wife Sofi withdraws money from a spousal RRSP within three years of the last contribution by John to any spousal plan, the withdrawal will be taxed in John's hands.

An exception to this rule occurs when the spousal RRSP accumulations are transferred into a Registered Retirement Income Fund or RRIF. In that case only the amounts in excess of the minimum amount you are required to withdraw will be taxed in the hands of the contributor to the spousal RRSP.

If John in our example above had turned 72 this year, he could no longer contribute to his own RRSP even though he still has unused RRSP contribution room of $5,000. His wife Sofi is 65, though. John can choose to make a spousal RRSP contribution, thereby depositing the money into Sofi's RRSP. He can then take the deduction on his return.

The pension income splitting rules may impact the amount of contributions some taxpayers make to the family's RRSPs. These rules will be discussed later. But remember, double digit returns by way of tax savings will often result from an RRSP contribution; so it's good to weigh that in to every investment decision.

ESSENTIAL TAX FACT | Any amounts contributed in the year and not deducted are considered to be "undeducted RRSP contributions." These amounts may be carried forward and deducted in future years if this is advantageous.

The point of all of this is, of course, to increase your wealth for use in retirement income planning. An RRSP deduction on Line 208 of the return creates new money for savings with an increased tax refund; you'll save more because tax on investment income is deferred, and you'll increase entitlements to refundable tax credits or social benefits like the Old Age Security or Employment Insurance as a result of your reduced net income.

ESSENTIAL TAX FACT | You can also save the RRSP deduction for a future year, perhaps when an unusual spike in income occurs.

Consider this example: Terry is out of work and not taxable, but he has maximized his RRSP contribution every year. He knows that he does not need to take the tax deduction, but can save his "undeducted RRSP contributions" for next year, when he expects a taxable severance package of over $80,000. He will get a bigger bang for his RRSP buck that way.

It can really pay off in a big way to claim your RRSP deduction when your marginal tax advantage is highest. But suppose you just don't have any cash to contribute to an RRSP? Here's more good news: RRSP contributions may be made in cash or in kind. That is, you may transfer an eligible investment from your non-registered investments to your RRSP and may claim a deduction for the fair market value of the asset at the time of the transfer.

ESSENTIAL TAX FACT | Investments that have declined in value should not be transferred to an RRSP as the loss in value will not be deductible.

If the fair market value at the time of the transfer is higher than the cost of the asset, you will have to report the capital gain in income for the year.

ESSENTIAL TAX FACT | When RRSP contributions are made by transferring capital property into the account, you are deemed to have disposed of the property at the time of the transfer.

However, there's a trap: if the fair market value of the asset is less than its cost, then the loss will be deemed to be nil. That is, it will not be claimable. Therefore, if you want to transfer an asset which has decreased in value to your RRSP in order to create a tax deduction, it's best to sell the asset, contribute the proceeds to the RRSP and then have the RRSP repurchase the asset. This method allows you to deduct the capital loss on your tax return. Also, be aware that any income accrued prior to the transfer of assets, such as interest, must be reported on the tax return as of the date of transfer to the RRSP.

Note, there are other new rules to ensure the taxpayer does not receive an advantage when assets are swapped from a non-registered account to a registered one, so check with your tax advisor before transferring assets back and forth. Non-compliance can result in expensive penalties.

Withdrawing RRSP accumulations. Your RRSP accumulations can be taken out in a lump sum; however this is not usually a good idea as the amounts will be taxed at the highest marginal rate at that time. You can also choose to create a periodic pension—monthly, quarterly, semi-annually, etc. This is important if you wish to qualify for the pension income amount and pension income splitting, which is possible once you have reached age 65 (or are receiving the amounts as a result of the spouse's death).

Withdrawals from an RRSP will be reported on a T4RSP slip, recorded as periodic income on Line 115 of your tax return if they represent a periodic pension withdrawal or otherwise, use Line 129. Withdrawals will be subject to withholding tax at the following rates (which will differ in Quebec):

Up to $5,000	10%
$5,000 to $15,000	20%
Above $15,000	30%

Especially when you take a lump sum from your RRSP, it is important for you to take this withholding tax into consideration before you make a withdrawal, to ensure you end up with the exact amount of funds you need for the purpose you have in mind.

ESSENTIAL TAX FACT | Tax withholdings can be minimized by taking several smaller withdrawals from your RRSP, rather than one large one. You might also consider, for example, taking them over two tax years for a better after-tax result.

Sometimes you'll want to withdraw money from an RRSP because you have undeducted contributions, or over-contributions. Such withdrawals are not taxable.

RRSP over-contributions and excess contributions. Over-contributions often happen when you instruct your employer to make RRSP contributions on your behalf through a payroll deduction plan, but forget to mention a change in your contribution room due to a tax reassessment. To cushion errors in contributions due to fluctuating RRSP room, an over-contribution limit of $2,000 is allowed without penalty, provided you are at least 18 in the preceding taxation year.

Many taxpayers, in fact, use this rule for tax planning purposes. They purposely contribute the amount allowed under their contribution room plus $2000. This is a great way to earn even more tax deferred income within your RRSP.

Debbie, for example, has RRSP contribution room of $5,000, which she has contributed. But she is allowed to contribute a total of $7,000 without penalty, and decides to do so to earn tax-deferred investment income while the money is in the plan.

> **ESSENTIAL TAX FACT** | Avoid making "excess contributions". These are RRSP contributions which exceed your contribution room plus $2,000. If you do, you need to create contribution room or pay the penalty.

That's important, because without the benefit of the RRSP contribution, leaving excess amounts in an RRSP will result in double taxation and expensive penalties. Discuss the following opportunities in managing your RRSP withdrawals with your tax and financial advisor:

- **Withdrawal of undeducted contributions.** Amounts contributed to your RRSP and not yet deducted may be withdrawn tax-free and with no withholding taxes by filing Form T3012A, *Tax Deduction Waiver on the Refund of Your Undeducted RRSP Contributions*. The amount withdrawn will be included on a T4RSP slip and must be reported as income. You may, however, claim an offsetting deduction on your tax return. Taxpayers who withdraw undeducted contributions without using Form T3012A will have tax withheld but may use Form T746 to calculate their allowable deduction on line 232.

- **Contributions in excess of overcontribution limits.** Excess RRSP contributions are subject to a penalty tax of 1% per month. A complicated form called a *T1-OVP* must be completed in that case and the penalty must be paid by March 31 of the year following. Penalties will accrue until the excess contributions are withdrawn from the RRSP. You'll want to ask a professional to help you with this form.

Tax-free transfers to an RRSP. You have learned that tax efficiency in retirement includes moving money into the right "buckets" so that layering of income sources is planned to average down the overall taxes paid. The following capital sources may be transferred to your RRSP on a tax-free basis over and above the normal RRSP contribution limits plus the $2,000 allowable over-contribution:

- **Eligible retiring allowances.** Amounts received on job termination as a severance package may be rolled over into an RRSP on a tax-free basis depending on certain conditions. For service after 1995, no RRSP rollover is allowed. For service after 1988 and before 1996, a single limit of $2,000 per year of service can be rolled into an RRSP. And for service before 1989, it is possible to roll over $2,000 for each year of service plus another $1,500 for each year in which the employer's contributions to the company pension plan did not vest in you. The eligible amount will be shown on the T4A from the former employer. In applying these rules, a single day in a calendar year counts as a "year" of employment.

- **Funds from another RRSP.** You may request a direct transfer of RRSP accumulations from one RRSP to another RRSP under which you are the annuitant. Form T2033 may be used to effect the transfer.
- **Funds from a spouse's RRSP.** On the breakdown of a marriage or common-law relationship, where the terms of a separation or divorce agreement require that the funds from one spouse's RRSP be transferred to the other, the funds may be transferred tax-free. Form T2220 must be used.
- **Registered Pension Plan (RPP) amounts.** If you cease to belong to an employer-sponsored RPP, the funds from the RPP may be transferred to your RRSP. Form T2151 must be used.
- **Deferred Profit Sharing Plan (DPSP) accumulations.** You may transfer funds from your DPSP to your RRSP. Form T2151 must be used.
- **Foreign pension receipts.** Lump sum amounts received from a foreign pension plan in respect of a period while you were a non-resident may be transferred to your RRSP. Amounts that are exempt from tax under a tax treaty with the foreign country may not be transferred.
- **Saskatchewan pension plan amounts.** A lump sum payment out of the Saskatchewan pension plan may be transferred to your RRSP tax-free.

Tax-free transfers from an RRSP. Funds from your RRSP may be transferred on a tax-free basis to:

- A Registered Pension Plan (only possible if the RPP terms allow this). Form T2033 may be used.
- Another RRSP.
- The RRSP of a spouse or former spouse on breakdown of marriage or common-law relationship.
- A RRIF. You may transfer funds from your RRSP to a RRIF under which you are the annuitant. Form T2033 must be used.
- The RRIF of a spouse or former spouse on breakdown of marriage or common-law relationship. Form T2220 must be used.
- An annuity. Amounts can be transferred from your RRSP to an annuity contract for your life or jointly for the life of you and your spouse or common-law partner with or without a guarantee period. If there is a guarantee period, it may not be for a period longer than until you (or spouse or common-law partner) are 90 years old.

- RRSP of spouse or former spouse or dependant on death.
- RDSP of surviving child or grandchild. Effective March 5, 2010 rollovers to an RDSP may be made on a tax-free basis if the surviving child or grandchild has sufficient RDSP contribution room.

Creating Your RRSP-Funded Pension. When it comes time to create your periodic pension withdrawals from an RRSP, the accumulations will generally be transferred into one of two investment vehicles that will enable a periodic taxable income, that is properly blended for tax efficiency:

- an annuity (which provides for equal monthly payments over a period of time)
- a Registered Retirement Income Funds (RRIF), which provides for gradually increasing payments over time.

> **ESSENTIAL TAX FACT** | Under a RRIF, a minimum amount must be withdrawn according to a predetermined schedule based on your age. The payments are taxable in the year received.

However you can withdraw more than this as required. As with RRSP payments, the amounts will qualify for the $2,000 pension income amount on Line 314 if you are over age 64 or receiving the amounts as the result of a spouse's death.

Before you withdraw, speak to your tax advisors about planning your income sources, taking into account the following concepts:

- Equalizing income between spouses—who should withdraw first or most—the higher income earner or the lower?
- Can other income sources be split between spouses—Canada Pension Plan benefits for example?
- Should dividends be reported by the higher earner (a possibility only if a Spousal Amount is thereby created or increased)?
- Should one spouse be earning more or less interest, dividends or capital gains from non-registered sources to reduce family net income?
- How will the clawback of the Age Amount or Old Age Security be affected by your pension withdrawals?
- How will your quarterly instalment payments be affected by your RRSP withdrawals?
- If you will be in a higher marginal tax bracket at death, should you withdraw more during your lifetime?
- The goal for couples is two equal incomes. Have you accomplished that?

CHAPTER 32

FOREIGN SHORES

Canadian residents may be subject to tax on foreign pension income sources, and tax treaties with foreign countries are put into place to help avoid double taxation. Even if your foreign pension income is deposited in an account offshore, know that because Canadian residents are taxed on world income in Canadian funds, all foreign pension income received—no matter where in the world—is taxable in Canada. A foreign tax credit may be claimed if the "source country" withholds taxes.

Certain tax exemptions are available to Canadian tax filers; of recent note:

Tax exemption on U.S. Social Security. Recipients of U.S. Social Security will claim a 15% deduction on Line 256 of the Canadian tax return.

> **ESSENTIAL TAX FACT** | U.S. Social Security benefits received after January, 2010, will be eligible for a 50% deduction, if they relate to pre-1996 service.

This change should be reviewed with executors of estates receiving qualifying benefits as well.

German Social Security. German social security benefits became taxable in Canada in 2003. For pensions which began in 2005 or earlier, the portion of the pension that is non-taxable is 50%. For pensions which begin after 2005, the percentage that is non-taxable in Canada is set in the year that the pension starts. The 50% rate for 2005 increases by 2% each year for the period 2006 to 2020, and then increases by 1% each year until the taxable percentage reaches 100%.

This percentage is used in the pension begins and in the subsequent year. For each year thereafter, the non-taxable portion is fixed at the amount (in Euro) that was non-taxable in the first full year that the pension is received.

Snowbirds. Canadians who live in the U.S. for the winter may have both Canadian and U.S. tax filing consequences, depending on whether they are considered to have resident alien status, which requires the filing of a U.S. tax return. A "closer connection" declaration must be made on June 15 every year to avoid this. Follow the Snowbird Tax Guide below to ensure you don't put yourself into an unintended tax filing position by overstaying your winter visit:

Snowbird tax guide: Key questions to be discussed with your advisors

1. **What does it mean to be a U.S. resident or to have a U.S. resident alien status?**

   Answer: To avoid U.S. taxation on world-wide income, it is necessary for the snowbird to avoid U.S. resident alien status. This occurs when the "substantial presence test" is met.

2. **What is the "substantial presence test"?**

   Answer: Calculating the Substantial Presence Test: Each day:
   - in current year counts as a full day;
   - last year counts as one-third of a day; and
   - year before that counts as one-sixth of a day.

   If your total is at least 183 days, you are considered a resident alien for U.S. filing purposes in the year. If your total is less than 183 days, you are considered a non-resident alien. Even if you a resident alien because you meet the substantial presence test, you can be considered a non-resident alien if:
   - you were present in the U.S. for less than 183 days
   - your tax home is in Canada; and
   - you had a closer connection to Canada than to the U.S.

3. **Are there tax implications to renting our winter vacation home to others?**

   Answer: Rental income on a U.S. property owned by a Canadian will automatically have a 30%, non-refundable withholding tax applied on the income. To avoid this withholding tax the Canadian can file a U.S. tax return.

4. **What do U.S. estate taxes include and when would U.S. estate taxes be triggered?**

   Answer: U.S. estate taxes are first based on worldwide assets. If worldwide assets are significant, even if the U.S. assets are not, U.S. estate taxes could still be payable. U.S. estate taxes would be applied on real estate, U.S. securities or certain other property that is deemed to be situated in the United States (collectively referred to as "U.S. situs assets") that total greater than $60,000 in aggregate. As estate tax rates and exemptions are expected to change in 2013, it is essential to get tax advice before buying U. S. property.

5. **What are gift taxes and why are they important?**

   Answer: If you "gift" a U.S. property to another family member, U.S. Gift Taxes could apply. These could be significant; again a reason to seek tax advice.

6. **If the intent is to break all ties with Canada, and become a non-resident, how does one go about doing this and what are the departure taxes?**

   Answer: If your intent is to break all ties with Canada and become a non-resident you will need to consider both the "primary" ties as well as the "secondary" ties, and the impact of departure taxes. CRA could still deem you as a Canadian resident and thus charge penalties and taxes if you have not clearly "broken" all of your ties with Canada. There are a number of assets and investments that are "deemed" to have been sold the day one breaks their ties with Canada: non-registered investments, certain rental, vacation properties and farmland to name a few. This could result in a significant capital gains tax paid on departure. However, provisions are in place to defer this tax under certain situations.

7. **How are CPP, OAS, RRSP and RRIF Income Payments impacted by departure from Canada?**

   Answer: Pensions, RRSP investments and Canadian real estate are not considered to have been sold for tax purposes upon departure from Canada.

CHAPTER 33

PENSION INCOME SPLITTING

With our progressive tax system, the more evenly you can spread your household income amongst family members, the more likely it is that you'll pay the least amount of income tax as a family. During the active earning years, the opportunities for splitting earned income are limited, but several opportunities exist to split retirement income and thereby reduce your total tax bill. We have discussed some of these opportunities already; to review:

Spousal RRSPs have been available for some time. When one spouse has higher earned income than the other, the spousal RRSP provides an opportunity for both the self-employed and those who will not be receiving a pension income to split RRSP income in retirement with their spouse. The spouse with the higher earned income claims the RRSP deduction, thereby reducing their income tax bill but the spouse (in whose name the contribution is made) will report the RRSP income when it is withdrawn as retirement income.

Where the spouses are different ages, use of a spousal plan can defer the time when the plan must be matured and a retirement income is taken until the year that spouse turns 71. A spousal plan can therefore provide a longer tax-free accumulation period than would otherwise be available.

Where neither spouse belongs to a RPP, the spousal RRSP may be the only way to split pension income before age 65.

Splitting of Canada Pension Plan benefits is beneficial if one spouse receives significantly more CPP benefits than the other. Through a simple application to Human Resources Development Canada, CPP benefits earned while the couple was together may be split between them. Be sure to review Chapter 30 of this book for upcoming changes to the CPP which may affect seniors who wish to continue working after age 60 while drawing benefits.

Splitting of qualifying pension income became possible starting in 2007. Spouses or common-law partners may elect to each report a portion of "eligible" pension income received. Essentially this is income that qualifies for the $2,000 pension income amount. Up to one-half of such pension income received can be reported by the recipient's spouse.

What is the Pension Income Credit? The Pension Income Credit is a $2,000 tax credit that is applied to the taxpayer's income tax return. This credit is multiplied by 15% on the federal tax return and therefore can reduce taxes payable by $300 each year for each spouse. A similar credit is available on the provincial return and its value varies by province.

To receive the pension income credit, you must first be receiving eligible pension income. To maximize the benefit of this credit, it is extremely important and valuable to split at least $2000 to a spouse's tax return so that this benefit could be doubled for the family, each and every year. Therefore, by first creating sources of income that would qualify for pension income splitting, and then by ensuring that at least $2000 of the eligible pension income is shared each and every year between spouses, taxpayers can create significant tax savings in retirement.

What is eligible pension income? "Eligible" pension income—that which can be split—is pension income that qualifies for the pension income credit, a $2,000 amount found on Schedule 1 of the tax return. The eligible income must be regular and systematic income. It generally falls into two qualifying categories:

1. **For those under 65:** periodic pension receipts of a life annuity from a registered pension fund or superannuation, or the amounts in (B) below if received as a result of a spouse's death.

2. **For those age 65 or over:** periodic annuity payments from an RRSP, RRIF, LIF, LRIF, PRIF, spousal RRIF, registered annuity or non-registered annuity and / or GIC income from an insurance company investment

A good example of this is a government worker who retires at 45 with an employer-sponsored pension benefit. Up to 50% of pension income received could be split for tax purposes with the spouse, regardless of the age of the pensioner or their spouse.

However, the rules for the other sources of income in (B) are different. The income can only be split once the annuitant reaches age 65.

Specifically excluded from the definitions of pension and qualified pension income are:
- Old Age Security,
- Canada or Quebec Pension Plan Benefits,

- a death benefit
- foreign pension income which qualifies for a deduction or exemption (example: US Social Security)
- a payment received out of or under a salary deferral arrangement, a retirement compensation arrangement, an employee benefit plan, an employee trust or the Saskatchewan Pension Plan.

Splitting of pension income between spouses can be beneficial but not for all taxpayers. The following should be taken into account when planning for splitting of retirement income:

- the effect on the Age Amount and OAS clawback on both the transferor and the transferee (could be detrimental);
- the effect on total non-refundable credits available to the family unit, considering specifically the Age Amount, the Pension Amount, the Spousal Amount and other credits transferable;
- the potential for moving the transferor to a lower bracket and the impact of potentially moving the transferee to a higher bracket, together with requirements to make quarterly tax instalment payments.

Planning a pension for RDSP beneficiaries. A disabled person who is a beneficiary of a Registered Disability Savings Plan (RDSP) must begin to take retirement benefits from it in the year he or she turns 60. Those benefits will not affect any other means-tested support delivered through the income tax system including the OAS.

Each payment made from a RDSP is considered to be comprised of grants, bonds and investment income and each such part is included in the beneficiary's income when received effective the 2008 and subsequent tax years.

There is an annual limit on the amount paid equal to the value of the assets of the plan at the beginning of the year divided by a factor equal to three plus the remaining number of years the beneficiary is expected to live ("life expectancy") as determined by Statistics Canada. Special rules apply when there is a shortened life expectancy to provide access to the funds.

Payments from an RDSP can be one of three types:

- a disability assistance payment made to the beneficiary or the beneficiary's estate,
- a transfer to another RDSP or
- a repayment that is required to be made to the government.

It may be a good idea to receive assistance from a tax and legal advisor in planning these payments to ensure all other tax preferences and social benefits available to the disabled taxpayer can be maximized.

CHAPTER 34

LAYERING INVESTMENT INCOME

ESSENTIAL TAX FACT | When retirees use available tax preferences in structuring retirement income so that they pay less tax year over year, they can continue to build wealth, and keep the taxman from encroaching on their capital.

The retired taxpayer, with money saved in a variety of different tax efficient "buckets" can thwart the taxman, who is first in line in receiving income from employment earnings. In fact, retirees recoup their economic power in retirement: you decide when to realize income for tax purposes. Therefore you continue to increase your wealth by maximizing the time value of money.

Tax efficient retirement income planning, therefore, evolves from a deliberate strategy to save and withdraw money in a careful order, in registered and non-registered accounts such as RRSPs, RRIFs and TFSAs. This order of investing and withdrawal matters in difficult investment climates, and requires prioritization:

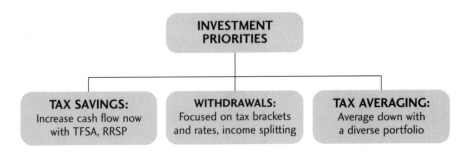

Benefits from public pension sources and accessibility to refundable tax credits can all help to provide the cash flow you need in retirement and through a variety of economic cycles. This is simply a return of your hard earned tax dollars paid while income was high throughout your earnings career. Maximize them in the present with all the tax preferences and deductions available to you. Then withdraw taxable income, efficiently.

Remember, investments in *non-registered accounts* can supplement required cash flows, but they will produce taxable income, in the form of interest, dividends, rental and royalty income.

> **ESSENTIAL TAX FACT** | The dispositions of income-producing capital in non-registered accounts can produce *capital gains or losses*—increases or decreases in the original value of capital invested.

Generally that will occur on the sale of the asset, but deemed dispositions are also possible: on emigration or death for example.

Finally, you can also supplement cash flow by withdrawing a return of your own tax-paid capital, but this depletes your ability to earn income from those investments in the future. Think carefully about this. Still, if such withdrawals are gifted as part of an estate planning strategy, your diverse portfolio can benefit enormously. You'll learn more about this in the next section of the book.

SOURCES OF CASH FLOW IN RETIREMENT

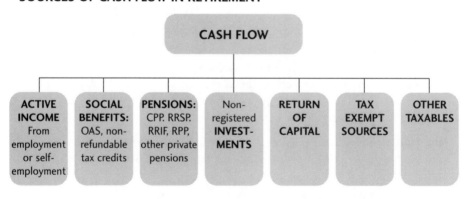

1. **Registered investment pools:** Because you have control over when the money in RRSPs and, in some cases RPPs is generated for tax purposes, plan a longer withdrawal period to average out the taxes payable. Split income with spouse if possible.

2. **Non-registered investments.** Plan to add to your retirement income with income sources that are taxed at lower marginal tax rates; splitting this income with family members where possible.

3. **Return of capital.** If you are short of money, principal withdrawals or a "return of capital" are not subject to tax. This is important as return of capital can often supplement taxable income when returns are temporarily too low to cover needs. However, this option should be viewed as a temporary fix, unless depleting a particular capital pool is a part of the plan.

RRSP drawdown strategies: There are two possible ways to draw down RRSP portfolios in a tax-efficient manner. Each option may require the client to take on more risk than what they should at this stage in their life.

- **Split income with spouse:** If you have not yet attained age 65, and therefore cannot yet make an election to split up to 50% of retirement income from an RRSP or RRIF with your spouse, have the lower earning spouse withdraw taxable funds from his/her own RRSP first; depleting that source if necessary while keeping the higher earner's RRSP intact. Alternatively (or in addition), withdrawals from a spousal RRSP can be made, keeping the three year holding rules in mind.

- **Withdraw up to bracket strategy:** Another important approach is to make additional RRSP withdrawals, in retirement, up to the next highest tax bracket or clawback zone. This income is going to be taxed at this same level at some point in time, so it may be prudent to withdraw the money now and reinvest it more tax-efficiently going forward. Further, accumulations may be taxed at higher marginal tax rate when the second surviving spouse dies.

- **Age-ineligible investing.** When a taxpayer reaches age 72, RRSP accumulations are required to generate taxable income. Accumulations are generally transferred into a RRIF or annuity or both prior to age 72 to achieve the desired effect on the tax return. Discuss the timing of taxable income under these options with your retirement income planner. After this try to maximize TFSA savings as a tax shelter.

Non-registered investments. Review the output of income-producing assets available for pre-retirement planning when assets are held outside an RRSP. Some options include:

- **Debt instruments, generating interest:** This income source is not tax efficient when held outside an RRSP; 100% of accrued earnings are added to income. This means that even if you don't receive the money from a compounding investment, you dip into your own pocket to pay the tax first. It should be earned within a registered account if possible.

- **Dividends from preferred and common shareholdings:** Extremely tax efficient, depending on where you live, dividends can even offset taxes payable on other income of the year, depending on your marginal tax bracket. However, be careful; an overweighting in dividend income can cause a clawback of Old Age Security benefits and other tax credits.

- **Accrued gains in income-producing assets:** Very tax efficient, as those gains will not be taxed until disposition. At that time, they will then be offset by capital losses of the year, and after this only 50% of the net amount is added to taxable income. Additional planning with charitable donations can render capital gains on certain securities completely tax-free.

- **Prescribed annuities and TSWP mutual funds:** This income can be tax efficient as it is made up of a combination of tax paid capital and earnings. These tools enable the client to receive the income they need, while also minimizing the tax paid.

- **Mutual fund distributions:** Regular distributions from the fund: capital gains, interest and dividends have a variety of tax consequences. Generally you'll want to buy these investments at the beginning rather than the end of the previous year to avoid receiving all the distributions for the year over a short ownership period.

- **Corporate class mutual funds:** The capital class structure will allow you to protect against declining markets by shifting capital into another class of shares of the corporation without triggering a capital gain. Those tax-efficient strategies will make a big difference in building net worth and this opportunity can allow for cash flow management in a variety of positive ways.

Don't forget the TFSA. Significant protection against inflation and taxation can be achieved when you take advantage of investment opportunities in a Tax-Free Savings Account, especially if all other tax deferral opportunities have expired. Otherwise, the return of your tax-paid capital can supplement taxable income, as discussed above, but at the expense of a diminishing balance on which to earn future income.

Minimize tax remittances. Know the present and future value of every dollar you earn as you structure income in retirement. You can make today's dollar work for you immediately by investing it… but only if it is in your possession in the first place. That's why you need to plan to keep of the first dollars you make by being vigilant about tax overpayments at source, or through quarterly instalment payments.

At the start of every calendar year, new forms TD1 Personal Tax Credits (Federal and Provincial) and T1213 Request for Reduction in Tax Withholding at source should be reviewed to ensure you are not taking money out of the marketplace to pay taxes you don't really owe.

ESSENTIAL TAX FACT | You can also reduce your withholding for the Old Age Security Recovery Tax (your clawback) with a T1213 (OAS) *Request To Reduce Old Age Security Recovery Tax at Source.*

For 2008 and subsequent years, the quarterly instalment threshold, used to determine whether instalments are payable by individuals was increased from taxes owing of $2,000 ($1,200 for Quebec filers) to taxes owing in excess of $3,000 ($1,800 for Quebec filers). If you expect your income will drop over prior years, change your remittances.

ESSENTIAL TAX FACT | It is not mandatory to follow the instalment notices sent by CRA. You can request to change your payments based on your prior year results or an estimation of current year income.

It is your responsibility to ensure that you pay enough tax throughout the year rather than leaving a large tax bill for the end of the year. So long as you adjust withholding taxes on various sources of income so that you do not have a large year-end tax bill, you do not need to make tax instalment payments.

However, if your taxes owing exceed $3,000, then you may be penalized. Use the forms mentioned above to increase taxes withheld at source. Never overpay your taxes just so that you can get a refund at the end of the year.

RETIREMENT INCOME LAYERING SUMMARY

SOURCE	TAX STATUS	TAX REPORTING
Employment	Taxable	Report on Line 101.
Old Age Security	Taxable to recipient. Clawed back when individual's net income on Line 236 exceeds indexed income thresholds	Call 1-800-277-9914 to apply. Report income on Line 113 from T4A(OAS) slip. Report income tax deducted on Line 437.
Guaranteed Income Supplement and Allowance	Report as income (line 146) for purposes of reducing tax credits—these sources increase individual net income	Deduct on Line 250 so that income is not taxable.
Canada Pension Plan	Taxable to recipient (except survivors benefits paid to minors, which are received by widow/ widower but taxed to child)	Report on Line 114 from T4A(P) slip, remember to take into account the ability to split income with spouse through a benefit assignment.

RETIREMENT INCOME LAYERING SUMMARY (Continued)

SOURCE	TAX STATUS	TAX REPORTING
Retiring Allowances (Severance Pay)	Taxable but portions may qualify for tax-free rollover to an RRSP or Registered Pension Plan (RPP)	Report amounts on T4A or T3 slips. Amounts in Box 026 of TA can be transferred to an RRSP or RPP on a tax-free basis. Qualifying amounts on T3 slip are in Box 47.
Superannuation (Periodic Pension Benefits)	Taxable but up to 50% of income may be split with spouse	Report amounts from T4A or T3 on Line 115; to split income complete form T1032 and follow reporting instructions.
Foreign Pension Income	Taxable in Canadian funds, however some are non-taxable due to a tax treaty.	Report gross amounts on Line 115, but take treaty deductions available on Line 256. Certain periodic pensions qualify for the pension income amount, too.
Annuity payments	Amounts from general annuities, Deferred Profit Sharing Plans (DPSPs) are taxable.	Depending on age some of these amounts may qualify for the offsetting pension income amount and income splitting.
Retroactive Lump Sums	Taxable if received for years after 1977, but may qualify for lump sum averaging. Includes employment income, damages, wage loss replacement, support from a spouse, RPP benefits, EI	Attach form T1198 *Statement of Qualifying Retroactive Lump-Sum Payments.*
Interest Income	From bank accounts, term deposits, GICs, etc. are taxable on an annual accrual basis	Report on Line 121. Note that in the case of T-Bills, a capital gain or loss may occur on disposition before maturity.
Capital Gains and Losses	Partially taxable. Income from the disposition of capital property is included at 50%.	Report on Line 127 if gains exceed losses for the year. Carry losses back 3 years or forward in offsetting capital gains in the future.
Dividend Income	Taxable. Income can be received from "eligible" or "other than eligible" dividends; the latter coming from small business corps that qualify for the small business deduction.	The actual dividend is grossed up by 25% in the case of ineligible dividends and 41% in the case of eligible dividends on Line 120. Then an offsetting dividend tax credit is taken in the amount of 13.33% and 16.43% respectively on Schedule 1 (2011 rates).

SOURCE	TAX STATUS	TAX REPORTING
RRSPs	Taxable. Both principal and earnings are taxable but qualify for pension income amount if taxpayer is at least age 65 or receiving amounts due to death of spouse	Claim on Line 129; if not eligible for the pension income amount on Line 314; otherwise claim on Line 115. Watch over and excess contributions. Amounts that qualify for the pension income amount also qualify for pension income splitting.
Spousal RRSP	Taxable in hands of contributor if holding period of 3 years from last spousal RRSP contribution is not met.	As above. Pay attention to designation of benefits at death; tax-free transfers on marriage breakdown.
RRIF	Taxable in hands of recipient.	As above. Note in case of spousal plan, transfers of RRSP accumulations to a RRIF results in minimum payments that are taxable to the annuitant. Amounts over this are taxed to spouse until holding period is over.
Self-employment	Proprietors are taxed on net business income and must make CPP contributions unless drawing benefits from the plan	File a Business Income Statement. Incorporated taxpayers lose CPP pension building opportunity if drawing dividends only.
Retirement Compensation Arrangements (RCA)	When making a withdrawal from an RCA the income is fully taxable. The income comes from two parts: refundable tax from CRA and the RCA investment itself.	Income reported on a T4A-RCA slip is reported on line 130 of the recipient's return. This income is classed as "other income" not eligible for any offsetting deductions or credits. RCA income is not eligible for pension income splitting.
Individual Pension Plans (IPP)	Taxable based on same rules followed for RRSP and RRIF.	See prior information regarding pension income splitting.

Insurance: In the event you have one of more of the following insurance policies additional income may be available in times of need:

SOURCE	TAX STATUS	TAX REPORTING
Disability Income	If premiums were paid by the employee, the income received is tax-free. Any amount paid by the employer, renders the entire income taxable. Disability income plans, whether they are group or individual, pay to a maximum of age 65.	Report only taxable amounts on line 104 (other employment income). Deduct premiums paid by employee if the amount is taxable.
Long Term Care Income	The income received is as a monthly tax-free benefit. The benefit is paid in the event the insured is unable to complete one or more "daily activities" as defined by the policy. Can be used for any purpose, based on home or facility care expenses.	Form T2201 *Disability Tax Credit* may assist with eligibility.
Critical Illness Insurance	These plans can be available up to the insured's age 75 or 80. A lump sum tax-free benefit would be received in the event the insured was diagnosed of having a critical illness.	The conditions covered under each plan vary, the three conditions found under all plans relate to heart attack, stroke or cancer.
Life Insurance Policies	Many life insurance plans accumulate cash on a tax-free basis, which can be withdrawn at any time. The tax implications at the time of the withdrawal will depend on the amount withdrawn and the "adjusted cost basis" of the contract.	As a general rule, the cost base will decline to zero, making the cash withdrawal 100% taxable. Report taxable amounts on line 130 (Other Income). Amounts do not qualify for pension income splitting.
Line of Credit	A line of credit can often be secured for up to 75% of the cash value of a life insurance policy. This income is tax-free; —considered to be a loan.	No tax implications.

CHAPTER 35

CLAIMING NON-REFUNDABLE
TAX CREDITS

ESSENTIAL TAX FACT | Since 2002, seniors who are eligible to claim
the Disability Amount and who live in a retirement home can claim
attendant care expenses as a medical expense.

This is just one of the important tax facts many taxpayers don't know about
when it comes to claiming additional non-refundable tax credits in retirement.
Medical expenses will be covered in more detail later in the book.

The following additional tax credits should be considered as part of the "Tax-Free
Zone" retirees can accumulate, when their tax preferences are maximized:

Amounts transferred to spouse: Taxpayers may be able to claim all or part of the
following amounts for which their spouse or common-law partner qualifies, if that
person did not need the whole amount to reduce his or her federal tax to zero:

- the age amount (line 301) if the spouse or common-law partner was 65
  or older;
- the amount for minor children (line 367);
- the pension income amount (line 314);
- the disability amount (line 316); and
- tuition, education, and textbook amounts (line 323) that the spouse or
  common-law partner designates to you. The maximum amount that the
  spouse or common-law partner can transfer is $5,000 minus the amounts
  that he or she uses, even if there is still an unused part.

The spouse or common-law partner cannot transfer to the taxpayer any tuition or education amounts carried forward from a previous year. In addition, spousal transfers may not be made if the couple was separated because of a breakdown in their relationship for a period of 90 days or more that included December 31 of the current tax year.

> **ESSENTIAL TAX FACT** | The election to split pension income may decrease the amounts available for transfer.

Disability Amount: This claim may be made for a taxpayer with "a severe and prolonged impairment in mental or physical functions." The Disability Amount is available to all taxpayers who qualify.

> **ESSENTIAL TAX FACT** | The basic Disability Amount is subject to indexing from year to year. Form T2201 *Disability Tax Credit Certificate* must be signed by a medical practitioner to qualify.

For those supporting a disabled minor, this Disability Amount is enhanced by an indexed supplement ($4,282 for 2011). This amount is reduced by amounts claimed under child care expenses on Line 214 and the Disability Supports Deduction on Line 215 in excess of a Basic Child Care Amount of ($2,508 for 2011).

There are some special rules in making this claim:

- The Disability Amount and the deduction for attendant care expenses under the Disability Supports Deduction may both be claimed on the tax return. However, the deduction for attendant care expenses could limit the Disability Amount Supplement claimed for minor children.
- The taxpayer is restricted from claiming both the costs of nursing home care or full-time attendant care in excess of $10,000 as a medical expense, together with the Disability Amount. One or the other can be claimed but not both.
- Those who pay someone to come into the home to provide care for the sick may claim expenditures up to $10,000 ($20,000 in the year of death) as medical expenses without interrupting the claim for the Disability Amount.

Individuals who qualify for the Disability Amount will also be considered to be infirm for the purposes of the Amount for Eligible Dependants, the Amount for Infirm Dependants, and the Caregiver Amount.

Taxpayers may send in the completed T2201 form before they file their return to minimize the delays in sending refunds caused by review of the form.

ESSENTIAL TAX FACT | Fees for the completion of the T2201 form are considered to be medical expenses.

Caregiver Amount: A taxpayer who supports and lives with an infirm dependant adult in a home which the taxpayer maintains may claim a specified amount for that dependant as a non-refundable credit against taxes payable. To qualify, the dependant must meet these three criteria:

- be at least 18 years old,
- be either
  - the child or grandchild of the taxpayer or the taxpayer's spouse or common-law partner, or
  - the parent, grandparent, brother, sister, uncle, aunt, niece or nephew of the taxpayer or the taxpayer's spouse or common-law partner and resident in Canada at any time in the year, and
- be either
  - the taxpayer's parent or grandparent and at least 65 years old or
  - dependent on the taxpayer because of mental or physical infirmity

ESSENTIAL TAX FACT | More than one person can be eligible to claim this credit. The claim can be split between eligible persons, so long as the total amount claimed does not exceed the limit.

However, there are some additional limitations to know about:

- If the dependant was claimed as an "eligible dependent" at line 305 ("equivalent-to-spouse"), only that supporting individual can make the Caregiver Amount claim.
- The Amount for Infirm Dependants over 18 on line 306 cannot be claimed for an individual for whom the Caregiver Amount is claimed. The Caregiver Credit may be more valuable, as the income threshold for clawback is higher than it is for an Infirm Dependent.

Use Schedule 5 *Details of Dependant* to list the dependants and the claims being made; calculate the amount on the *Federal Worksheet*; and claim the amount on line 315 of Schedule 1 *Federal Tax*.

CHAPTER 36

TAX PLANNING:
AVERAGING DOWN TAX BURDENS

End-of-year protests by average taxpayers on Wall and Bay streets, brought to light inequalities in incomes earned by the rich and the poor. However, an important take-away is this: those who become rich invest, taking advantage of tax preferences on the various income sources they earn. There are no tax breaks for indebted consumers.

> **ESSENTIAL TAX FACT** | The tax system rewards investors. The high net worth individual keeps more of what is earned because capital gains and dividends are taxed more advantageously than employment income.

To be successful, it's important that one's investment portfolio is filled with appreciating assets that knock out the wealth eroders: taxes, fees and inflation, while producing income taxed at low marginal rates. However, that's also risky, hence the tax breaks.

It's important to pay yourself first, to preserve your savings. Slash expensive user fees, interest costs and MERs; reduce tax withholdings and instalment payments, too. Remember, it's your legal right to arrange your financial affairs within the framework of the law to pay the least taxes legally possible.

You have learned two ways a retiree's returns are directly affected by taxes: on annual taxable distributions or taxable withdrawals, and as a result of the additional tax penalties paid when social benefits like the Old Age Security and other refundable and non-refundable tax credits are clawed back.

ESSENTIAL TAX FACT | In planning retirement income, stay clear of the next marginal tax bracket, and manage the clawback income zones at the same time.

Then, plan retirement income withdrawals to minimize taxes every year in the future:

- **Split retirement and investment income** with your spouse.
- **Diversify income source withdrawals.** Avoid net income spikes with investment income diversification. (You have learned that dividends for example can artificially gross up net income, which in turn can increase per diem fees at nursing homes, and public pharmacy care plan deductibles, while reducing monthly social benefits like OAS and other tax credits found on your tax return.)
- **Always look back.** Be sure to recover errors and omissions on prior filed returns (up to 10 years back). This includes missed capital losses that can help you decrease capital gains earned in non-registered accounts in the future. That's important because when it comes time to tap into your asset pools in retirement, you must pay close attention to a third, more powerful tax enemy, which lurks in the future… the taxes paid on disposition of your income-producing assets—either during your lifetime or upon "deemed disposition" at death. That tax is fortified by its hidden partner: inflation.

Manage purchasing power. We discussed inflation briefly in the introduction to this book. Know that inflation erodes the purchasing power of your dollar. At an inflation rate of 2%, the future value of $1.00 today will be 67 cents in 20 years. That means the purchasing power of $500,000 in savings will be about $334,000. Yikes! You'll need to protect every dollar you earn even more… and one way to do this is by looking out for the best real rates of return over time, taking into account both inflation and taxes.

While inflation robs your money of its purchasing power over time, the taxman wins in the future by taxing your inflated values. This happens because your original cost base, upon which your capital gains are calculated, is not indexed to inflation. To play defensively: it's important to transfer assets into the right hands, at the right time, *and keep saving money if you can.*

ESSENTIAL TAX FACT | To minimize tax encroachment on your accumulated assets, manage taxes paid on your savings along the way; then keep an eye on the adjusted cost base, your proceeds of disposition and your unused capital losses to transfer assets into the right hands at the right time.

The trick to financing retirements is to keep more of today's valuable dollars intact, by investing them for as long as possible in assets that will appreciate more than the rate of tax and inflation combined, in a tax sheltered environment.

It is entirely appropriate to continue to accumulate and grow your retirement portfolios, while you withdraw required income, so a multi-pronged approach to wealth management is important.

ESSENTIAL TAX FACT | Always maximize the time value of money. A dollar in your pocket today is more valuable than a dollar to be received in the future. When you compute present value, you calculate what your cash flow in the future will be worth in today's dollars. When you calculate future value, you determine how large an investment today will grow to be in the future.

This is the perfect bridge to our next section: Tax efficient investing.

Part VI
Tax Efficient Investing

CHAPTER 37

WHAT IS
TAX EFFICIENT INVESTING?

The first goal in building sustainable family wealth—no matter what the economic cycle of the day brings—is to accumulate enough capital to provide your family with income for life. This process begins with anticipating how much capital you need to generate that income. For how long? By when? According to Statistics Canada, the average age of retirement is 62 years, the average length of retirement 15 years for men and 19 years for women.

So, that's what you are planning for and you have seen from our discussion on Tax Efficient Retirements, that the process begins with the first dollar you can afford to invest. When you add tax efficiency to your quest, you can multiply your wealth exponentially. So what is tax efficient investing?

> **ESSENTIAL TAX FACT** | Tax efficient investing is the process of taking advantage of tax rules to pay the least amount of taxes on income and capital, thereby accumulating the most after-tax wealth for the family over time.

This implies not just a one-time process, but a long-term strategy to govern your investment activities. In fact, when you pay less tax on income along the way, you'll have more money for savings, which builds capital faster. That's a basic principle of tax efficient investing.

A focus on after-tax results is also the first step in preserving the future purchasing power your savings will have. A tax efficient investment approach will provide direction in managing income as well as capital accumulation and your withdrawal activities. It will also help you better manage your own investment behaviors better, as you work with both tax and investment advisors to get the results you need.

To increase your after-tax income produced by savings, you need to know your marginal tax rates on your investments. These were briefly defined earlier in this book.

> **ESSENTIAL TAX FACT** | The marginal tax rate is the rate of tax paid on the next dollar earned or saved on the next dollar deducted. Income source and income level both factor into your MTR.

To be completely accurate, marginal tax rates should take into account the effect of the next dollar of income on refundable tax credits and, of course, the provincial taxes. The most effective way to determine the marginal tax rate is to calculate the income taxes payable on the return, plus refundable credits, and then add $100 of the type of income that will next be earned. Note the new taxes payable plus the revised amount of refundable credits receivable. The difference is the marginal tax rate as a percentage.

The marginal tax rate will depend on the type of income you earn and how much other income you have. Most types of capital gains attract one-half of the marginal tax rate for interest income, for example. The MTR for dividend income is not as easily calculated, as the dividend gross up and dividend tax credit vary with the type of dividend, and there are variations in the dividend tax credits by province. Generally, however, dividends attract a lower rate than interest, business or property income.

The MTR is an effective tool in comparing the after-tax rate of return on different investment income sources as well as calculating the after-tax return on investments which reduce taxable income, such as RRSP contributions. See Chapter 8 of this book for an example.

> **ESSENTIAL TAX FACT** | Tax efficient investment product selection is important too, when you take a long term approach to investing. It offsets inflation erosion.

Recently, worried investors have flown out of the stock market to what they consider to be "safe" havens: Guaranteed Investment Certificates (GICs) and other interest-bearing debt obligations, like Canada Savings Bonds. The guaranteed return of principal and income resulting from the use of your money by government is attractive to many.

Although the name implies that these debt obligations are bonds, Canada Savings Bonds do not have many of the characteristics of other bonds. They are issued by the Government of Canada, are non-marketable and redeemable on demand. After the first three months, they pay interest up to the end of the month prior to cashing; otherwise interest is paid on November 1 each year, in the case of regular bonds. Compound bonds are also available, where interest accrues but is only paid on redemption.

ESSENTIAL TAX FACT | Many Canadians buy CSBs on a payroll deduction plan. In that case, be sure to claim the interest you pay in financing the purchase on Line 221 as a carrying charge.

Unfortunately, when you take taxes and inflation into account, most investors will actually lose principal and purchasing power on their CSB investment because it is neither tax efficient nor inflation-proof, as demonstrated below:

REAL AFTER-TAX RETURN OF $1000 COMPOUNDING CSB*

Year	Interest Earned	Taxes	Inflation Adjustment	Principal and Earnings Left**	Real After Tax Return
Principal	$1000.00				
0	Plus:	Less:	Less:		
1	$ 18.00	($ 5.58)	($ 30.00)	$982.42	(1.76%)
2	$ 18.32	($ 5.68)	($ 29.47)	$965.59	(1.71%)
3	$ 18.65	($ 5.78)	($ 28.97)	$949.49	(1.67%)
4	$ 18.99	($ 5.89)	($ 28.48)	$934.11	(1.62%)
5	$ 19.33	($ 5.99)	($ 28.02)	$919.43	(1.57%)
6	$ 19.68	($ 6.10)	($ 27.58)	$905.42	(1.52%)
7	$ 20.03	($ 6.21)	($ 27.16)	$892.08	(1.47%)
8	$ 20.39	($ 6.32)	($ 26.76)	$879.39	(1.42%)
9	$ 20.76	($ 6.44)	($ 26.38)	$867.34	(1.37%)
10	$ 21.14	($ 6.55)	($ 26.02)	$855.90	(1.32%)
Total	**$1195.30**	**($60.54)**	**($278.86)**	**$855.90**	**(14.41%)**

* Assumes 1.8% interest rate, inflation at 3% and a 10-year hold period. Taxpayer is in 31% tax bracket.
** Amounts shown in current-year dollars (i.e. adjusted for inflation from year 0).

Your return after taxes and inflation, after 10 years is actually a loss of 14.41% in real dollar terms. Could another type of investment be more tax efficient and build more sustainable wealth? Yes, quite possibly. To keep your eye on "real" returns—after tax, after inflation and after taking into account the costs associated with the investment—consider the following strategies for tax efficient investing, and then link the appropriate investment products to the strategy:

#1 – Avoid tax

#2 – Defer tax

#3 – Earn tax-preferred income

#4 – Plan inclusion of fully taxable income carefully

#5 – Blend income and capital for tax-preferred cash flow

#6 – Reduce net and taxable income with tax deductions

#7 – Shift taxes to lower earners or alternate tax structures

#8 – Reinvest any tax savings and minimize capital withdrawals

#1 – Avoid tax. It all begins with keeping more of the first dollar you earn. If you are employee, reduce withholding taxes. If you are an investor or proprietor avoid overpaying your quarterly instalment remittances. As discussed in previous chapters, review your anticipated income level for next year carefully. With the financial turbulence experienced recently, you may find that your overall income from investments, employment and business activities may have taken a hit. Don't add insult to injury by withdrawing capital out of the marketplace at exactly the wrong time to overpay your tax instalments. Adjust your instalments to reflect your income reality.

Invest in a TFSA. As discussed in Chapter 10, the most tax efficient investment you can make is within the Tax-Free Savings Account. To refresh your memory, a maximum of $5000 can be invested into this account for each adult resident of Canada; there is no tax on the earnings inside the account, which can be withdrawn at any time for any reason. Your TFSA contribution room grows automatically with each year of adulthood. You don't even have to file a tax return to build it.

The plan started in January 2009 and so including 2012, there is $20,000 in contribution room available if you have not yet contributed. This is very important, as all earnings are completely tax-free. When you compare this to the CSB investment, here's the difference in how your money will grow:

REAL AFTER-TAX RETURN OF $1000 COMPOUNDING CSB IN A TFSA*

Year	Interest Earned	Taxes	Inflation Adjustment	Principal and Earnings Left**	Real After Tax Return
Principal	$1000.00				
0	Plus:	Less:	Less:		
1	$ 18.00	$0	($ 30.00)	$988.00	(1.20%)
2	$ 18.32	$0	($ 29.64)	$ 976.68	(2.33%)
3	$ 18.65	$0	($ 29.30)	$ 966.03	(3.40%)
4	$ 18.99	$0	($ 28.98)	$ 956.04	(4.40%)
5	$ 19.33	$0	($ 28.68)	$ 946.69	(5.33%)
6	$ 19.68	$0	($ 28.40)	$ 937.97	(6.20%)
7	$ 20.03	$0	($ 28.14)	$ 929.86	(7.01%)
8	$ 20.39	$0	($ 27.90)	$ 922.35	(7.76%)
9	$ 20.76	$0	($ 27.67)	$ 915.44	(8.46%)
10	$ 21.14	$0	($ 27.46)	$ 909.12	(9.09%)
Total	**$1195.30**	**$0**	**($286.17)**	**$909.12**	**(9.09%)**

* Assumes 1.8% interest rate, inflation at 3% and a 10-year hold period. Taxpayer is in 31% tax bracket.
** Amounts shown in current-year dollars (i.e. adjusted for inflation from year 0)

Because the 1.8% return does not exceed the inflation rate of 3%, your capital will be eroded, even in the TFSA, but because the income is earned tax-free, you save the $60.54 in taxes and your money's purchasing power is only eroded by 9.09%. Your net after-tax return, therefore, is 5% more if the CSB is held within the TFSA.

Choosing the right investments and the right rates of return within the TFSA is important. Consider that when $5000 is invested each year over a productive lifetime of 45 years (age 20 to 65) the amount saved is $225,000. With the right rate of return and no taxes to pay, this can multiply exponentially.

If the investments chosen have increasing rates of return over time inflation losses can be recovered as illustrated below:

**REAL RETURN OF A $1000 INVESTMENT
IN A TFSA WITH INCREASING RETURN RATE***

Year	Return Rate	Interest Earned	Taxes	Inflation Adjustment	Principal and Earnings Left**	Real After Tax Return
Principal	$1000.00					
0		Plus:	Less:	Less:		
1	1.0%	$ 10.00	$0	($ 30.00)	$ 980.00	(2.00%)
2	1.5%	$ 15.15	$0	($ 29.40)	$ 965.75	(3.43%)
3	2.0%	$ 20.50	$0	($ 28.97)	$ 957.28	(4.27%)
4	2.5%	$ 26.14	$0	($ 28.72)	$ 954.70	(4.53%)
5	3.0%	$ 32.15	$0	($ 28.64)	$ 958.22	(4.18%)
6	3.5%	$ 38.64	$0	($ 28.75)	$ 968.11	(3.19%)
7	4.0%	$ 45.70	$0	($ 29.04)	$ 984.77	(1.52%)
8	4.5%	$ 53.47	$0	($ 29.54)	$ 1008.70	0.87%
9	5.0%	$ 62.09	$0	($ 30.26)	$ 1040.53	4.05%
10	5.5%	$ 71.71	$0	($ 31.22)	$ 1081.02	8.10%
Total		**$375.56**	**$0**	**($294.54)**	**$1081.02**	**8.10%**

** Assumes inflation at 3% and a 10-year hold period.
** Amounts shown in current-year dollars (i.e. adjusted for inflation)

With the increasing rate of return, once the return rate exceeds the inflation rate, losses to inflation are recovered and your investment begins to show real returns. Over the ten-year period shown, your savings grow by 8.1%.

#2 – **Defer tax.** Whenever you can defer paying tax, you should, to take advantage of the time value of money.

> **ESSENTIAL TAX FACT** | By investing your money at its present value, before it is eroded by taxes and inflation, its ability to earn more future income increases. Investing sooner counts too: invested sooner your money will grow faster and bigger than if you wait and invest later.

Your money grows exponentially when invested on a tax-deferred basis. A common way to do so is to invest in "registered" accounts. Although we have made reference to these investment products throughout this book, this is a good place to revisit their definitions and features. That's because, regardless of age or experience, the difference between a "registered" and a "non-registered" account is often misunderstood by novice investors.

The most common of the registered investments, the Registered Retirement Savings Plan (RRSP), and for employees who belong to an employer-sponsored plan, or Registered Pension Plan (RPP), both provide for a tax deduction when principal is invested, thereby reducing net income on the T1 Return. This will bring further gains in some tax brackets by way of increased social benefits and refundable tax credits, as previously described.

When you invest in a **registered investment**, there is no taxable income inclusion on the investment earned as long as the capital and earnings remain inside the registered plan. However, withdrawals of the earnings, and in the case of the RRSP and RPP the principal invested on a pre-tax basis, a full income inclusion in the year of withdrawal, as described below:

- Taxable principal and earnings: RRSP, RRIF, RPP
- Taxable earnings only: RESP, RDSP

Astutely timed to be withdrawn when the taxpayer is in a lower tax bracket (for example, upon retirement), taxes payable will be lower. Income splitting with the spouse, withdrawing over longer periods and up to the top of the taxpayer's current tax bracket can all improve tax efficiency.

Other registered investments defer tax without the benefit of a deduction for capital invested or the special no-tax treatment the TFSA offers. This includes the Registered Education Savings Plan (RESP) and the Registered Disability Savings Plan (RDSP).

However, these are still important investment vehicles because they allow for a deferral of tax on income earned within the plan, they generate grants and bonds from the federal government to increase capital in the plan and they allow taxpayers to choose the best time to generate the income subject to tax. In some cases, income can be transferred to other family members, or split between family members.

You will notice reference to a relatively new type of investment: the **Registered Disability Savings Plan (RDSP)**. This plan provides for the opportunity to save for a private pension, specifically designed to suit the needs of disabled people who qualify for the Disability Tax Credit.

ESSENTIAL TAX FACT | Ask your tax and investment advisors about this as the investment, structured much like an RESP (Registered Education Savings Plan), features lucrative government contributions by way of Registered Disability Savings Grants and Bonds that sweeten the pot considerably.

#3 – Earn tax-preferred income. We are now going to move into a discussion of investments made in a "non-registered" account. In this case, taxes will be payable on income sources earned. That requires some planning. You can arrange your affairs to:

- shelter your income from tax in the present
- defer taxation of your income into the future
- earn the types of income which attract the least amount of tax
- take advantage of our progressive tax system by splitting income with other family members

To do this, you should know when investment earnings are "realized" or reportable for tax purposes, and that not all income sources are taxed alike. To begin, there are two broad classifications of income of your investment activities noteworthy for tax purposes: (a) Income from property: interest, dividends, rents, royalties and (b) Capital gains and losses.

CHAPTER 38

REPORTING INTEREST
AND DIVIDENDS

The fourth rule in tax efficient investing is to plan the inclusion of fully taxable income sources carefully. Interest income is one such source, making it the least efficient investment income source.

> **ESSENTIAL TAX FACT** | The full amount of accrued income must be reported annually—so you pay tax on compounding earnings before you receive them. For this reason, taxpayers often plan to earn interest income inside registered accounts.

Interest income is common to most investors. It can often accrue on a compounding basis (that is, interest is reinvested rather than paid out to the investor during the term of the contract). The following are examples of "debt obligations" which are investment contracts that pay interest income:

- A Guaranteed Investment Certificate which features a fixed interest rate for a term spanning generally one to five years.
- A Canada Savings Bond.
- A treasury bill or zero coupon bond which provides no interest, but is sold at a discount to its maturity value.
- A strip bond or coupon.
- A Guaranteed Investment Certificate offering interest rates that rise as time goes on. These are also known as deferred interest obligations.
- An income bond or debenture where the interest paid is linked to a corporation's profit or cash flow.

- An indexed debt obligation instrument that is linked to inflation rates, such as Government of Canada Real Return Bonds.

ESSENTIAL TAX FACT | The anniversary date of an investment contract will be either one year from its date of issue less a day, the anniversary of that date in each subsequent year, or the day of disposition. That's when accrued interest must be reported.

The issue date is important—reporting stems from that date rather than the date of ownership. Also, because of the annual reporting rules, which apply to investments acquired after 1989, an issue date in November of one year, for example, does not require interest reporting until the following year. In other words, the accrual of interest for the period November to December 31 is not required.

You should be aware that for investments acquired in the period 1981 up to and including 1989, a three-year reporting cycle was required, but you could switch to annual accrual reporting if desired.

Interest reporting follows two basic tax rules:

1. You must report the interest in the taxation year when it is actually received or receivable.

2. Compounding investments allow you to earn interest on interest during the term of the contract. In this case, you must report all interest income that accrues in the year ending on the debt's anniversary date. Although you pay tax on income you have not yet actually received with money from other sources, you have effectively reinvested the whole amount of the earnings generated.

Interest income reporting is often obvious: you will receive a T5, T3 or T600 slip, depending on the investment. Interest received or accrued each year must be reported as investment income on Schedule 4 – *Statement of Investment Income*, and Line 121 of the tax return. Note: you must report interest income earned even if you did not receive a T-slip.

Things get a little trickier when investment contracts have unique features:
- they may be non-interest bearing and sold at a discount to their maturity value
- the interest rates may be adjusted for inflation over time
- the rate of interest may increase as the term progresses
- interest payments may vary with the debtor's cash flows or profits
- where the instrument is transferred before the end of the term, a reconciliation of interest earnings must take place.

Here are some examples:

Coupon Bonds. Regular government or corporate bonds can also be called "coupon bonds" and pay a stated rate of interest. If the interest is from a Canadian source it will be reported on a T5 slip and entered on the tax return in the calendar year received in the normal manner. If from a foreign source, interest is reported annually in Canadian funds on Schedule 4 and may generate a foreign tax credit if taxes have been withheld at source in the foreign country.

Further complications arise when the bond or coupon is sold before maturity. In that case, the new investor receives interest on the next payment date, as usual, even though some of the interest may have accrued prior to the purchase. An adjustment must be made to ensure each bond owner reports the correct amount of interest up to the date of ownership change. In addition, a capital gain or loss might arise on the disposition.

> **ESSENTIAL TAX FACT** | Over time, fluctuations in the rate of interest will affect the value of bonds. In general when interest rates rise, the value of a bond or debenture paying a fixed rate of interest will decrease, and vice versa. In those cases, a capital gain or loss may result on disposition.

How do you report income when there is an interest component and you later sell the asset for more than its cost base? Some illustrations follow:

Treasury Bills. These are short-term government debt obligations, generally available in three, six or twelve month terms. If the T-Bill's term exceeds one year, the normal annual interest accrual rules would apply.

T-Bills are similar to strip bonds (discussed below) because they are acquired at a discount to their maturity value and have no stated interest rate. On maturity you will receive their face value, which will include the accrued interest amount. This is generally reported on a T5008 slip. If you sell the T-Bill before maturity, a capital gain or loss could result. This is how you would calculate the tax consequences:

1. Calculate the interest that has accrued in the period of ownership. Report this as interest income on the tax return. This would be a pro-rata portion of the difference between your cost and the face value of the T-Bill.

2. Calculate the proceeds of disposition less the interest accrued.

3. Reduce this figure by the adjusted cost base.

4. Subtract any outlays and expenses, such as brokerage fees.

5. The result is the capital gain or loss.

For example, a T-Bill with a face value of $10,000 is acquired for $9,600 and a brokerage fee of $50. The T-bill matures 365 days after it was acquired. The bill was disposed of before end of term for $9,900, and a brokerage fee of $40 was paid. It had been held for 188 days.

1. Interest to be reported = $10,000 − $9,600 = $400 x 188/365 = $206.03. The brokerage fee of $50 is claimed as a carrying charge on Line 221.

2. Calculate Adjusted Cost Base: $9,600 + $206.03 = $9,806.03.

3. Capital Gain on Disposition: $53.97, calculated as follows: Proceeds of Disposition = $9,900 less ACB $9,806.03 less Outlays and Expenses $40 = $53.97.

Strip bonds. These are also known as zero-coupon bonds as they do not pay interest during the period of ownership. They are purchased at a discount and if held to term will yield a future value that is higher. The difference between the present and future value is considered to be the interest paid over the period to maturity. The resulting interest must be reported annually on the anniversary date of the bond's issue date each year.

> **ESSENTIAL TAX FACT** | If a strip bond is sold prior to its maturity date, a capital gain or loss may result. The Adjusted Cost Base (ACB) used in the calculation of the gain or loss will be the original amount paid for the strip bond plus the interest accrued from the date of purchase to the date of disposition.

Here's an example: The yield on a 5 year bond sold at a discount of 20% of the face value is 4.564% $[(10,000/8,000)^{(1/5)} − 1]$ so the interest accrued on the bond would be:

Year	Interest	Value
0		$ 8,000.00
1	$365.12	$ 8,365.12
2	$381.78	$ 8,746.90
3	$399.20	$ 9,146.10
4	$417.42	$ 9,563.52
5	$436.48	$10,000.00

If the bond sold for $9,000 with three years remaining, the yield to maturity would be 3.5744% $[(10,000/9,000)^{(1/3)} − 1]$ so the interest accrued after the sale to the new owner would be:

Year	Interest	Value
0		$ 9,000.00
1	$321.70	$ 9,321.70
2	$333.19	$ 9,654.89
3	$345.11	$10,000.00

On disposition before maturity, accrued interest is added in calculating the adjusted cost base, outlays and expenses are deducted to compute the capital gain or loss. The adjusted cost base for the new owner is the cost of the property ($9,000 in this case).

Indexed debt obligations include, in addition to interest paid on the amount invested, a payment (or deduction) on maturity that represents the decrease (or increase) in the purchasing power of the investment during the term of the investment. This additional payment is reported according to the normal annual accrual rules. If in the year of disposition or maturity it is determined that interest has been over-accrued the overaccrual can be deducted as a carrying charge on Schedule 4.

Income bonds and income debentures. A special type of bond or debenture may be issued with a term of up to 5 years by corporations that are in financial difficulty and under the control of a receiver or trustee in bankruptcy. A return on such an income bond is paid only if the issuing corporation earns a profit from its operations. Such amounts paid or received by the investor are then treated as a dividend for tax purposes.

Exchanges of debentures for securities. When a bond or debenture is exchanged for shares of a corporation, the exchange is not considered to be a disposition for tax purposes, providing that the share is received directly from the corporation which issued it. Therefore there are no tax consequences. This is also true when one debenture is exchanged for another bond or debenture, providing that the principal amount is the same.

Dividends

A return of the after-tax profits of a corporation to its shareholders is known as a "dividend". Dividends received from Canadian corporations are subject to special rules, as an adjustment must be made to compensate for the taxes already paid by the corporation. The adjustment varies depending on the rate of tax the corporation paid on the income from which dividend is paid.

If the dividend is paid from income that attracted a high rate of corporate tax, the dividend is called an "eligible dividend" and is grossed up by 41% for 2011

(38% for 2012 and later years). Public corporations almost invariably issue eligible dividends. The grossed up dividend is reported directly at line 120.

If the dividend is paid from income that attracted a low rate of tax (generally within a private corporation), the dividend is grossed up by 25% and reported at line 180. Dividends reported at line 180 are included in total dividends reported at line 120. These are sometimes called "ineligible dividends" or "other than eligible dividends".

The grossed up dividend generates a "dividend tax credit", both federally and provincially. These credits reduce taxes otherwise payable. If the dividend is eligible, the federal dividend tax credit is 16.43% for 2011 (15.02% for 2012 and future years) of the grossed up dividend. If the dividend is not eligible, the federal dividend tax credit is 13.33% of the grossed up dividend. The federal dividend tax credit is claimed on Schedule 1.

Provincial dividend tax credits vary by province, and are calculated on the related provincial tax calculation form.

You have learned that because the dividend "gross up" artificially increases net income, it may reduce your refundable or non-refundable tax credits, such as:
- The Canada Child Tax Benefit
- The GST/HST Credit
- The Working Income Tax Benefit
- Provincial refundable tax credits
- The Age Amount
- The Spousal Amount
- Amount for Eligible Dependant
- Medical expenses
- Amounts for Other Adult Dependants.

It may also negatively affect other financial transactions that are dependent upon the size of net income on the tax return:
- Old Age Security Clawbacks
- Employment Insurance Clawbacks
- Guaranteed Income Supplements
- Provincial per diem rates for nursing homes
- Certain provincial medical/prescription plans.

Obviously, eligible dividends have a greater impact on your ability to claim these credits or to avoid clawback, as they are grossed by a larger amount. But, the dividend tax credit for such dividends is also greater than it is for ineligible dividends.

If your income is high enough that you are not eligible for these tax credits and you are already fully clawed back, eligible dividends attract a lower rate of tax. If you can claim the credits or are subject to clawback, eligible dividends will attract a fairly high overall MTR. On the other hand, the MTR on eligible dividends for lower income taxpayers is often negative (because the dividend tax credit exceeds the taxes owing on the dividend income).

ESSENTIAL TAX FACT | A taxpayer can earn a significant amount of eligible dividends on a tax-free basis, depending on the province of residence. This is an example of a tax-efficient income source for some taxpayers.

Therefore income planning around investment options is important, especially for seniors, and should take into account all these rules.

You should be aware of the tax consequences of the following types of dividends:

- **Capital dividends.** Sometimes a shareholder in a private corporation may receive a Capital Dividend. Such dividends are not taxable. To qualify as a Capital Dividend, the dividend must be paid out of the Capital Dividend Account (CDA) of a private Canadian corporation. This account is set up to accumulate the non-taxable (50%) portion of any capital gains realized by the corporation, capital dividends received from other corporations, untaxed portions of gains realized on the disposition of eligible capital property, and life insurance proceeds received by the corporation.

- **Capital gains dividends.** These are dividends received from a mutual fund company. They are reported on a T5 Slip and Schedule 3. Capital gains dividends are considered to be capital gains and not dividends (that is, they are taxed at 50%, are not grossed up and are not eligible for the dividend tax credit).

- **Stock dividends.** This type of dividend arises when a corporation decides to issue additional shares to its existing shareholders, instead of paying a cash dividend. Like regular dividends, stock dividends must be included in income, and are subject to gross-up, and the dividend tax credit. The amount of the dividend is the amount that the corporation adds to its capital accounts on issuing the share. Where the stock dividend is paid by a public company, this is usually the fair market value of the shares issued.

ESSENTIAL TAX FACT | A special rule allows the transfer of dividends from one spouse to another if by doing so a Spousal Amount is created or increased. The dividend income is left off the lower-income spouse's tax return and is reported by the higher-income spouse, who can then use the offsetting dividend tax credit.

CHAPTER 39

REPORTING RENTAL INCOME

Many have invested in real property to get a lift out of their investment dollar, and increase personal net worth. If that investment is in a principal residence, a tax-free gain on the sale of your home is possible. This is so even if you earn income from that tax exempt residence—by renting out a room or rooms, for example, or by running a business from your home. We'll dig deeper into the tax consequences of primary and secondary residences or rental properties later, but our mandate here is to discuss revenue properties held for investment purposes.

Those who collect rental income from a property rented to tenants will have tax consequences in operating the property and usually upon the disposition of the property as well. In the first year, it is important to set up the tax reporting for a revenue property properly:

- A *Statement of Real Estate Rentals* (Form T776) must be completed.
- Income and expenses will be reported on a calendar year basis. Technically, a landlord is supposed to use accrual accounting in reporting revenues and expenses. As a practical matter, there are generally few major differences between cash and accrual accounting for individual landlords, and most individuals report rental income on a cash basis. The CRA will accept cash accounting so long as the cash income does not differ significantly from accrual income.
- Gross rental income must be reported. It is best to open a separate bank account to keep this in. If you rent to someone you are related to, you must report fair market value rents if you rent for less.
- Advance payments of rent can be included in income according to the years they relate to.

- Lease cancellation payments received are included in rental income.
- In order to deduct operating expenses from rental income, there must be a profit motive (i.e. you must be renting to make a profit).
- Fully deductible operating expenses include maintenance, repairs, supplies, interest, taxes.
- Partially deductible expenses could include the business portion of auto expenses and meal and entertainment expenses incurred.

ESSENTIAL TAX FACT | If an expenditure extends the useful life of the property or improves upon the original condition of the property, then the expenditure is capital in nature.

- Expenditures for asset acquisition or improvement cannot be deducted in full. Rather Capital Cost Allowance (CCA) schedules must be set up to account for depreciation expense.
- As land is not a depreciable asset, it is necessary to separate the cost of land and buildings on the CCA schedule.
- CCA is always taken at your option. It is possible to forego making any claim at all in one year to preserve it for the future. A rental loss cannot be created or increased with a CCA claim.
- Not deductible are any expenses that relate to personal living expenses of the owner, or any expenses that relate to the cost of the land or principal portions of loans taken to acquire or maintain the property.

ESSENTIAL TAX FACT | Rentals to family members can be tricky.

When you rent a portion of your home to a family member for a nominal rent you may not claim a rental loss, as there is no profit motive. In this case, you need not include the rent in income.

Deductible expenses. Expenses are usually deducted on a cash basis as paid, so long as this does not result in a material difference from accrual basis accounting. If you account on an accrual basis, expenses are to be matched with the revenue to which they relate, so that expenses prepaid in one year are not deducted then but in the later year to which they relate.

Common deductible operating expenses include:
- **Advertising**—Amounts paid to advertise the availability of the rental property
- **Capital Cost Allowance**—Special and important rules apply regarding restorations improvements. Improvements that extend the useful life of the

property (new roof, new fence or new carpeting for example) must be listed on the Capital Cost Allowance schedule, resulting in only a portion of the expenditure being currently deductible under the CCA rules. On the other hand, a repair that returns the property to its original state, such as replacing a piece of the carpet, is a current expense, which is 100% deductible.

ESSENTIAL TAX FACT | A deduction for Capital Cost Allowance cannot increase or create a rental loss. In the case of multiple property ownership, this rule is applied to the net profits of all properties together.

- **Condominium fees**—Amounts applicable to the period when the rental condo was available for rent may be deducted.
- **Insurance**—If the insurance is prepaid for future years, claim only the portion that applies to the rental year, unless you are using cash basis accounting.
- **Landscaping costs** may be deducted in the year paid.
- **Legal, accounting and other professional fees**—There are unique rules to consider in deducting fees paid to professionals:
  - Legal fees to prepare leases or to collect rent are deductible.
  - Legal fees to acquire the property form part of the cost of the property.
  - Legal fees on the sale of the property are outlays and expenses which will reduce any capital gain on the sale.
  - Accounting fees to prepare statements, keep books, or prepare the tax return are deductible.
- **Maintenance and repairs**—Costs of regular maintenance and minor repairs are deductible. For major repairs, it must be determined if the cost is a current expense or capital in nature.
- **Management and administration fees**—If you pay a third party to manage or otherwise look after some aspect of the property, the amount paid is deductible. Note that if a caretaker is given a suite in an apartment block as compensation for caretaking, a T4 Slip must be issued to report the fair market value of the rent as employment income.
- **Mortgage interest**—Interest on a mortgage to purchase the property plus any interest on additional loans to improve the rental property may be deducted. Note:
  - If an additional mortgage is taken out against the equity in the property and the proceeds are used for some other purpose, the mortgage interest is not deductible as a rental expense, but may be deductible as a carrying charge if the proceeds were used to earn investment income.

- Other charges relating to the acquisition of a mortgage (banking fees, for example) are not deductible in the year paid, but can be amortized over a five-year period starting at the time they were incurred.
- If the interest costs relate to the acquisition of depreciable property, you may elect to add the interest to the capital cost of the asset rather than deduct it in the year paid. This will be beneficial if, for example, the property generates a rental loss and you cannot use that loss to reduce your taxes owing.
- **Motor vehicle expenses**—Travelling expenses are generally considered to be personal living expenses of the landlord. And, if you own only one rental property, then motor vehicle expenses to collect rent are not deductible. However, if you personally travel to make repairs to the property, then the cost of transporting tools and materials to the property may be deducted.

> **ESSENTIAL TAX FACT** | If you own rental properties at two or more sites away from your place of residence, CRA will allow motor vehicle costs to collect rent, supervise repairs or otherwise manage the properties.

- **Office and office supplies**—Office and other supplies used up in earning rental income are deductible as are home office expenses in situations where you use the office to keep books or serve tenants.
- **Property taxes**—These are deductible.
- **Renovations for the disabled**—Costs incurred to make the rental property accessible to individuals with a mobility impairment may be fully deducted.
- **Travel costs**—The same rules apply here as for motor vehicle costs. Also travel costs to supervise a revenue property do not include the cost of accommodation, which CRA considers to be a personal expense.
- **Utilities**—If costs are paid by the landlord and not reimbursed by the tenant, they will be deductible. Costs charged to tenants are deductible if amounts collected are included in rental income.

Multiple owners. When two or more taxpayers jointly own a revenue property, it is necessary to determine whether they own the property as co-owners or as partners in a partnership. If a partnership exists, CCA is claimed before the partnership income is allocated to the partners. In effect, all the partners are subject to the same CCA claim. If a co-ownership exists, each owner can claim CCA individually on their share of the capital costs. The next chapter covers the consequences of revenue property dispositions.

CHAPTER 40

REPORTING CAPITAL GAINS
AND LOSSES

Wealthy people invest their money to build new wealth on a tax exempt, pre-tax or tax-deferred basis, and then pay tax at the lowest marginal rates on the increases in values of their assets. *The Income Tax Act* supports this because when you invest you take risk, and you put your own money on the line first, before you earn any income.

There is no immediate tax on the increase in value of your capital assets. However, when an income-producing asset is disposed of for an amount greater than its cost base on acquisition, a capital gain will arise. Fifty per cent of that gain is taxable. However, if an asset is disposed of for less than its cost base, a capital loss is the result. That loss will offset capital gains of the year, and if unabsorbed, can be used again in "carry over" periods, which we will explain below.

Although it is usually income-producing assets like stocks, bonds and real estate that fall within the capital gains provisions, certain personal items may also be subject to capital gains tax. This can include second homes, coins, and rare jewelry.

Specifically, the amount of a capital gain (or loss) is the difference between the proceeds from disposing of the asset and the adjusted cost base (ACB) of that asset, less any outlays and expenses. These terms are foreign to most, but are important, so that you can understand how to transfer assets back and forth between family members and maximize your tax advantages, too. Use this equation to compute your capital gains or losses:

$$\text{Proceeds of Disposition} - \text{Adjusted Cost Base} - \text{Outlays and Expenses} = \text{Capital Gain or Loss}$$

ESSENTIAL TAX FACT | The proceeds of disposition will normally be the actual sales price received. But proceeds can also be a "deemed" amount (the fair market value, for example) in cases where there is a taxable disposition but no money changes hands—on death, gifting or emigration, for example.

The adjusted cost base starts with the cost of an income-producing asset when acquired. This could be the cash outlay, or in the case of acquisition by way of a transfer by gift, inheritance, etc., the fair market value at the time of transfer. The ACB may also be increased or decreased by certain adjustments: the cost of improvements to the asset, for example, or in the case of land, non-deductible interest or property taxes.

For example, Jonas buys shares for $100 plus $10 commission and sells them six months later for $200 less $20 commission.

- The "Adjusted Cost Base" of the shares is $110 (price paid, including commissions).
- The "Proceeds of Disposition" are $200.
- The $20 commission on sale is an "outlay and expense" of sale.
- The "Capital Gain" is $200 − $110 − $20 = $70.

The amount of capital gain that is included in income is called the "taxable gain" and this is determined by the capital gains inclusion rate. This has changed a number of times since the introduction of capital gains taxes in 1972, as outlined below:

History of Capital Gains Inclusion Rates

- 1972-1987 and Oct. 18, 2000 to date: 50% (½)
- 1988-89 and Feb. 28, 2000 to Oct. 17, 2000   66.67% (⅔)
- 1990-Feb. 27, 2000   75% (¾)

Because the capital gains inclusion rate changed in 2000, it was possible to have a "blended capital gains inclusion rate" for that year, varying from 50% to 75% depending on when any capital gains or losses were experienced during the year.

In certain cases, when you dispose of capital assets, you may not have to include the capital gain in your income. For example, when you donate publicly traded shares to a registered charity or private foundation, your capital gains inclusion rate is deemed to be zero—you get a donation credit for the value of the shares but you don't have to pay any tax on the gain! See our later chapter on strategic philanthropy for details.

In cases where you dispose of a capital asset that is being used in a business and replace the asset with another, you may be able to defer any capital gains on the original asset until the replacement is disposed of.

Why do you need to know this? Simply stated, to apply your tax advantages properly to the decisions you make in your life.

Working with losses. When a capital disposition ends in a loss, it must first be applied to reduce all other capital gains income of the year on Schedule 3. If a taxable capital gain remains, it is reported as income at Line 127 of the return. When you bring forward an unused loss from a prior year (incurred in the period 1972 to present) it may be necessary to adjust the loss to today's capital gains inclusion rate—50%.

> **ESSENTIAL TAX FACT** | Capital losses may only be used to reduce capital gains in the current year. If losses exceed gains in the current year they may be carried back to reduce capital gains in any of the previous three years or in any subsequent year.

The *Income Tax Act* gives CRA the power to refuse loss recognition if you don't record them on a timely basis. So, you'll always want to recognize those losses on your tax return in the year they occur even though you may not be able to take advantage of the loss in that year. Form T1A *Request for Loss Carryback* is available to help you carry over a loss, and to complete it properly, seek expert tax advice.

> **ESSENTIAL TAX FACT** | Losses that are applied to capital gains of prior years will usually generate a tax refund. That can immediately help to stabilize your financial position.

More good news: CRA will begin paying interest on any refund owed to you 30 days after the later of:
- The day on which an application is received
- The day on which an amended return is filed
- The day on which a written request is received
- The first day immediately following the year after the year a loss was incurred.

Losses at death. Note that when the taxpayer dies, unused capital losses can no longer be carried forward so the unused capital losses (reduced by any capital gains deduction previously claimed) may be used to offset other types of income in the year of death or the immediately preceding year.

Limited partnerships. A special rule applies when investors lose money on disposition of (units in) a limited partnership. Limited partnership income is generally reported to the investor on Form T5013 and transferred to the tax return on Line 122 or as rent or other investment income, depending on its source. The partner's "at-risk" amount is shown on the T5013 slip, together with the partner's income or loss from the partnership. This slip will also note what portion of that loss is a limited partnership loss.

Limited partnership losses up to the partner's "at-risk amount" may be deducted against other income. However, when losses exceed the at-risk amount, they cannot be used to offset other income or be carried back. Instead, they must be carried forward until the taxpayer reports limited partnership income. In that year, limited partnership losses of other years are deducted on Line 251 of the tax return.

Now that you know the basics about reporting capital gains and losses, let's talk about your investments in publicly traded companies.

Identical properties. It is necessary to determine whether you owned "identical properties," for example, shares in public companies or units in a mutual fund that have identical rights and which cannot be distinguished one from the other, to properly calculate gains and losses. If you do, add the cost of all identical shares in the group and divide the sum by the number of shares held to determine the average cost per share.

For example, assume Leila purchased 1,000 shares of XYZ company on June 1 and then another 800 shares on August 31. In the first case she paid $10 per share and in the second she paid $12.00 per share. She now owns 1,800 shares for an average cost of $10.89 ([1,000 x $10 + 800 x $12] / [1,000 + 800]).

Leila needs this information in October of the same year, when she decides to sell 500 shares to finance her Christmas shopping. At that time she gets $15.00 per share and earns a capital gain $2055 before deducting her brokerage fees: $7,500 ($15.00 x 500 shares) less $5,445 ($10.89 x 500).

Tax loss selling. Leila may have wanted to time her winners and losers in her portfolio before year end to maximize her tax advantages. That is, she could plan to offset her capital gains from this transaction with capital losses generated through "tax loss selling"—selling property which has an unrealized capital loss before year end, so that the loss may be used to offset realized capital gains. You may hear your financial advisors speak about this option, and you will want to see how the numbers shake out to make a proper decision.

In Leila's case, she might choose to sell her shares in another company held in a non-registered account, ABC Company, which she bought for $9 a share and which are currently worth $6 per share. That capital loss generated will be offset her gains from XYZ company if both dispositions occurred in the same year.

Superficial losses. There is no restriction to this type of transaction, except where property identical to the property which is sold at a loss is purchased within 30 days prior to the disposition, or within 30 days after the disposition. Such a "superficial loss" will be disallowed and is generally added to the Adjusted Cost Base of the replacement property.

ESSENTIAL TAX FACT | When it comes to your mutual funds, reinvested income realized along the way can affect your gain or loss when you sell the units.

Mutual funds. When you acquire a mutual fund in a non-registered environment, it is important to record the cost and number of units acquired for use in calculating the Adjusted Cost Base. Start a spread sheet and record each investment's cost, including commissions and the number of units acquired. The total adjusted cost base is divided by the number of units to arrive at the cost per unit.

Example: Units acquired: 1,000. Adjusted Cost Base: $10,000. Per unit: $10.00

Tax treatment of distributions. Your adjusted cost base and unit costs will likely be adjusted during the holding period of your investment as mutual funds are required to distribute all interest, dividends, other income and net capital gains to their unit holders at least once every year. With the exception of any return of capital, these distributions are taxable. In the year you acquire a mutual fund, you will usually receive a full annual distribution, even if you invested late in the year.

A T3 Slip (from a mutual fund trust) or a T5 Slip (from a mutual fund corporation) will report these distributions in the proper income categories. Rarely is this income received in cash. Rather, it is used to buy more units in the fund and those reinvested amounts are added to the Adjusted Cost Base.

> **ESSENTIAL TAX FACT** | Accounting for increases in the ACB will ensure that you report the minimum capital gain (or maximum capital loss) when you sell the units in the future. Your financial advisors can help provide the information.

Switches and exchanges. In general, when you exchange an investment in one fund for another (e.g. from an equity fund to a balanced fund), a taxable disposition is considered to have occurred, with normal tax consequences—if your investment is in a mutual fund trust. There are no tax consequences when you switch from one class or series to another class or series of funds—if the investment is in corporate class funds.

Tax consequences upon disposition of the units. Mutual fund units or shares are classified as "identical properties" for tax purposes. As you have learned previously, the average cost of the shares/units must be calculated each time there is a purchase by dividing total units owned into the adjusted cost of the units/shares including all reinvested earnings, as illustrated above. This provides you with the cost per unit required to calculate the capital gains or losses properly. Note that dispositions do not affect the adjusted cost base of the remaining units.

Income trusts. Income trusts are trust entities set up in recent years to manage the affairs of a business and flow the profits of the business to the investors (or unit holders) directly rather than having the business pay corporate taxes and then pass the remaining profits to the shareholders as dividends. For most income trusts, these rules will be changing beginning in 2011 when the trust will be required to pay the equivalent of corporate income taxes on the income before flowing it through to the unit holders. See Chapter 41 *Deductions for Investors* for more details on recent changes.

In some cases, income trusts may pay a return of capital to the unit holders. As with mutual funds, the return of capital portion of the income is not taxable, but will reduce the adjusted cost base of the trust units and therefore increase any capital gain on their disposition. This too can be difficult to keep track of, so work with your tax advisor to keep those ACB balances current.

Segregated funds. A segregated fund is similar to a mutual fund in that it is a pooled investment. However it is established by an insurance company and the funds invested are segregated from the rest of the capital of the company. The main difference between a segregated and a mutual fund is in the guarantee—that a minimum amount will always be returned to the investor regardless of the performance of the fund over time.

Income that is allocated out to segregated fund unit holders is reported on a T3 Slip, as the insurance company will have set up a trust for the purposes of creating the segregated fund. Dividend income received from the fund will be eligible for the dividend tax credit, interest will be taxed in the normal manner and any foreign taxes paid on foreign income allocations will qualify for the foreign tax credit.

When income—interest, dividends or capital gains or losses—is distributed as a result of investment performance, it will be received in the hands of the trust, which then allocates the income out on the basis of units to the investors.

Such income allocations do not affect the value of the segregated fund. This is not the case when you receive distributions out of a mutual fund, as these will affect the value of the mutual fund (it will generally go down on the day of distribution).

> **ESSENTIAL TAX FACT** | Unlike a regular mutual fund, a segregated fund can allocate a loss to the unitholder. This can be used to offset other capital gains of the year, or the carry-over years.

Another important investment and tax planning feature of segregated funds is that allocations made from such a fund can take into account the length of time the investor has owned the units.

> **ESSENTIAL TAX FACT** | When a mutual fund distributes income, all unit holders receive a share of the distributions as of the day of the distribution, even if they have only held the funds for one day. This can generate a large and unwanted tax liability if the unit holder is not aware.

Segregated funds may also offer maturity and death guarantees on the capital invested and, specifically, reset guarantees—which is the ability to lock in market gains. This can be from 75% to 100% of the amount invested, which will be returned to the taxpayer on death or maturity.

Depending on the insurer, a reset can be initiated by the investor two to four times per year. The guaranteed period on maturity is usually 10 years after the policy is purchased, or after the reset. There are no tax consequences at the time the accrued gains in the investment are locked in by way of reset. This can be a very attractive feature of this investment type. The tax consequences are as follows:

- **Guarantee at maturity.** If at maturity the value of the fund has dropped, the insurer must top up the fund by contributing additional assets to bring the value up to the guaranteed amount. There are no tax implications at the time of top up. However, there will be when the taxpayer disposes of the fund. This will be the difference between the ACB (which includes allocations of income over time) and the proceeds received.

- **Guarantee at death.** The policyholder is deemed to have disposed of the contract at its fair market value at time of deemed disposition—death or emigration for example. If the value of the assets in the fund increases, the gain will be taxable to the policyholder when the policy matures or to his estate if the policy owner dies. If the value of the assets in the fund decreases, the taxpayer is deemed to have acquired additional notional units in the fund so that no gain is incurred, even though the taxpayer receives more than the value of the notional units. A capital loss may occur if the guaranteed value is less than 100% of the investment.

Other asset classifications, and the tax treatment of gains and losses on disposition will be discussed in later chapters.

CHAPTER 41

DEDUCTIONS FOR INVESTORS

ESSENTIAL TAX FACT | One of the most missed tax deductions for investors is the safety deposit box.

Fortunately, you can request an adjustment to your tax return for up to ten years back to recover an omission like this under the Taxpayer Relief provisions available.

The difference between good and bad debt often lies in its tax deductibility. Those who leverage their assets as part of their strategic plan to build wealth, will often do so successfully by earning more income and increasing their net worth. However, in a world awash in debt, claiming tax deductible interest is often the only consolation for the eroding effect that the costs of debt can have on personal wealth.

In Canada, "carrying charges" such as safety deposit box fees and interest expenses may be deducted when there is a potential for income. In the case of investments, that means income from property: interest, dividends, rents and royalties. You will note, capital gains are specifically excluded. Interest is not deductible unless you acquire an income-producing asset. In the case of shares, it is CRA's policy that the interest paid on money borrowed to purchase the shares will be deductible even though no dividends are received, unless the company has a stated policy that no dividends will be paid.

Also, when you incur expenses to invest your money, a tax deduction is only allowed if the potential to earn income is in a non-registered environment. That means interest on loans used for the purposes of investing in an RRSP, TFSA, RESP or RDSP is not deductible. Nor is interest paid on a tax exempt property, like your principal residence, unless there is an expectation rental income will be earned.

Eligible carrying charges are all reported on Schedule 4—Statement of Investment Income. The total carrying charges are then deducted on Line 221 and serve to offset all other income of the year, so they can be an important way to reduce overall tax burdens and increase eligibility for social benefits and credits. Consider the following list of deductible amounts carefully to be sure you haven't missed any.

Summary: Deductible carrying charges

- The safety deposit box.
- Accounting fees relating to the preparation of tax schedules for investment income reporting.
- Investment counsel fees. These do not include commissions paid on buying or selling investments. These commissions form part of the adjusted cost base of the investment, or reduce proceeds of disposition from the investment.
- Taxable benefits reported on the T4 Slip for employer-provided loans that were used for investment purposes. (Often missed.)
- Canada Savings Bonds payroll deduction charge.
- Life insurance policy interest costs if an investment loan was taken against cash values.
- Management or safe custody fees.
- Foreign non-business taxes not claimed as a federal or provincial foreign tax credit.
- Interest paid on investment loans if there is a reasonable expectation of income from the investment, even if the value of the investment has diminished.
- Brokerage fees* paid to secure debt obligations such as strip bonds may be claimed as a deduction. In addition, fees paid for investment counsel are deductible as a carrying charge. To be deductible, these investment counsel fees must be specific to buying and selling specific securities or to manage those securities. If they are charged by a stockbroker who also may be charging a commission for the trades themselves, the investment counsel fees must be separately billed.

*Note that if brokerage fees are paid to buy shares or other securities, they are treated as part of the Adjusted Cost Base (ACB) of the securities and reported on Schedule 3 Capital Gains and Losses when the securities are sold. When brokerage fees are paid to sell securities, they are deducted from the proceeds so that brokerage fees to sell securities reduce the net proceeds. This will either decrease a capital gain realized, or increase a capital loss.

Leveraging to invest. Now that you know what can be deducted, know this: many investors wonder if they should leverage existing capital assets in order to invest more into the marketplace. Often they are approached to consider different leveraged loan arrangements, particularly if they believe they have not saved enough for retirement.

Be sure to crunch the numbers over the life of the loan. The potential for investment income must be present, not just from a tax point of view, but also in order for you to pay off your interest (before tax). You will need cash flow to do this. The investment must be able to pay real dollars on a guaranteed basis before your risk can be properly assessed. Otherwise you will have to dip into other funds to pay your loans. You need to assess those possibilities with your financial advisor, so that you can sleep at night.

> **ESSENTIAL TAX FACT** | When income-producing assets diminish in value, interest on the loan is still tax deductible.

Have your assets diminished in value since you acquired them with a loan? Will your interest still be deductible in that case? Special tax rules do allow for this.

During the time that you own an investment, the full amount of interest paid to purchase them is a deductible carrying charge. After you disposed of the investment, if the proceeds were not enough to pay off the loan, the interest on the remaining balance remains a deductible carrying charge. You can continue to deduct the interest until the loan is fully repaid. If you did not use the proceeds to pay down the loan, then you can deduct only the portion of interest that would have been paid had you done so.

Specified investment flow-through trusts. Rules for the deductibility of interest paid to own specified investment flow-through trusts (SIFTS) are being tightened. These trusts are commonly known as income trusts and publically-traded partnerships.

You may recall that on October 31, 2006, the government suddenly changed the tax rules for income trusts. Simply put, these structures allowed income to flow through to the taxpayer who held in units in them, rather than being paid by the trust itself, thereby offloading the tax liability to investors. The 2006 changes resulted in SIFTS being taxed as if they were corporations, with income distributions subject to tax at that level.

In addition, income distributed to unitholders is taxed as eligible dividends. These changes came into effect on January 1, 2011 for SIFTs already in existence on October 31, 2006. Real Estate Investment Trusts (REITs) were not affected by these new rules as they fall outside the definition of SIFT.

Publicly traded stapled securities. At least partially in response to these changes, a new class of investment was created by the SIFTs: the publically traded stapled security. This is a combination of a debt and equity investments that must be transferred together. These stapled securities offer some of the tax advantages of income trusts. They are also used to allow REITs to hold property or carry on business that might otherwise cause them to lose their status, therefore falling under the SIFT definition.

Through the use of the stapled security, the trust could effectively transfer income to the unitholders by paying interest on the debt portion of the stapled security and deduct the amount paid from its income. However, on July 20, 2011 the government announced proposed changes to the Income Tax Act that would disallow any deduction for interest paid or payable on the debt portion of the stapled security. This was effective as of the day of the announcement. For existing stapled securities, the change will become effective on July 20, 2012, unless the stapled security existed on October 31, 2006, in which case the change is effective January 1, 2016.

With these changes, SIFTs are expected to begin the process of unstapling the debt and equity portions of the securities, as the income flowed through the debt portions would no longer be deductible to the SIFT but would remain taxable to the investor (unitholder). Discuss the implications on your portfolio with your advisors.

For REITS, the use of stapled securities was used to flow income to unitholders that would normally not be allowed to the REIT. If this income cannot be flowed through (because the distributions would no longer be tax deductible), REITs are expected to divest themselves of the property or business that would otherwise cause them to lose their status as REITs.

CHAPTER 42

STRATEGIC PHILANTHROPY

"Do you wish to sell your shares?" That's a question you should ask your investment advisor to change. Instead, you want to be asked, "Do you want to sell or transfer your shares?" The reason, is so that you can have the option of transferring publicly traded shares upon which you have an accrued gain directly to your favourite charity, to take advantage of the opportunity to avoid capital gains tax when you do so. You'll also get a tax receipt for the donation, too.

Strategic philanthropy is important within many families, and it comes with tax benefits, like the one above. Done well, a plan around your charitable giving can help teach your family members about your values and specific principles for investing and also introduce them to the concept of tax efficiency. That's a good way to discuss financial matters and rally around a cause too.

Practicing tax efficient philanthropy. Most Canadians give to charities at some point in the year. Those gifts, usually of money, will be claimed on the tax return, first on Schedule 9 *Donations and Gifts*, and then on Schedule 1. The amounts donated to Registered Canadian Charities must be supported by receipts that have official registration numbers.

The claim for donations is a two-tiered federal credit: 15% on the first $200 and 29% on the balance. The real dollar value is higher than this, when provincial taxes are factored in. Because the rate is higher on donations over $200, it will be advantageous to group donations between spouses, or common-law partners who are allowed to claim each other's donations. You may carry forward donations for up to five years, for a better claim.

As mentioned above, there are lucrative tax rules for those who transfer publicly traded shares to their favourite charity or private foundation, but in the latter case, there may be some restrictions.

ESSENTIAL TAX FACT | A transfer of shares of a private Canadian controlled corporation to a charity is ignored at the time of the donation. The donation credit is claimed if the security is disposed of within five years. This includes disposition by death of donor; however, the donations credit will be allowed at that time if the donor dies before the five-year period is up.

This all began in 2006, when the capital gains inclusion rate for the donation of publicly traded securities to a registered charity was reduced to nil. Parallel changes effectively removed from employment income the net taxable portion of the gain on the exercise of a stock option where the employee donated the shares to a charity.

In the case of private foundations, gifts made on or after March 19, 2007 to a private foundation also qualify for the zero inclusion rate. The February 26, 2008 federal budget then extended the capital gains exemption on the donation of publicly-traded securities to include capital gains on the exchange of unlisted securities that are donated within 30 days of an exchange for publicly traded securities. This will include exchanges after February 26, 2008 of a partnership interest or shares in a private corporation for publicly traded shares if these shares are donated to a qualified donee within 30 days of the exchange.

Therefore taxpayers will receive an advantage in earning tax exempt capital gains and a donation receipt when qualifying investments are donated, too.

Charitable gifts may also be made to registered charities, registered Canadian amateur sports associations, a Canadian municipality or province, or Canada, charities outside Canada to which the Government of Canada has made a donation in the prior 12 months, the United Nations and its agencies, and to certain U.S. charities, but in this case, the donations claim limit is 75% of U.S. source income for U.S. charities that do not otherwise qualify.

The taxpayer may claim the least of the total charitable gifts to a maximum of 75% of the individual's net income for the year plus 25% of certain other amounts including capital gains and recapture on gifts of depreciable property. Additional tax advantages arise when an individual donates certain cultural and ecological gifts, or makes gifts to the Crown.

Watch for gifts made through employment which will be on the taxpayer's (or their spouse's) T4 slip rather than an official receipt. Cultural gifts and ecological gifts must also be certified as such to be eligible for the credit.

ESSENTIAL TAX FACT | Total charitable gifts include gifts made in the current year or in any of the immediately preceding five years.

This means a taxpayer may elect not to claim an amount in respect of charitable gifts made in the year and carry the unclaimed gifts forward for five years. This would be advantageous where the taxpayer is not taxable or where claiming the total gifts would create a non-refundable credit in excess of the taxpayer's taxable income.

Recent budget changes. Budget 2011 introduced the following changes that will affect individuals who make charitable donations, of interest especially to investors:

Gift of Non-Qualifying Securities

A donor will not receive a donation receipt for a donation of a NQS (non-qualifying security i.e. share in a private corporation) until, within five years of the donation, the shares have been sold for consideration that is not another NQS. In other words, there will be no receipt until the real value of the donation has been realized. This rule will apply to securities disposed of by donees on or after March 22, 2011.

Granting of options to qualified donees

The donation of an option to acquire a property is allowed and, in the past, a receipt has been issued immediately. New rules will delay the receipt until the option has been exercised. As well, the donation receipt will be issued for the difference between any amount paid for the property and/or option by the donee (the advantage) and the Fair Market Value of the property at the time the option is granted. If the advantage exceeds 80% of the FMV then it is not considered a gift and there will be no receipt. This measure will apply in respect of options granted on or after March 22, 2011.

Donations of flow-through shares. Flow-though shares are shares in an oil and gas exploration company with eligible exploration, development and project start-up expenses that are renounced by the corporation and flowed through to investors, who deduct them on their tax returns. These flow-through shares are deemed to have a cost base of zero, with the result that on disposition, a capital gain (or loss) is calculated on the full amount of the proceeds. If such shares are donated to charity, the combination of the flow-through deductions, charitable donation credit and the exemption from taxes on the capital gains results in significant advantages for investors who donate their flow-through shares after claiming the deductions for the flow-through credits.

ESSENTIAL TAX FACT | The tax advantages of donating flow-through shares has been reduced significantly for flow-through shares acquired after March 22, 2011.

For donations of flow-through shares acquired after March 22, 2011, the portion of the capital gain that is exempt is reduced to the actual increase in value of the shares over the cost of the shares to the investor. This means that the donor will have to pay capital gains tax on the lesser of the value at the time of donation and the original cost of the flow-through shares.

Where some of the shares are sold and the remainder donated, more complicated rules are in place to determine the exempt portion of the gain on the donated shares. Be sure to consult with your tax advisor if you are considering donating flow-through shares that were acquired after March 22, 2011.

CHAPTER 43

PRINCIPAL RESIDENCES

ESSENTIAL TAX FACT | In most cases, any capital gain on the disposition of a principal residence will be exempt from tax.

Under Canadian tax law, the principal residence is a very important concept. Under current rules, each household (adult taxpayer and/or spouse) can designate one principal residence to be tax exempt on sale. A principal residence is classified to be "personal-use property", which means that any losses on disposition are deemed to be nil (that's right, not claimable on the tax return).

ESSENTIAL TAX FACT | One tax exempt principal residence can be owned per household.

A principal residence can include a house, cottage, condo, duplex, apartment, or trailer that is ordinarily inhabited by you or some family member at some time during the year. Except where the principal residence is a share in a co-operative housing corporation, the principal residence also includes the land immediately subjacent to the housing unit and up to one-half hectare of subjacent property that contributes to the use of the housing unit as a residence. If the lot size exceeds one-half hectare, it may be included in the principal residence if it can be shown to be necessary for the use of the housing unit.

ESSENTIAL TAX FACT | If you have had only one principal residence, used solely for personal use, no tax reporting is required at the time of disposition, even if a capital gain results.

Where a family owns only one property and lived in the property every year while they owned it, the calculation of the tax exemption on disposition of the property is very straightforward. In these cases there won't be any taxable capital gain on the property.

Where more than one property is owned, and the family uses both residences at some time during the year, the calculation of the principal residence exemption becomes slightly more difficult when one property is disposed of.

ESSENTIAL TAX FACT | Starting in 1982 only one property per year can be designated as a principal residence for the family.

For periods including 1971 to 1981, each spouse can declare one of the properties as their principal residence. This means that any capital gain that accrued in this period can be sheltered on both properties provided that each was owned by a different spouse.

This effectively means that after 1981 any accrued capital gain on one of the properties (that isn't designated as a principal residence) will be ultimately subject to tax when sold.

The following are important dates to know when assessing the tax consequences of the disposition of family residences:

- Pre 1972: no tax will be levied on accrued gains on any capital assets
- 1972 to 1981: one tax exempt principal residence allowed in the hands of each spouse
- 1982 to date: one tax exempt principal residence allowed to each family unit where there was legal married status
- 1993 to date: one tax exempt principal residence allowed to each conjugal relationship (common-law)
- 1998 to 2001: same-sex couples could elect conjugal status, thereby limiting their tax exempt residences to one per unit
- 2001 to date: same-sex couples required to recognize one tax exempt principal residence per conjugal relationship.

In a nutshell, the capital gain on the property is first calculated using regular rules for capital gains and losses. Once this has been done, the exempt portion is calculated, and this exempt portion is subtracted from the capital gain. The exempt portion of the gain is calculated as:

$$\text{Total Gain} \quad \times \quad \frac{\text{(Number of years designated as principal residence} + 1)}{\text{Number of years the property was owned}}$$

To calculate the exempt portion of gains on your principal residences, you need a special form: Form T2091—*Designation of a Property as a Principal Residence by an Individual*. It's complicated, so get some help from a tax pro to do it right.

For example, assume the Smith family sold a cottage last year. They designated it to be their principal residence for nine of the ten years in which they owned it. As a result, they paid no taxes on the gain they earned on disposition. This year, however, they are selling their home in the city. This property will be designated the principal residence for 11 of the 20 years they owned it, as the cottage was designated the principal residence in the other nine years.

To calculate the exempt portion of the gain on the second property, the capital gain is multiplied by the formula: 11 years of designated ownership plus one year divided by 20 years (the number of years the property was owned). Form T2091 would be used to make this calculation and the resulting capital gain would be reported on Schedule 3 of the tax return.

ESSENTIAL TAX FACT | It's most important for anyone who made a capital gains election on capital assets in 1994 to keep a copy of Form T664 Capital Gains Election with their will so that executors can take that 1994 valuation into account on the disposition of assets on the final return.

Mixed use of principal residence. When you start using a principal residence for income-producing (rental, home office) purposes, "change of use" rules must be observed for tax purposes. The fair market value of the property must be assessed in this case. This is because for tax purposes you are deemed to have disposed of the property and immediately reacquired it at the same fair market value, changing its classification from a personal-use property to an income-producing property.

Any resulting capital gain, if any, is nil if the home is designated in each year as a principal residence. However, any taxable gain would be calculated on Form T2091 if you owned and designated a second property to be your principal residence at any time the first property was owned. An election can be made to defer paying tax.

ESSENTIAL TAX FACT | If you have elected to defer recognizing the change in use of the property, any capital gain or loss will only be accounted for when you actually sell the property, or when you choose to rescind the election.

If at some time in the future, if the property is used as a principal residence, the same FMV assessment must be made, as you are deemed to have disposed of and reacquired the property for this new use. Tax consequences are then assessed, again possibly resulting in a capital gain or a loss.

Employer-required moves. You can choose to designate the property as your principal residence for up to four years after moving; longer if it was a requirement of your employer that you relocate to a temporary residence that is at least 40 kilometres away. This extension will be allowed where you move back into the home on which the designation is being made before the end of the calendar year in which employment is terminated.

ESSENTIAL TAX FACT | A property may be designated a principal residence for up to four years after moving out; sometimes longer.

How do you accomplish all of this? Simply attach a letter to the tax return in the year the property changes to an income-producing use, noting that a S. 45(2) Election is being made. Attach a description of the property itself and sign the election. And be very careful to observe these additional rules:

- Any rental income earned on the property while you are absent must be reported in the normal manner.
- Capital Cost Allowance must not be claimed on the property. If it is, you will lose your principal residence exemption on the portion of the property upon which this deduction is claimed.
- No other property can be designated as a principal residence at the same time.
- You must have been a resident or deemed resident of Canada.

Similarly, you can defer accounting for the deemed disposition when an income-producing property converts to personal use, by making a similar election. This is only allowable, however, if no capital cost allowance was claimed on the property since 1984. Follow the same election procedures as described above, but cite S. 45(3).

Other taxable real estate holdings. During a real estate boom, the disposition of real property can be very lucrative, often depending on its timing and its use. So, it can pay off handsomely to know the tax rules before you act. The term "real estate" usually includes buildings and land, but can also include a leasehold interest in real property.

When you hold real estate for your personal use and enjoyment, for example, it will generally not earn income, and any gain on sale may be entirely tax exempt if it has always been used as a principal residence, as explained above. In the case of second or subsequent residences that do not produce income, a capital gain would generally be reportable on disposition.

The disposition of income-producing real estate, therefore, can produce either:

- a capital gain (or loss—but only on land) which is 50% taxable under current rules, if property has been used to produce income (generally rents) or
- income from a business, which is fully taxable. This might occur when the property itself is classified as inventory, as in the subdivision and sale of lots. But it can also occur if the CRA considers you are in the business of buying and selling real estate, given the number of times you have flipped properties to make a profit. Discuss this with your tax advisor.

> **ESSENTIAL TAX FACT** | The more closely your business or occupation (e.g. a builder, a real estate agent) is related to real estate transactions, the more likely it is that any gain realized from such a transaction will be considered to be business income rather than a capital gain.

The big question is this: will resulting gains be considered income (100% taxable) rather than capital (50% taxable) in nature? In deciding on whether a transaction is "income" or "capital" in nature, the courts have considered the following facts on a case-by-case basis:

- the taxpayer's intention with respect to the real estate at the time of its purchase,
- feasibility of the taxpayer's intention,
- geographical location and zoned use of the real estate acquired,
- extent to which these intentions were carried out by the taxpayer,
- evidence that the taxpayer's intention changed after purchase of the real estate,
- the nature of the business, profession, calling or trade of the taxpayer and associates,
- the extent to which borrowed money was used to finance the real estate acquisition and the terms of the financing, if any, arranged,
- the length of time throughout which the real estate was held by the taxpayer,
- the existence of persons other than the taxpayer who share interests in the real estate,
- the nature of the occupation of the other persons who share interest as well as their stated intentions and courses of conduct,

- factors which motivated the sale of the real estate, and
- evidence that the taxpayer and/or associates had dealt extensively in real estate.

ESSENTIAL TAX FACT | It is CRA's view that the subdivision of farmland or inherited land in order to sell it will not necessarily constitute a conversion to inventory.

In summary, if your intention is to earn income from the sale of real estate, the profit is fully included in income from business. However, if the property is held for use in the business (i.e. to produce income, such as from a rental property or office building) the gain on sale is capital in nature.

Note: Vacant land that is capital property used by its owner for the purpose of gaining or producing income will be considered to have been converted to inventory (and therefore subject to business income computation) at the earlier of:

- the time when the owner commences improvements with a view to selling the property, and
- the time an application is made for approval of subdivision into lots for sale, provided that the taxpayer proceeds with the development of the subdivision.

Mortgage take back arrangements. Sometimes when a property is sold, the vendor takes back a mortgage. The entire transaction must be reported in the year of disposition, but if the full proceeds of sale are not received, a "reserve" can be created to exclude from income the amount due in the future. The basic calculation works as follows and is made on Form T2017 *Summary of Reserves on Dispositions of Capital Property* before the figures are entered on Schedule 3 of the tax return:

$$\frac{\text{Proceeds not due until after the tax year}}{\text{Total proceeds of disposition}} \quad \textbf{X} \quad \text{Capital Gain} \quad = \quad \text{Reserve}$$

The capital gains reserve you can claim for amounts not yet received is limited to 5 years for all properties other than family farm or fishing property and small business corporation shares (see below).

ESSENTIAL TAX FACT | There are specific rules available for claiming a reserve, which defers the gain for the amounts not yet due in the current year, to save you lots of money!

The maximum percentage of the gain that may be claimed as a reserve is 80% in the first year, 60% in the second, 40% in the third, 20% in the fourth, and in the fifth year, no reserve may be claimed. In each year, the reserve claimed cannot exceed the reserve claimed in the previous year.

For family farm and fishing property and small business corporation shares transferred to a child, the maximum reserve period is 10 years. The maximum percentage of the gain that may be claimed as a reserve is 90% in the first year, decreasing by 10% each year so that in the tenth year, no reserve may be taken.

CHAPTER 44

TAX PLANNING:
BUILDING WEALTH

The first goal in building wealth is to accumulate enough to provide income for life. The second is to preserve the savings set aside for that purpose from its significant eroders: taxes, inflation, fees, market volatility and even inappropriate investor behaviors.

At The Knowledge Bureau, we have developed a framework for accumulating, growing, preserving and transitioning wealth, called *Real Wealth Management*™. It is a strategic process using accountable principles that strike a balance between the use of net income and capital to establish build sustainable family wealth, with purchasing power.

A Real Wealth Management focus will help you and your financial advisors make sound investment decisions that focus on how well your financial activities contribute to you net wealth.

- **Tax efficiency:** Focus on the tax return and how to increase your ability to save today.
- **Risk management:** portfolios designed to protect families against declines in standards of living.
- **Evaluation: Changes in net worth statement:** are you wealthier than last year?

The accumulation of wealth begins by keeping more of the first dollar earned. Because taxes erode both income as it is earned, and capital that has accumulated, tax efficiency can significantly enhance your ability to accumulate. If your objective is to plan for a long retirement withdrawal period, while maximizing the purchasing power of your money, it's important to follow a specific order of investing.

Tax efficient investing evolves from a careful order of investing in registered and non-registered accounts such as RRSPs, RRIFs and TFSAs. The goal is to maximize the value of pre-tax dollars, compounding time and the opportunities to defer taxes on savings into the future. Upon withdrawal the challenge is to average down the taxes we pay over a longer time horizon, if possible.

Different sources, different tax rates. Each of these opportunities for building income and capital can be subject to a series of specific tax rules, which may, at the outset appear complicated. Your challenge is to make more tax efficient investment decisions by moving your focus to a long-term tax savings strategy, and matching investment products accordingly.

Professional advisors can help by working with you as educators showing you the after-tax values of income and capital and how to maximize tax preferences—tax deductions, credits and benefits—linked to your marginal tax rates.

Economic power: Family income splitting. Remember that taking a family and inter-generational viewpoint can maximize the relationship between time and money, when it comes to tax savings. When planning for multiple economic cycles available in a family—starting with the lifespan of the youngest member and moving to the oldest—a holistic investment strategy is possible. From a tax point of view, family income splitting leaves more cash flow for use in the family.

Managing asset accumulation. Transferring income-producing assets into the right family member's hands at the right time, reduces the tax on the increase in value of those assets. And that's a great way to preserve capital that continues to produce income for generations to come. We will discuss this in greater depth in the next section.

Summary—Understanding the impact of choices: How you invest, when you invest and for how long has significant impact on wealth accumulation—which determines whether you'll have income for life and beyond. Retirement income adequacy, according to research by the Department of Finance[1] "critically depends on:

- the tax assistance for savings (RRSP versus non–RRSP),
- timing of investments and
- the type of investment.

It will pay you to start early, invest consistently and tax-efficiently to accumulate, grow, preserve and transition sustainable wealth in your future.

---

[1] *Investment Performance and Costs of Pension and Other Retirement Savings Funds in Canada: Implications on Wealth Accumulation and Retirement*, Dr. Vijay Jog, December 2, 2009

Part VII
Taxes and Life Events

CHAPTER 45

TAKE A LIFECYCLE APPROACH

The majority of Canadians who live today will die in old age—that is after age 65. We are lucky in our longevity, but it does require financial preparation. Most of us will qualify for some type of public pensions, such as Old Age Security and the Canada Pension Plan. Most will also want to, and be able to supplement those public income sources with personal savings, to cope with unknowns like market volatility, taxes and inflation.

Do you need to worry about that at age 24? Not really, but if you understand the power of the time value of money, and resolve to pay only the correct amount of tax in your lifetime—not one cent more—you will be able to focus on the benefits of long term investing, with more money, sooner. Your future financial success can be guaranteed if you consistently save some portion of every dollar you make along the way. A tax efficient strategy to do so will help you do so.

Your goal is to keep more of the first dollar you earn; hold on to it the longest and get the most purchasing power—after tax—when you need it.

It is the young that have the most potential to accumulate the most wealth, too. They have time on their side to weather economic cycles, they can work and invest longer, so their recovery time is less rushed. They will likely inherit money and invested capital and they will benefit from compounding time: the number of years they have to reinvest the money they earn, again and again.

That's why it's so important to know how your age affects your tax filing opportunities. Consider the following lifeline approach to your tax planning, which can help you ask the right questions of your advisors. You will learn more about the powerful opportunities for income splitting with families, in our next chapter, too.

SUMMARY: A TAX EFFICIENT LIFECYCLE, BY AGE

AGE	TAX PLANNING MILESTONES
Birth	• Open savings account to invest Universal Child Care Benefit and the Canada Child Tax Benefit. Resulting earnings are taxed in the hands of the child. Open a non-registered account for transfers of capital that results in capital gains. • Open an RESP and apply for the Canada Education Savings Bond is you qualify.
Age 5	• Last year for UCCB
Under 7	• Increased child care expense deductions available
0-17	• Invest in Registered Education Savings Plans and earn Canada Education Savings Grants and Learning Bonds • File tax returns if the child has earned income to build up RRSP contribution room. • A "kiddie tax" may apply to certain earnings from private corporations • The child is a dependant for the purpose of Canada Pension Plan disability and survivor benefits • The child is a dependent child for the purposes of the Child Amount • The child's activities may qualify for the Arts and Fitness Tax Credits, Public Transit Amounts • Disabled children may qualify for the enhanced Disability Tax Credit.
Age 15	• Last year for eligibility for the Canada Fitness/Arts Tax Credit, and child care expense claims, unless disabled • May qualify for education amount only if courses are taken at a post-secondary level
Age 16	• Last year of eligibility for Child Care Amounts, unless disabled
Age 17	• File a tax return to claim the refundable GST Credit (first payment following 19th birthday)
Age 18	• Eligibility to contribute to the Canada Pension Plan • Eligibility to open a TFSA—Tax-Free Savings Account • Contributions to a Registered Disability Savings Plan are based on beneficiary's net income • Transfer tuition, education &textbook credits to parents, grandparents or spouse • A $2000 over-contribution to an RRSP is allowed.
Age 21	• Income earned on deposits of personal injury awards become taxable; Canada Learning Bond must be transferred into an RESP.
Age 31	• Age eligibility for contribution to an RESP ends
Age 35	• Age eligibility for contribution to an RESP ends for a disabled beneficiary
Age 49	• Registered Disability Savings Grant and Bond eligibility ends

Age 18 to 55	• Earning and investing years: file a tax return every year
	• Invest in a TFSA every year
	• Make RRSP contributions every year
	• Open non-registered accounts for other surplus or "redundant" savings
	• Buy a tax exempt principal residence
	• Manage debt and non-deductible interest costs
	• Grow your personal net worth (Assets – Liabilities)
Age 55	• Eligibility for a phased in retirement: take company pension early
Age 59	• Eligibility for contribution to a Registered Disability Savings Plan ends
Age 60	• Eligibility for early withdrawal of Canada Pension Plan Benefits
Age 65	• Old Age Security benefits begin; eligibility for Age Amount
	• Canada Pension Plan Benefits begin unless late start election is made
	• In home Caregiver Amounts may be claimable
	• Conversion of RPPs and RRSPs to pension benefits may begin in order to benefit from pension income splitting
Age 70	• Last year for contributing to the Canada Pension Plan
Age 71	• Conversion of RRSP to RRIF or annuity; maturation of deferred profit sharing plans
	• IPPs must be converted to income according to RRIF rules beginning in 2012
Age 90-100	• Maximum RRIF payout age, terms of several types of annuities end.

Life's most important asset: your tax exempt home

When you buy a home that does not burden you with too much debt, you will be taking a giant step towards wealth creation. This investment has the potential to provide you with:

1. Tax exempt capital appreciation

2. Protect your wealth as a hedge against future inflation

3. Provide a potential base for income (from rentals or home office use)

4. Provide equity that can be leveraged to acquire other income-producing assets

Buying a home can, however, provide some real risk as well. Aside from the taxes you pay throughout your lifetime, a mortgage on your home can be your most significant lifetime debt. The risk of loss is also present, especially if you have to move because you lose your job, are transferred, are getting divorced, or find the renewal of your mortgage brings with it substantially higher—and unaffordable—interest costs.

ESSENTIAL TAX FACT | While capital gains enjoyed on the sale of your principal residence are not taxable, losses incurred are not tax deductible, either.

While losses on the sale of your personal residence are not tax deductible, if you must sell because your employer requires you to move, the employer may be able to cushion your losses on a tax-free basis.

> **ESSENTIAL TAX FACT** | The cost of interest paid on your home mortgage is generally not tax deductible unless the home is used for an income-earning purpose by you as a self-employed individual.

Therefore you need to manage carefully the repayment of mortgage principal (the quicker the better) and mortgage interest payments (the lower the rate the better). Your mortgage interest rate is the next most significant factor in managing your costs, and while homeowners have been lucky with low interest rates recently, you can see from the chart below how small differences in interest rates can significantly increase your costs

COMPARISION OF COSTS WITH VARYING INTEREST RATES

$500,000 Home, $125,000 down payment; $375,000 Mortgage; 25 year amortization

Rate	Monthly	Total*	Interest	Savings over
		P + I	Only	10% rate
4%	$ 1,972.58	$ 591,773	$ 216,773	$ 414,525
5%	$ 2,181.02	$ 654,306	$ 279,306	$ 351,992
6%	$ 2,399.27	$ 719,782	$ 344,782	$ 286,516
7%	$ 2,626.56	$ 787,968	$ 412,968	$ 218,330
8%	$ 2,862.05	$ 858,612	$ 483,615	$ 147,683
9%	$ 3,104.92	$ 931,475	$ 556,475	$ 78,823
10%	$ 3,354.33	$1,006,298	$ 631,298	n/a

*Assumes same rate and monthly payment throughout full amortization period. Figures are estimated.

Therefore, one of the first rules of lifecycle planning is to manage the non-deductible debt you incur with your home mortgage. The second is to anticipate and plan how to pay that debt down. Making an RRSP contribution is a good place to start!

Assume you are in a 42% marginal tax bracket, and you contribute your maximum contribution to an RRSP this year, which your Notice of Assessment states is $12,000. Making the contribution will save you $5,040 on your tax return. Assume you will apply your tax savings, (which you are receiving monthly because you have wisely requested a reduction of taxes withheld at source), to your mortgage. This equates to $420 a month.

If you have a $375,000 mortgage, currently amortized over 25 years, at an interest rate of 5%, you would be paying approximately $2,181 a month. If you bumped this payment up by $420, you'd cut your amortization period by almost 7 years. (Monthly payments of $2,601 on a $350,000 mortgage at 5% will pay it off in 18.25 years.)

Therefore by making your annual RRSP contribution you will create the following opportunity:

1. Accumulate tax sheltered earnings from principal of $12,000 for ten years. At a compounding rate of 9% this would grow to $198,724

2. Save 7 years on your mortgage amortization.

25 years x $2,181 x 12 months	=	$654,300
18.25 years x ($2,181 + 420 = $2,601) x 12 months	=	$569,619
Difference		$ 84,681

3. Total accumulations by making annual RRSP contributions of $12,000 and investing them in the home mortgage over a 10-year period   = $283,405

The numbers speak for themselves, even in a low interest environment! (Ask your financial advisor to do the example above using a variety of compounding rates of return.)

Financing Your Home Purchase. Especially when under pressure, many people think about withdrawing money from their RRSPs first. This may or may not be the best place to start to pay down unmanageable mortgage debt. However, it's possible the RRSP is the right place to go when you qualify as a first time homeowner.

> **ESSENTIAL TAX FACT** | When you withdraw money from an RRSP, both principal and earnings must be added in full to your income in the year of withdrawal, unless you withdraw under a Home Buyers' Plan or Lifelong Learning Plan.

You can tap into the RRSP on a tax-free basis, under either the Home Buyers' Plan or Lifelong Learning Plan. Details are explained below, to help you discuss options with your tax and financial advisors.

RRSP: Tax-free withdrawals

	Maximum Withdrawal	Repayment Schedule	Starts When?	To Qualify
Home Buyer's Plan	$25,000	15 years	2nd calendar year after withdrawal	Must purchase home and not have owned home in previous five years
Lifelong Learning Plan	$20,000	10 years	5th calendar year after withdrawal or year after ceasing to be a student	Must become full time student

CHAPTER 46

LOVE AND MARRIAGE

When you fall in love, and your single life turns to couplehood, it can be one of the most rewarding events of your life, not only for your emotional well-being but also for your financial strength.

> **ESSENTIAL TAX FACT** ⏐ You are considered to be spouses for tax purposes when you are legally married.

To start, your new living arrangements can generate a claim for the spousal amount. The spousal amount changes every year due to indexing. See Chapter 2 for details. Provisions relating to the spousal amount relate equally to common-law partners. In each case, we are referring to unions between the same or opposite sex.

> **ESSENTIAL TAX FACT** ⏐ If spouses or common-law partners are living apart at the end of the taxation year, then only the spouse's income for the period while the couple were living together is used in the calculation of the spousal amount.

So when does one enter a conjugal (rather than platonic) living arrangement with a spouse for tax purposes? First, and simplest, is the act of legal marriage.

It is possible that you will be able to claim a "spousal amount" for your new wife or husband in the year of marriage, but this will be based on their net income (Line 236) for the whole year, no matter when you get married—even December 31!

ESSENTIAL TAX FACT | If one spouse is required to pay spousal support for the other spouse, in the year of change, the payor may either claim the spousal amount or take the deduction for spousal support paid, but not both.

If you choose to live as common-law partners, you will be treated the same as spouses for tax purposes if you live together as at the end of the year and you have a natural or adopted child together. If there is no child, once you have lived together for a continuous period of 12 months and in that time have not separated for more than 90 days you will attain common-law partner status.

ESSENTIAL TAX FACT | In the year of death, the spousal amount may be claimed in full on the final return or on any of the optional returns filed for the deceased.

It is also important to note that no taxpayer may claim the spousal amount in respect of more than one spouse or common-law partner in the year and that only one individual may make the claim in respect of the other individual.

Where two (or more) individuals are qualified to make the claim in respect of another, they must agree who will be making the claim or neither claim will be allowed.

Non-resident spouses. In order for you to claim the amount for a spouse or common-law partner who is a non-resident it is necessary that the spouse be supported by or be dependent on you. The question of support or dependency is determined on the facts of each case.

ESSENTIAL TAX FACT | Gifts which enhance or supplement the already adequate lifestyle of a non-resident dependant do not constitute support.

If the non-resident spouse or common-law partner has enough income or assistance for a reasonable standard of living in the country in which they live, they are not considered to be supported by you or be dependent on you for support.

To support a claim for a non-resident spouse or common-law partner, you must provide proof of the amounts paid or given as support of the spouse or common-law partner.

ESSENTIAL TAX FACT | Remember, the higher earning spouse may transfer and claim five of the spouse's available credits—the age, pension, tuition, textbook and education and disability amounts, and the amount for dependent children if the lower earner is not taxable. Co-mingling of medical, charitable and political expenses is allowed, as are contributions to a spousal RRSP. These are first steps to consider in tax planning within conjugal relationships.

Adoption Tax Credit. Taxpayers may claim a non-refundable tax credit for their eligible adoption expenses to a maximum of $11,128 (for 2011), a claim which may be split between adoptive parents. The claim is made in the year in which the adoption becomes finalized but may include expenses that were incurred in prior taxation years.

Co-mingling pensions and other assets

When individuals become a couple, opportunities open up for tax savings by splitting of income between two taxpayers which can often lead to a lower family tax bill. These include the opportunity for spousal RRSP contributions, ability to split eligible pension income between spouses, the ability to split CPP benefits with your spouse and, through careful planning, the splitting of investment income between spouses. See Chapter 14 for the rules that apply to family income splitting.

On the down side, becoming a couple means that only one residence may be designated as a principal residence rather than the ability to each designate a residence. Where both spouses have their own residences, the ability to shelter one of those residences will be lost. Rules applicable to couples may also limit the value of deductions and credits, like child care expenses which, with some exceptions, may only be claimed by the lower-income spouse and refundable credits such as the GST/HST Credit and CTB which are now calculated based on family net income.

CHAPTER 47

SEPARATION AND DIVORCE

Departure from an existing lifestyle, can give rise to a capital disposition; this can happen as a result of a number of personal changes including:

- Separation or divorce
- Death of the taxpayer (discussed in Chapter 53).

In each case there is a deemed disposition of capital assets. However, in the case of marriage breakdown, a tax-free rollover is available.

> **ESSENTIAL TAX FACT** | The Income Tax Act allows for a tax-free rollover of capital assets to a former spouse on breakdown of the marriage.

When spouses or common-law partners have lived apart for a period of at least 90 days because of a breakdown of their conjugal relationship, then from the beginning of that 90-day period they are no longer treated as spouses.

In the year of such a breakdown, there are numerous significant tax rules to observe including:

- the division of assets
- spousal or common-law partner RRSPs
- the claiming of child care expenses
- support payments made and received
- legal fees paid

- federal non-refundable credits such as claims for dependent children under the dependent child amount and the amount for eligible dependants and refundable credits including the Child Tax Benefit, Universal Child Care Benefit, and the Working Income Tax Benefit, and
- provincial credits.

Division of assets. On the breakdown of a marriage or common-law relationship, where the terms of a separation or divorce agreement require that the funds from one spouse's DPSP, RESP, RPP, RRSP, or RRIF be transferred to the other, the funds may be transferred on a tax-free basis.

> **ESSENTIAL TAX FACT** | Upon relationship breakdown, spouses may elect that gains or losses realized on the disposition of capital property transferred while the taxpayers are living apart should not be allocated back to the other spouse or common-law partner.

Cost of transferred property. The transfer of depreciable property between spouses as a result of a relationship breakdown takes place at the Undepreciated Capital Cost of the property. As a result, no recapture, terminal loss, or capital gain is incurred on the transfer. For other property, the transfer takes place at the Adjusted Cost Base of the assets so no capital gains are triggered.

Attribution rules. When one spouse transfers assets to the other, the Attribution Rules generally attribute any income earned by the transferred assets back to the transferor. However the Attribution Rules do not apply to income earned during the period when the former spouses are living apart because of a breakdown in the relationship. Capital gains or losses, however, continue to attribute back unless the spouses elect otherwise.

> **ESSENTIAL TAX FACT** | The minimum holding period requirement is not observed on spousal RRSPs when the taxpayers are living apart as a result of a breakdown in their relationship.

Spousal RRSPs. Withdrawals from spousal or common-law partner RRSPs made by the annuitant are generally reportable by the contributing spouse if any RRSP contribution has been made in the current year or the previous two years. However, this rule is waived for separated/divorced couples.

Child care expenses. Child care expenses must normally be claimed by the lower income spouse but may be claimed by the higher income spouse during a period where the taxpayer was separated from the other supporting person due to a breakdown in their relationship for a period of at least 90 days as long as they were reconciled within the first 60 days after the taxation year. If the taxpayers were not reconciled within 60 days after the taxation year, then each spouse may claim any child care expenses they paid during the year with no adjustment for child care expenses claimed by the other taxpayer.

Legal fees on separation or divorce. Legal fees to obtain a divorce or separation agreement are normally not deductible. However, as of October 10, 2002, CRA considers legal costs incurred to obtain spousal support relating specifically to the care of children (not the spouse) under the Divorce Act or under provincial legislation, as well as the costs incurred to obtain an increase in support or make child support non-taxable, to be deductible.

> **ESSENTIAL TAX FACT** | Alimony or support payments made to a spouse or common-law partner are taxable to the recipient and deductible by the payor. In the year of separation or divorce, however, the payer may claim either the deduction for support or the spousal amount, but not both.

Federal refundable tax credits. The Child Tax Benefit (CTB) and Goods and Services/Harmonized Sales Tax Credit are forward-looking amounts. That is, they are received as a redistribution of income for the purpose of assistance with the current expenses of mid and low income earners in the next "benefit year"—July to June, but they are calculated based on net family income from the prior tax year.

> **ESSENTIAL TAX FACT** | When a family breakdown occurs, CRA should be immediately notified so that the calculation of the credits for the next CTB or GST/HST Credit payment may be made without including the estranged spouse or common-law partner's net income.

Immediate notification of change in marital status is most important to supplement monthly income, especially in the case of the CTB. Also, be sure to do so because the statute of limitations for recovery of missed or underpaid credits is generally only 11 months, although some leniency may be available.

The *Income Tax Act* assumes that the eligible CTB recipient is the female parent. However, "prescribed factors" will be considered in determining what constitutes care and upbringing and who is fulfilling that responsibility.

For example, where, after the breakdown of a conjugal relationship, the single parent and child returns to live with his or her parents, the single parent will continue to be presumed to be the supporting individual unless they too are under 18 years old. In that case, the grandparents may claim the Child Tax Benefit for both their child and their grandchild.

Where both parents share custody of a child, CRA now allows the parents to share the CTB and GST/HST Credit beginning with the first payment for the 2010/2011 benefit year (July 2010).

Provincial tax credits. Many provinces have tax reductions or refundable credits that are based on family net income. In most cases, in the year of separation, it is not necessary to include the estranged spouse or common-law partner's income in the family income calculation and normally no credits or reductions on behalf of the estranged spouse or common-law partner will be allowed. Each partner will claim the credits or reductions to which he or she is entitled.

Separation and divorce. A couple need not be legally or formally separated for their tax status to change. A couple is considered to be separated if they cease co-habitation for a period of at least 90 days. When a couple separates:

- Each person will be taxed as an individual
- Income and assets will be separated
- Refundable and non-refundable tax credits will be allocated based on individual net income levels
- Spousal RRSP contributions will no longer be allowed
- Income attribution becomes a non-issue. That is, income attribution ends when there is a separation, providing that an election to this effect is made in the year of separation or after separation, and providing that the couple continues to live apart. Therefore the new owner of the property after a relationship breakdown is responsible for all subsequent tax consequences on the earnings and capital appreciation (depreciation) of the property.
- RRSP accumulations can be split. Funds that have accumulated in RRSPs may be rolled over on a tax-free basis to the ex-spouse when the parties are living apart and if the payments follow a written separation agreement, court order, decree or judgment. The transfer must be made directly between the RRSP plans of the two spouses and one spouse cannot be disqualified because of age (over age 71). The same rules for tax-free transfer of funds apply to RRIF accumulations. Form T2220 is used to authorize the transfers between the plans.
- TFSA accumulations can also be split on a tax-free basis. The funds from one party's TFSA may be transferred tax-free to the other party's TFSA. This will have no effect on the contribution room of either of the parties.
- Property brought into the marriage by one of the spouses will be considered owned by that person. Generally the property is assigned to that person during the negotiation of the separation agreement.

- Transfer of other property. Property can be transferred on relationship dissolution at its adjusted cost base, (or Undepreciated Capital Cost in the case of depreciable property) so that there are no tax consequences at the time of transfer. This applies to property transferred in settlement of marital property rights as well as any other voluntary transfers. These rules effectively transfer any accrued gains on the property to the transferee.

ESSENTIAL TAX FACT | By special election, assets may be transferred at their Fair Market Value. This could result in significant tax savings if, for example, the transferor had unused capital losses to apply to gains on the transferred property.

Where this election is made, the transferee receives a significant tax benefit in that future capital gains will be calculated based on the FMV at the time of transfer. Further, if the FMV of the property is less than its ACB, it may be advantageous to trigger the capital loss. This would allow the transferor to offset other capital gains of the year, the previous three years or capital gains realized in the future.

Also remember to take into account any capital gains election the individuals may have made in February 1994 and apply the increased adjusted cost base in calculating the tax consequences of property transfers resulting from the relationship breakdown.

- After separation, CRA recognizes two family units, and therefore it is possible for each to own one tax exempt principal residence.

CHAPTER 48

PARENTHOOD

The tax system delivers three primary tax preferences to parents, which you should look into immediately after a baby is born:

- Refundable credits. Child Tax Benefits and GST/HST Credits
- Social benefit. Universal Child Care Benefit
- Non-refundable credits. Claims for the amount for eligible dependant, the amount for dependent children, the children's fitness amount, children's arts amount, medical expense for the child, disability amount for the child, amount for public transit passes
- Deductions. Claims for child care expenses

In addition, you should plan to save for your child's education immediately by tapping into generous tax-assisted savings provisions under the Registered Education Savings Plan (see Part III). As a minimum, try to save the Universal Child Care Benefits and the Child Tax Benefits received in a separate account in the name of the child—resulting investment earnings will be taxed to the child rather than in your hands and therefore will accumulate on a tax-free basis.

> **ESSENTIAL TAX FACT** | Tax credits are tax preferences which are deducted from taxes owing or in some cases refunded to you, even if no taxes are owing. It is therefore important to understand your rights to "non-refundable" and "refundable" credits.

Claiming your tax credits. Both the federal and provincial governments provide tax credits to certain taxpayers to promote social and economic policy goals. Part One covered this topic in detail. Be sure to file a return to cash in.

> **ESSENTIAL TAX FACT** | Every dollar invested in an RRSP or other deduction which reduces net income, reaps a higher marginal benefit for many low to middle income earners than for some high income earners.

A point of confusion for tax filers is how tax credits differ from tax deductions. Non-refundable tax credits provide equal benefits to all taxpayers, whereas tax deductions benefit taxpayers in higher tax brackets more than taxpayers in lower tax brackets.

Also note that non-refundable credits found on Schedule 1 are of no benefit to those with no taxes owing.

> **ESSENTIAL TAX FACT** | Refundable tax credits will benefit even those with little or no income—they are a redistribution of income through the tax system. So you don't have to have income to receive them, but you must file a return to report family net income on Line 236—that is, your own income and that of your spouse or common-law partner.

Child Tax Benefit. This federal refundable tax credit is composed of the National Child Tax Benefit and two supplements, the National Child Tax Benefit Supplement for lower-income families and the Child Disability Benefit for families with disabled children. Certain provinces and territories also offer child benefit and credit programs administered by CRA.

The CTB is paid each month to an eligible individual for a qualified dependant, who is a person who was:

- under 18
- not claimed as a spouse or common-law partner by another individual

The recipient of the benefit must also:

- reside with the qualified dependant
- be the parent who is primarily responsible for the care and upbringing of the qualified dependant (the female parent who lives with the child is generally considered to be that person)
- be a resident of Canada or the spouse or common-law partner of a resident of Canada

The amounts paid monthly are calculated for a "benefit year"; that is, the period July 1 to June 30. The level of benefits is based on the net family income reported by the parents for the tax year ending before the benefit year.

> **ESSENTIAL TAX FACT** | Once eligibility for the Child Tax Benefit is established, both the eligible individual and the spouse or common-law partner must file an income tax return each year to maintain eligibility. If the spouse or common-law partner is a non-resident, Form CTB9 must be filed to report their income.

When the family situation changes, that is the parent marries, starts living common-law, separates or divorces, CRA should be notified as soon as possible so that the correct family net income can be taken into account in the calculation of the next child tax benefit amount. Use Form RC65 to notify CRA of such changes in marital status.

The Child Tax Benefit has several lucrative components you may qualify to receive:

- The National Child Tax Benefit. This consists of a basic amount plus an additional amount for the third and subsequent dependants.
- The National Child Tax Benefit Supplement. This is an additional payment for the first child, the second child, and for the third and subsequent children. The annual amount is reduced by a different percentage of the family net income in excess of a base amount, depending on the number of dependants.
- The Child Disability Benefit. This special amount is paid for each qualified dependant who is eligible for the disability amount.

Most provinces and territories also include a supplement for residences of their province. This amount is included in the cheque from the federal government.

The Child Tax Benefit is one of the most lucrative provisions in the *Income Tax Act* for Canadian children. Be sure you maximize it by keeping an eagle eye on the size of your net income (try to keep it below income-testing thresholds with an RRSP deposit).

> **ESSENTIAL TAX FACT** | The $100 per month Universal Child Care Benefit must be reported as income by the spouse or common-law partner with the lower net income.

The Universal Child Care Benefit (UCCB). If you are eligible to receive the Child Tax Benefit you are also eligible to receive a benefit of $100 per month for each child under the age of 6 years. The UCCB does not depend on your income level so if you do not receive the CTB because your family net income is too high you are still eligible to receive the UCCB. To apply for the benefit use Form RC66 Canada Child Tax Benefit Application. If your spouse or common-law partner is a non-resident, Form CTB9 Canada Child Tax Benefit Statement must be filed to report their income.

This benefit must be reported as income (on line 117) by the lower-income spouse or common-law partner. Beginning in 2010, if the UCCB is received by a single parent, the UCCB may be included in the income of the recipient or the child for whom the Amount for an Eligible Dependant is claimed.

Although taxable, the UCCB is not to be taken into account for the purposes of calculating income-tested benefits delivered through the income tax system such as the Child Tax Benefit and GST/HST Credit (see below). Receipt of the UCCB will also not increase the clawback of Employment Insurance or Old Age Security benefits.

The UCCB does not affect the amount that may be claimed for Child Care Expenses.

ESSENTIAL TAX FACT | If the total GST/HST Credit for the year exceeds $100 then one- quarter of the amount will be paid in July, October, January, and April. If the total credit is $100 or less, it is paid in July.

The Goods and Services/Harmonized Sales Tax Credit. Similar to the CTB, the GST/HST Credit is not considered to be income to the recipient. Rather it is a way to reimburse low earners, who must pay the Goods and Services or Harmonized Sales Tax, which is levied on consumption rather than ability to pay.

The GST/HST Credit is paid quarterly to eligible individuals in respect of themselves, their spouses or common-law partners and qualified dependants. It is based on the family income reported on the income tax return for the year ending before the July 1 benefit year. Note that if the taxpayer has a balance due to CRA, the GST/HST credit may be applied to such outstanding taxes.

ESSENTIAL TAX FACT | Because an individual will become eligible in the quarter following the 19th birthday, it is important that 18-year-olds file an income tax return.

Who is eligible to receive it? This is someone who in a particular payment quarter:
- is at least 19 years old at the beginning of the quarter,

- was a parent who resided with their child, or
- was in a marriage or common-law partnership.

ESSENTIAL TAX FACT | Individuals who become residents of Canada in the year should file Form RC151 to apply for the GST/HST Credit. The credit will be paid starting the quarter after the individual becomes a Canadian resident.

Where two eligible individuals are cohabiting spouses or common-law partners then only one of the eligible individuals may apply for the GST/HST Credit.

A qualified dependant for GST/HST Credit purposes is a person who:
- is the child of the individual or dependent for support on the individual or the individual's spouse or common-law partner
- resides with the individual
- is under 19 years of age

The following individuals are not eligible for the GST/HST Credit:
- deceased individuals
- persons confined to a prison for at least 90 days which includes the first day of the quarter.
- persons for whom a special allowance under the Children's Special Allowances Act is paid
- non-residents, except those who are married or living common-law with a resident of Canada or who were a resident before the quarter.

ESSENTIAL TAX FACT | If the marital status of an eligible individual changes, CRA should be notified either by letter or using Form RC65.

To apply for the Goods and Services/Harmonized Sales Tax Credit, mark the box labelled "Yes" next to the question "Are you applying for the GST/HST credit?" on page 1 of the T1 return.

ESSENTIAL TAX FACT | If a qualified individual does not have a cohabiting spouse or common-law partner but does have at least one qualified dependant, an additional amount is payable under the GST/HST Credit.

The **Working Income Tax Benefit** (WITB) was introduced in 2007 for low income taxpayers who have employment or self-employment income. In order to qualify, you must be a resident in Canada and you must not have been a full-time student or in prison. See Part I for details.

Claim for dependent children. If you have children under 18 living at home, you can claim a non-refundable credit of $2,131 (for 2011) for each child. This credit is not reduced if the child has income. The amount may be claimed by either spouse or may be shared between spouses.

Where custody is shared, only one parent may make the claim for each child. Where one parent is claiming the child as an eligible dependant, only that parent may also make the claim for that child as a minor dependant.

A special non-refundable tax credit for single parents. Singles should also be interested in a particular non-refundable tax credit available if there is a child in the family. This is known as the Amount for an Eligible Dependant and it brings an "equivalent-to-spouse amount" into the family, based on the dependant's net income.

The credit is found first on Schedule 5 and is transferred to Schedule 1 of the tax return, line 305. It is available if you did not claim the spouse or common-law partner amount and:

- you were not married or living common-law or
- you were married or living common-law but
  - did not live with a spouse or common-law partner and
  - did not support or were not supported by a spouse or common-law partner

and you support and live with a dependant in a home which you maintain.
To qualify, the dependant must be:

- your child,
- your parent or grandparent, or
- a child under 18 years of age or a person wholly dependent on you because of mental or physical infirmity.

These qualifications need not be met throughout the year but must be met at some time during the year. In addition the following rules must be observed:

- Only one person can claim the amount for an eligible dependant in respect of the same dependant.
- No one may claim the amount for an eligible dependant if someone else is claiming the amount for spouse or common-law partner for that dependant.
- Only one claim may be made for the amount for an eligible dependant for the same home. Where more than one taxpayer qualifies to make the claim, the taxpayers must agree who will make the claim or no one will be allowed to.

- If a claim for the amount for an eligible dependant is made in respect of a dependant, no one may claim the amount for infirm dependants or the caregiver amount in respect of the same dependant.

Child Care: A special tax deduction for working parents. When you have a child, it is quite likely you may at some point have to pay child care expenses while you work or go to school. Eligible expenses will be claimed as a deduction on the tax return and will reduce your net income—which in turn can increase the refundable tax credits we discussed above. Calculate this lucrative deduction on Form T778 and on Line 214 of the T1 Return.

See Chapter 26 for a complete description of the claim for Child Care Expenses.

CHAPTER 49

DEBT AND DEBT FORGIVENESS

Taxpayers often borrow money to make investments that produce income. Is the interest deductible? There are specific tax rules to note.

ESSENTIAL TAX FACT | Interest incurred when money is borrowed to make an investment in a capital asset is only deductible when the property is acquired for the purposes of earning income (interest, dividends, rents or royalties) or where there is potential for such income to be earned.

Other important tax facts to note on interest deductibility include the following:

- Interest on money borrowed to invest in property generating tax-exempt income or an interest in a life insurance policy is specifically not deductible.
- Interest paid on money borrowed to invest may not be deductible at all if there is no reasonable expectation of profit from the investment.

CRA's views on interest deductibility are set out in an Interpretation Bulletin (IT-533). This should be required reading for all taxpayers who borrow money for business or investment purposes and pay interest costs.

Here are the Essential Tax Facts to know:

- **Tracing/linking.** The onus is on you to trace funds to a current and eligible usage.

ESSENTIAL TAX FACT | Interest deductibility will hinge upon the direct and current use of the money borrowed and the identification of an income-earning purpose.

- **Chief source of income.** The investment loan that gives rise to the interest expense can be for an ancillary, rather than primary, income-producing purpose. This is a question of fact.
- **Borrowing to acquire common shares.** Interest on money borrowed to purchase common shares will be deductible unless the company has a stated policy not to issue dividends.

ESSENTIAL TAX FACT | A deduction for the costs of interest and property taxes paid on undeveloped land is limited to net income from the property. Should there be little or no income from the land, undeducted amounts may be added to the cost base of the land, which will affect the size of future capital gains or losses on disposition.

Debt forgiveness. Investors can sometimes get squeezed in hot real estate markets, running into difficulty with their lenders. The same thing can happen when market values of securities held dip significantly, leaving investors with diminished values. Where a debt is forgiven and a debtor is required to pay an amount less than the actual amount owing, there are a series of tax consequences. The forgiven amount is generally applied to reduce a number of other tax preferences (see below).

ESSENTIAL TAX FACT | It is also possible to transfer unused balances of forgiven debt to another taxpayer. Where this is done the debt forgiveness rules described here apply to the other taxpayer.

In order, the forgiven amount is used to reduce:
- Non-capital loss balances (except for allowable business investment losses)
- Farm losses
- Restricted farm losses
- Net capital losses
- Depreciable property's capital cost and UCC balances
- Cumulative eligible capital
- Resource expenditure balances

- Adjusted cost base of certain capital properties
- Current year capital losses.

After these applications are made, 50% of the unapplied forgiven amount is added to income, but a special reserve can be used to minimize tax consequences. When net income is less than $40,000 a year, a deferral of tax is possible. Speak to your tax advisor about these rules. Inquire about whether it is possible for you to continue to write off interest expenses on outstanding loans.

Pay off the debt—tax efficiently. Debt that is not forgiven must be repaid. If you are on the latter path, consider what "buckets" of money you'll tap into to do so. You may decide to draw from other tax-paid amounts; simply a return of capital. However, if you have accrued gains on the amounts withdrawn, you will be required to include a taxable portion in your income; which could make your problems worse in the next tax filing season.

You will want to be strategic before you generate losses. If the lump sum you need is smaller and based on a short-term but urgent need, (for example, you owe CRA an unexpected balance due, your credit cards are maxed, or you have to pay for a funeral) you may wish to first withdraw from your Tax-Free Savings Account. Then consider contributing to rather than withdrawing from an RRSP, thereby creating new capital with which to pay your bills, due to your tax savings.

This can work if you are age eligible and have the contribution room and may not require any new capital, as you may be able to flip assets held outside registered accounts into an RRSP to create the deduction. (Watch for unintended tax consequences before you do this however).

If, on the other hand, the sums you need are large, or if lifecycle changes require asset dispositions due to illness, death, divorce or moves to another city to take a job, you will want to know the special rules on how and when to report capital gains and preserve losses arising on the disposition of other assets.

> **ESSENTIAL TAX FACT** | The increase in value in capital assets held outside registered accounts will accrue on a tax deferred basis until the assets are disposed of. Then only 50% of the gain will be taxable. Losses incurred on most capital assets, however, are only deductible against capital gains, but will qualify for carryover provisions.

You may be able to control when you sell or transfer an asset (over two tax years for example) or choose investments that allow you to blend the withdrawal of tax-prepaid principal and taxable earnings—all with the goal of minimizing your overall tax cost.

Margin calls. Of course, tapping into those significant resources will only work if you are ready to sell, or if in fact, your asset is accessible to you within your required time lines. Investors who feel pressured to sell RRSP assets to shore up shortages in value in their non-registered accounts, for example, due to a margin call, should look to their various tax-efficient options before doing so. The RRSP withdrawal can in fact exasperate the situation, as it will be taxable, and that will make CRA a creditor, too.

In short, depending on the diversity of your portfolio, your marginal tax rate, and your family tax filing profile, there are several options for income and equity creation to discuss with your financial advisors when debt management is the issue.

CHAPTER 50

BUSINESS STARTS AND STOPS

It's possible that you are paying too much tax over your lifetime if your situation includes any one of the following circumstances:

- Earn the majority of their income from one source (e.g., employment or pensions)
- Have one person in the family who earns significantly more than the others
- Pay too much to the government through tax withholding or tax instalments
- Fail to build equity

These four key tax issues are often easier to diffuse through self-employment. Besides generating profits, every business owner has the potential to build equity. The technology, product, distribution method or client base you have invested in contains value that some other firm may wish to acquire some day. This is an opportunity that has significant tax advantages, and if set up properly, the structure of the venture can greatly enhance your family's wealth.

The problem is that many start-up entrepreneurs fail to anticipate just how quickly their business can take off. This is particularly true of those who start their enterprise due to negative circumstances—the loss of a job for example.

ESSENTIAL TAX FACT | A business must be run according to a business plan for best results, and tax compliance is an important part of the process, as you will be responsible for the remittance of source deductions like income tax withholdings, and sales taxes including the GST/HST.

Every business owner should be discussing the best structure for the business organization with his or her tax advisor regularly. For many, a key question is whether the business should be incorporated or whether you should simply keep operating your proprietorship?

The answer is often one of timing. For example, you may wish to earn start-up losses in a proprietorship, in order to offset other income of the year—perhaps from a severance package. Or, if there are excess losses in the start up years, you may wish to carry them back and offset employment income earned in the best of the last three tax years, to recover prior taxes paid.

You will also want to maximize your retirement savings opportunities, first through your RRSP contribution room, which as you have learned, is generated from actively earned sources like employment income from a full or part-time job, and self-employment income from a proprietorship.

As an unincorporated business grows, and start-up losses are absorbed, personal tax rates can become an expensive way to fund needs and save for retirement wants. That's where a corporate entity can provide absolute tax relief, allowing the business owner to fund expenditures with before-tax dollars or larger after-tax dollars. In addition, a small business corporation can help the business owner diversify remuneration to earn employment income, including tax-free and taxable perks, dividends and capital gains, while taking advantage of some excellent tax deferral and income splitting opportunities.

But of equal—or possibly even greater importance—is the fact that upon the disposition of the shares of a small business corporation, each shareholder can take advantage of a $750,000 capital gains deduction. For a family of four adult shareholders, this can amount to $3 million in tax-free gains… significant wealth, which we will discuss more below.

Proprietors should therefore discuss the opportunities incorporation may provide for them and when the best time to do so might be. Important questions to be asked include the following:

- Who will own the shares and what class of shares should each family member own?
- How do we determine who gets dividends and when?
- How do we protect the family business in case of marriage breakdown or a shareholder's bankruptcy?
- How are shares of the company valued on sale, transition and/or shareholder's death?
- Under what circumstances can shareholders tap into the Capital Gains Deduction?

Private Corporate Holdings. The *Income Tax Act* provides for unique tax treatment on the disposition of privately held shares of a Qualified Small Business Corporation (QSBC).

> **ESSENTIAL TAX FACT** | Should a disposition of a qualified small business corporation or farming/fishing enterprise result in a capital gain, a lifetime capital gains exemption of $750,000 may be available.

To qualify, the shares must be shares of a small business corporation that was owned by you, your spouse or common-law partner, or a partnership related to you, and:
- The corporation must have actively used at least 90% of its assets (on a fair market value basis) in the operation of the business,
- During the 24-month period prior to the disposition, at least 50% of the corporation's assets (on a fair market value basis) must have been used in an active business carried on primarily in Canada,
- During the 24-month period prior to disposition, the shares must have been shares in a Canadian controlled private corporation (CCPC).

The capital gain is reported in the first section of Schedule 3 and the deduction is claimed on Form T657 Calculation of Capital Gains Deduction for 2011 and Line 254 of the return.

> **ESSENTIAL TAX FACT** | In 1994 a $100,000 Capital Gains Exemption, available for most capital property was eliminated, but taxpayers were allowed to make an election to shelter any gains accrued prior to the elimination date of the deduction: February 22, 1994.

Farming and fishing. The $750,000 lifetime Capital Gains Exemption may also be available to offset a capital gain on the disposition of qualified farm and fishing properties. To be considered to be qualified property, the property must be one of the following:
- An interest in a family farm or fishing partnership owned by you or your spouse or common-law partner,
- Shares in a family farm or fishing corporation owned by you or your spouse or common-law partner,
- Real property (i.e. land, buildings) and eligible capital property (such as quotas) that were used

- in the business of farming or fishing by you, your spouse (or common-law partner), child, or parent in the preceding 24 months prior to disposition. Gross farming or fishing income must also exceed income from all other sources for at least two years, or
- by a family farm or fishing corporation or a family farm or fishing partnership of you, your spouse, common-law partner, child or parent that has farming as a principal business for at least 24 months prior to the disposition.

Losses on private company shares. Dispositions that result in losses are also eligible for special tax treatment. If losses arise on the disposition of shares in a small business corporation or due to its insolvency, 50% of these can be used to offset all other income of the current year, (use line 217 of the tax return).

Should excess losses remain, they can be carried forward back to offset other income of the previous three years or carried forward for a period of 10 years. Unapplied losses after this period become capital losses, which can be carried forward and applied against capital gains earned in the future.

These are very lucrative tax provisions that can substantially increase the wealth of corporate small business owners, or ease the pain of the loss if times go bad.

CHAPTER 51

ILLNESS AND INCAPACITY

In 1991, 11.6% of the Canadian population was aged 65 or over. This is expected to rise to 16% by 2016, and to about 23% in 2041[1]. Disability increases with age; the following stats show the percentage of people disabled next to their life cycles:

Age Range	Percent of Population Disabled
0 to 14	3.7%
15 to 64	11.5%
65 to 74	43.5%
75 and over	56.3%

Canadians with a disability increased by (+21.2%), reaching 4.4 million, between 2001 and 2006. In 2010, 1 in 11 Canadians over 65 live with dementia. Within a generation, this will more than double. Dementia increases with age: 11% for those 75 to 84; 35% for people aged 85 and over have it. Unfortunately, our primary caregivers, women are especially hard hit: 72% of all Alzheimer cases, and 62% of all dementia cases.[2]

Fortunately, there are a number of tax provisions that are available to recognize the costs of giving care, when there are gaps in the community in doing so. The

[1] Source: Statistics Canada, Participation and Activity Limitation Survey, 2006, Catalogue no. 89-628-x. Last modified: 2009-06-22 ; The Canadian Study of Health and Aging (CSHA)
[2] Canadian Study of Health and Aging (CSHA), 1991,1996,2001, Alzheimer Society of Canada. Statistics Canada 2008 Elder Care: What we know today

provisions below are available to families, but are discussed from the perspective of singles; as most of us will be single again one day.

> **ESSENTIAL TAX FACT** | If you are single, you may wish to claim an Amount for Eligible Dependant or the Caregiver Amount, whichever yields a better overall result. Claims can be split between caregivers, provided that the total amount claimed for the same dependant does not exceed one full claim.

It is possible to be single and give care, either alone or in conjunction with other caregivers. For example, two single siblings could be sharing the care of an aging, disabled parent. In that case, the Income Tax Act allows for the splitting of certain non-refundable tax credits. The significant credits you should be familiar with are:

• **Amount for eligible dependants.** If you maintained a dwelling in Canada and supported a person related by blood, marriage or adoption who was under 18 and lived with you in that dwelling you may claim the Amount for an Eligible Dependant (formerly known as the Equivalent-to-Spouse amount). Only one claim may be made for each dwelling and for each dependant.

• **Amount of infirm dependants 18 and over.** If you support a dependant who is 18 or over and mentally or physically infirm, a special credit is available based on that dependant's net income level. This will include income from Old Age Security, Guaranteed Income Supplements, Spouse's Allowances, CPP Benefits, EI Benefits, Workers' Compensation Payments and Social Assistance. Members of your extended family may qualify—parents, grandparents, siblings, aunts, uncles, nephews, nieces, and in-laws—if infirm and living in Canada.

• **Caregiver Amount.** If you care for an elderly parent or grandparent or other disabled dependant who is over 17 years old and living with you in your home, you may be eligible to claim the Caregiver Amount. This claim is also based on the dependant's net income, but is phased out at higher income threshold levels than the infirm dependant amount, making it possible to make a claim even if the dependant is receiving Old Age Security and Canada Pension Plan income. If a claim for an Amount for an Eligible Dependant was also made for this dependant, the Caregiver Amount will be reduced by that claim.

> **ESSENTIAL TAX FACT** | The Caregiver Amount will not be claimable unless the dependant is living with you—even if you provide substantially all supports to your dependant in their home.

- **Disability Amount.** This is possibly one of the most lucrative yet most frequently missed provisions on the tax return. It requires the signing of a form by a medical practitioner—Form T2201 *Disability Tax Credit Certificate.*

ESSENTIAL TAX FACT | To qualify for the Disability Amount, the taxpayer must suffer from a severe and prolonged ailment that is expected to last for a continuous period of at least twelve months.

Note, if a person was diagnosed with cancer in, even late in the year, and the condition of the disease became debilitating by the end of the year, the amount would be claimable for the whole year.

The condition must "markedly restrict" the patient. Examples are:
- blindness at any time in the year
- inability to feed or dress oneself (or situations in which this is possible but only after taking an inordinately long period of time to do so)
- inability to perform basic functions, even with therapy or the use of devices and medication. These can include:
  - perceiving, thinking, remembering or other cognitive functions
  - speaking to be understood by a familiar person in a quiet setting
  - hearing to understand a familiar person in a quiet setting
  - walking
  - controlling bowel and/or bladder functions

In addition, those persons who receive therapy to support a vital function—like kidney dialysis—for an average of at least 14 hours a week will qualify to claim this credit. A supplement is available for those who support disabled children. However, if child care expenses are claimed for the child, the supplement will be reduced. Since 2005, individuals who suffer from multiple restrictions that together have an impact on their everyday lives may also be eligible to claim the disability amount.

If the amount is not needed by the disabled person because that person is not taxable, the amount can be transferred to a supporting individual. If that person is a spouse, use Schedule 2; otherwise a special line is allocated for transfers from other dependants: Line 318. There are some special rules in making this claim to take note of, however:
- the Disability Amount and the Disability Supports Deduction may both be claimed on the tax return. However, that deduction could limit the disability amount supplement claimed for minor children.

- you cannot claim both the costs of nursing home care or full-time attendant care as a medical expense and the Disability Amount. One or the other can be claimed but not both.
- those who pay someone to come into the home to provide care for the sick may claim expenditures up to $10,000 ($20,000 in the year of death) and still claim the Disability Amount.

Note: Consider investing in the Registered Disability Savings Plan for disabled dependants in your life. The RDSP allows for leveraging of individual contributions through government contributions to the plan. See Part 1 for more details.

Rules for claiming medical expenses. Medical expenses can be claimed for the best 12- month period ending in the tax year. Medical expenses should be grouped in a twelve month period that bears the best claim. This could be February 1 to January 31, May 1 to April 30 and so on.

ESSENTIAL TAX FACT | In the year of death, the normal 12-month period for making the medical expense claim is increased to a 24-month period that includes the date of death. Medical expenses paid by the executor after death may be included.

The claim for medical expenses is one of the most common provisions on the return—it affects the majority of tax filers—yet it is most often under-claimed and misunderstood. Medical expenses may be claimed for:
- you, your spouse or common-law partner;
- a child or grandchild of you or your spouse who depended on you for support, and
- adult children or grandchildren, a parent, grandparent, brother, sister, uncle, aunt, niece, or nephew of you or your spouse who lived in Canada at any time in the year and depended on you for support.

In the case of expenditures for the first two groups of dependants, the total medical expenses are co-mingled and then reduced by 3% of your net income. The claim is made at Line 330 of the tax return. It is generally to your advantage to claim the medical expenses for these individuals on the return of the lower-income family member, because of this limitation, unless that person is not taxable.

Claims for other adults. Medical expenses for dependent adults may be added to the return of a supporting individual, but that claim is calculated separately on Line 331 of the return. Total medical expenses must be reduced by 3% of the dependant's net income. The former limit of $10,000 on such claims has been removed for tax year 2011 and beyond. The 3% net income limitation is applied separately to each individual claimed here. The claim must be for the same 12-month period chosen for medical expenses made at Line 330.

What's new in claiming medical expenses?

The March 2010 federal budget included changes that prohibit any claims for the cost of medical or dental services, or any related expenses, provided for purely cosmetic purposes, unless the services are necessary for medical or reconstructive purposes.

For 2008 and subsequent years, the following medical expenses may be claimed:
- for those who have severe autism or epilepsy, these expenses :
  - the cost of acquiring, caring for and maintaining an animal to assist the taxpayer
  - travel, board and lodging expenses for attending a school or other facility for training in the use and handling of such animals.
- various new devices including:
  - altered auditory feedback devices for those with speech impairments
  - electrotherapy devices designed to be used by a person with a medical condition or a severe mobility impairment
  - standing devices designed for those with a severe mobility impairment to undertake standing therapy
  - pressure pulse therapy devices designed for use by those with balance disorders

Other allowable medical expenses. If you have missed claiming any of the provisions below, do know you may be able to recover them, under the Taxpayer Relief Provisions:

Medical Practitioners
- a dentist, a medical doctor, an optometrist
- a pharmacist, a psychologist, a psychoanalyst, a psychologist
- a speech-language pathologist, an osteopath, a chiropractor, a naturopath,
- a therapeutist (or therapist), a physiotherapist, a chiropodist (or podiatrist)
- a Christian science practitioner
- a qualified speech-language pathologist or audiologist
- an occupational therapist who is a member of the Canadian association of occupational therapists
- an acupuncturist, a dietician, a dental hygienist
- a nurse including a practical nurse whose full-time occupation is nursing as well as a Christian science nurse
- an audiologist

Medical Treatments
- medical and dental services, attendant or nursing home care
- ambulance fees, transportation, travel expenses (see below)
- eyeglasses, guide dogs, transplant costs
- alterations to the home for disabled persons (prescribed)
- lip reading or sign language training
- sign language services, cost of training to provide care for an infirm dependant
- therapy provided by a medical doctor, psychologist or occupational therapist for a patient who qualifies for the disability amount
- tutoring services for a patient with a learning disability or mental impairment
- drugs prescribed by a medical practitioner (see left above) and recorded by a pharmacist, lab tests, private health plan premiums, including group insurance premiums paid through employment.
- Blue Cross premiums including travel costs

Medical Devices/Modifications
- an artificial limb, an iron lung, a rocking bed for poliomyelitis victims
- a wheelchair, crutches, a spinal brace, a brace for a limb
- an ileostomy or a colostomy pad, a truss for a hernia, an artificial eye, a laryngeal speaking aid, an aid to hearing, an artificial kidney machine
- incremental costs of building a new home for a patient who is physically impaired or lacks normal physical development where those costs are incurred to enable the patient to gain access to or be functional within the home.
- alterations to the driveway of residence of a person with a mobility impairment to facilitate access to a bus.
- moving expenses to more to a more suitable dwelling to a maximum of $2,000
- Lesser of $5,000 and 20% of the cost of a van that has be adapted for the transportation of an individual who requires a wheelchair
- incremental cost of gluten-free food products for persons with celiac disease
- The cost of talking textbooks

> **ESSENTIAL TAX FACT** | As long as you are a resident of Canada, medical expenses incurred abroad are also claimable, including Blue Cross and other travel or private health insurance premiums.

Blue Cross and similar private health insurance premiums are often deducted by the employer; the amount paid by the employer and included in the employee's income will be shown on the T4 slip; amounts paid by the employee will likely be shown on pay stubs.

ESSENTIAL TAX FACT | You may claim travel expenses for the patient and one attendant who must travel 40 km or more to receive medical services not available in your community; additional costs may be claimed when travelling 80 km or more.

— Note, when travelling to receive medical services, actual receipts can be used for costs of travel including gas, hotel and meals, or you can claim vehicle expenses using a simplified method based on a rate per kilometre. This method does not require receipts to be kept for vehicle expenses, only a record of the number of kilometres driven. If you are travelling from one province to another for treatment, the rate is calculated based on the province in which the trip began. For ongoing current rates, visit the CRA web site at: http://www.cra-arc.gc.ca/travelcosts.

New Family Caregiver Tax Credit

The March 2011 federal budget announced the implementation of a Family Caregiver Amount to be available for the 2012 and subsequent taxation years. This amount is not really a separate credit but rather an increase in the value of any of the following amounts is increased by $2,000 where the dependant is infirm:

- Spouse or Common-Law Partner Amount ($10,780 becomes $12,780)
- Child Amount ($2,182 becomes $4,182)
- Amount for Eligible Dependants ($10,780 becomes $12,780)
- Caregiver Amount ($4,385 becomes $6,385, maximum income increases by $2,000 as well)
- Infirm Dependant Amount ($4,385 becomes $6,385, maximum income increases by $2,000 as well)

Where the dependant is under age 18, they will be considered infirm only if they are likely to be, for a long and continuous period of indefinite duration, dependent on others for significantly more assistance in attending to the dependant's personal needs and care when compared generally to persons of the same age.

When the Child Amount and the Amount for Eligible Dependants is claimed in respect of the same child, only the Child Amount will be eligible for the Family Caregiver Tax Credit.

The $2000 Family Caregiver Tax Credit will be indexed to inflation beginning in 2013.

CHAPTER 52

ESTATE PLANNING— TRANSFERRING ASSETS

When you acquire assets outside of a registered account, you must classify the asset properly for tax purposes. These classifications are important upon later disposition—sale or transfer to others.

There are several categories of capital properties on Schedule 3 of the tax return, which is completed in the year you dispose of such assets. These include:

- Personal-use property
- Listed personal property
- Small business corporation shares
- Identical properties such as mutual funds, publicly traded shares, bonds
- Real estate and other depreciable property

Personal-use property. This is property you hold primarily for personal use and enjoyment, or the use and enjoyment of your family. This includes such items as a car, boat, cottage, furniture, and other personal effects.

> **ESSENTIAL TAX FACT** | Gains on the disposition of personal-use property are taxable as capital gains, but are subject to "The $1,000 Rule".

The $1,000 Rule states that both the proceeds and adjusted cost base of the property are recorded as at least $1,000. This rule effectively ignores accounting for gains on smaller personal-use items.

ESSENTIAL TAX FACT | When a part of a personal-use property is disposed of, the $1,000 minimum amount used for the proceeds of disposition and adjusted cost base must be allocated to the entire property and not to each part.

Losses on personal-use property (other than listed personal property) are deemed to be nil because they are considered to be a personal cost of owning the asset. For example, if you own a cottage for personal use and enjoyment, and sell that cottage at a loss, there are no tax consequences. Personal residence dispositions are discussed in more detail later.

There is a special rule that prevents you from claiming the $1,000 minimum ACB on each piece of a set of properties.

For example, assume a couple wishes to sell a set of silver goblets and cutlery to make enough money for a trip abroad. The set was acquired for $750 at a garage sale and the couple can now sell each piece for $50. There are 100 pieces in the set. The set is considered to be one property and the $1,000 rule will apply only once to the entire sales transaction, even if the pieces are sold to multiple buyers over a period of time. Thus, the minimum proceeds of disposition for the entire set will be $5,000 and the adjusted cost base of the entire set will be $1,000. When one piece is sold, the minimum numbers are $10 per piece so a sale of one piece for $50 will result in a capital gains of $40 ($50 - $10).

Listed personal property. This is a special subset of personal-use property which includes collectible pieces such as:

- a print, etch, drawing, painting, sculpture, or other similar work of art,
- jewellery,
- a rare folio, rare manuscript or rare book,
- a stamp, or
- a coin or coin collection.

As with other personal-use property, gains on listed personal property are taxable as capital gains on Schedule 3, and are subject to the $1,000 Rule. However, losses on these properties are treated differently.

Where losses on listed personal property exceed gains reported during the year from other listed personal property, unused balances may be carried back and applied against listed personal property gains in any of the prior three years or carried forward to apply against listed personal property gains in any of the following seven years.

ESSENTIAL TAX FACT | Losses on listed personal property are allowed, but may only be deducted from gains on other listed personal property.

Asset transfers: When lifecycles change

To everything there is a season… perhaps it is time to move your ailing parents into your home to better take care of them. Should you sell their home? Perhaps your parents have decided it is time to pass the cottage to you and your siblings. At what value will you inherit this now? Perhaps you have decided to leave the country to take a job overseas. How can you avoid departure taxes if you don't wish to sell your assets?

ESSENTIAL TAX FACT | Sometimes, assets are sold to strangers or transferred to relatives. In fact, assets can often be transferred without immediate tax consequences to spouses or children. This is called a "tax-free rollover" to a non-arm's length party.

Many of these real life scenarios result in taxable consequences without the exchange of money. So, to begin any discussion on wealth preservation in times of change, you will need to understand your obligations and opportunities when assets are transferred to family members. To do so, you need to understand some tax jargon:

- "Arm's length" transactions are those undertaken with an unrelated person.
- "Non-arm's length" persons are related to you by blood, marriage or adoption, or those affiliated with you, which can include a common-law partner, corporation, partnership or members of a group who are affiliated with one another.

ESSENTIAL TAX FACT | For most assets transferred to a spouse or common-law partner, tax consequences of disposition can be deferred until the asset is actually disposed of.

For example, when Tom sells his rental property to an unrelated third party, he is conducting business on an arm's length basis. If he sells the property to his wife, Samantha, it is a non-arm's length transaction. The disposal of your assets can be through an actual sale, or upon a "deemed disposition". A deemed disposition arises:

- On death
- When an asset's use is changed from business to personal
- When property is transferred to a trust or a registered account

- When you emigrate
- When an asset is given to another as a gift
- When one asset is exchanged for another
- When an asset is stolen, damaged, destroyed or expropriated
- When shares held are converted, redeemed or cancelled
- When options to acquire or dispose of property expire
- When a debt is settled or cancelled.

ESSENTIAL TAX FACT | When assets are transferred to the spouse, income from the property and gains or losses on disposition will be attributed back to the transferor unless the receiving spouse actually pays fair market value for the asset or a bona fide loan is drawn up.

For example, Marion needed to make an RRSP contribution but she had no cash. Instead, she opted to transfer 100 shares of ABC corporation to her self-directed RRSP. Marion will receive an RRSP receipt for the fair market value of the shares and must also report a capital gain—as she is "deemed" to have disposed of the shares at their fair market value.

At the time of sale or transfer, the Adjusted Cost Base of your asset (original cost plus or minus certain adjustments) will be subtracted from the proceeds of disposition to calculate the resulting gain or loss. As transfers between family members generally occur without the exchange of money, a deemed disposition occurs... but at what value?

At the time of such transfers to a spouse, it is only necessary to report the change of ownership on the transferor's return at the asset's adjusted cost base. This results in a "tax-free rollover" of the asset to the spouse.

ESSENTIAL TAX FACT | If you transfer capital property to your spouse during your lifetime, resulting capital gains or losses on disposition are taxed back in your hands, unless your spouse pays fair value. In general, no disposition will be considered to have taken place at fair market value at that time, unless you so elect.

You can also elect not to have those general rules apply by making an election when filing the return. In that case, the transfer will be reported at the property's fair market value (FMV). The tax consequences will then be addressed immediately on your return—that is, a capital gain or loss could result. Consulting with a tax advisor is wise.

This might be particularly advantageous, for example, if you want to use up capital loss balances. (The same strategy—electing FMV instead of ACB—may be used in transferring assets upon the death of one spouse.)

When you transfer an asset to your spouse at FMV and provided that the spouse pays FMV or a bona fide loan is drawn up:

- income earned from the property is reported by the spouse to whom the property is transferred
- later dispositions of the property will be taxed in the transferee spouse's hands
- interest paid on a loan drawn will be deductible if the resulting property is used to earn income, and interest is actually paid by January 30 of the following year
- you will report that interest received on your tax return.

Note that the gains or losses from the disposition of capital assets transferred to minor children will be included on their own returns—often resulting in nil tax. However transfers of assets to adult children are treated differently.

> **ESSENTIAL TAX FACT** | When you transfer property to your adult children during your lifetime, the property is always transferred at fair market value and the tax consequences are immediately reported. Timing is important.

For example, Harold and Edna want to transfer their cottage property to their adult son Jonathan and his wife Jesse this year. At the time of transfer, fair market value will be assessed, and Harold and Edna will use that figure as the "proceeds of disposition" on their tax return. This will normally produce a taxable gain; however, if the property is a principal residence, a special tax exemption may be tapped. See Chapter 43 for more about Principal Residences.

Taxable and tax-free rollovers may also arise on emigration, separation or divorce or death. Speak to your tax and financial advisors before these changes occur, wherever possible, and understand the tax calculations behind any resulting capital gain and loss applications.

This becomes even more important with the Tax-Free Savings Account, which can be transferred tax-free to a spouse on death or divorce.

In the case of the Registered Disability Savings Plan, where the beneficiary dies, or otherwise ceases to qualify for the RDSP, generally, any Canada Disability Savings Grant (CDSG) or Canada Disability Savings Bond (CDSB) funded by government to the plan within the ten years preceding death, and the income earned on such amounts, must be repaid. Amounts in excess of contributions, after taking into account the repayment, will be included in income of the beneficiary in the year of death.

CHAPTER 53

FINAL RETURNS
AND SURVIVORSHIP

No personal financial plan can be completed without a plan for transferring assets to the next generation, yet the majority of Canadians are reluctant to discuss the transfer of their assets with family members and many don't have a will. But to paraphrase Benjamin Franklin, death and taxes are perhaps the only two constants we can count on from the moment of birth... and it pays well to be prepared for the inevitable.

> **ESSENTIAL TAX FACT** | Wealth can be effectively passed along to others during your lifetime or upon your demise. But what's important is that you begin immediately to set up an estate plan with your financial advisors and that you have a will.

A lifetime of complicated personal relationships makes that more difficult, especially if you are wealthy. Whether you are already alone or preparing to be alone, protecting your assets at the time of death is an important obligation to your family as well as society. Consider the following checklist for starting an estate plan:

Objectives for starting an estate plan
- Identify financial institutions. Where are your assets held? Include key contacts.
- Identify advisors. Who are your professional advisors including banker, accountant, lawyer, stockbroker, insurance agent and what is their contact info?

- Identify proxies. Who will exercise Power of Attorney if you become disabled or cannot direct your own personal affairs?
- Identify heirs. List exact contact information, as well as their relationship to you. In the case of singles, these heirs could include your favorite charity. Discuss options for the transfer of assets and funds during your lifetime and at death.
- Identify gifts. Sketch out what you wish for each of your heirs to receive.
- Identify needs. Will any of your heirs require assistance with ongoing income?
- Identify executors. Prepare a list of possible executor(s) and make approaches.
- Identify guardians. Prepare a list of those to whom you would trust the care of your minor children, as well as those who should not have that responsibility.
- Identify business succession plans. How should your business interests be distributed, and who should step in to run the show?
- Plan for probate fees and capital gains taxes at death. Review life insurance policies that may be used for those purposes.
- Identify capital assets and their fair market value annually.
- Identify asset transfer instructions. Which assets should be transferred during your lifetime, and which should be transferred only upon your death?
- Make plans for safekeeping. Keep all important documents in a safety deposit box and identify the location.
- Deal with debt. Cleaning up spilled milk is no fun for anyone…especially if it's been there for awhile. List debt obligations and the order they should be repaid. Make a list of ongoing financial obligations that should be cancelled on death.
- Draw up your will. Tell your lawyer where it is to be kept.

Filing consequences at time of death. When you die, one mandatory final return must filed for the period January 1 to date of death, and this return must be filed by the later of:
- April 30 of the year immediately following the year of death
- six months after date of death

ESSENTIAL TAX FACT | There are several "elective returns" that can be filed on death, which will allow you to claim against certain personal amounts, to result in a substantial tax benefit.

Note, however, the final return from January to date of death is usually the only one most taxpayers will file. On that return, income earned up to date of death is reported. Certain income sources may have to be "prorated" to the date of death, including employment earnings, pension receipts, interest, rents, royalties, or annuity income. Offsetting expenses are accrued to date of death in a similar fashion.

ESSENTIAL TAX FACT | The most significant transaction on the final return could revolve around the disposition of capital assets. That's because a deemed disposition of your assets is considered to have taken place immediately before your death.

When you die, you are deemed to have disposed of your assets immediately before death, usually at Fair Market Value (FMV). However, the value of the deemed disposition can vary, depending on who will acquire the assets... your spouse (including common-law partner), child or another. Transfers to children or others are generally made at the property's FMV; transfers to spouse can be at the asset's adjusted cost base (or UCC in the case of depreciable assets) or FMV.

The use of "tax-free rollovers". The deemed disposition rules on death of the taxpayer therefore override the Attribution Rules that apply while living. That is, capital property transferred to the spouse on your death will not be taxed until your spouse disposes of the property. The spouse will use your adjusted cost base, and pay tax on the full gain from the time you acquired the asset, thereby completely postponing the tax consequences at the time of your death until your spouse dies or sells the property.

Depending on your taxable income at the time of your death, your executor may wish to roll over assets to the spouse on a tax-free basis, or have them transfer at fair market value. Fair value may make sense if your income in the year of death is low or if you have unused capital losses from the past that have been carried forward. Such balances can often be used to offset income created by the higher valuations that have accrued to the date of death. It will also provide your survivors with the opportunity to start with a higher adjusted cost base on the acquisition of your assets, which will save them money down the line as well.

ESSENTIAL TAX FACT | Be sure to provide your executor with a copy of the 1994 tax return and in particular Form T664 upon which a capital gains election may have been made to use up your $100,000 Capital Gains Exemption. This will affect the calculation of the deemed disposition of capital properties on the final return.

In the absence of those plans, capital gains or losses resulting from the deemed disposition of your assets on death must be reported, together with any recapture or terminal loss on depreciable assets, with the resulting tax payable (if any) on that return.

ESSENTIAL TAX FACT | Request a clearance certificate from CRA to relieve the executor of any further liability.

RRSPs and other pensions. Didn't spend it all? What happens when you die and leave unspent accumulations in your RRSP?

You are deemed to have received the fair market value of all assets in your RRSP or RRIF immediately prior to death. If there is a surviving spouse or common-law partner the assets may be transferred tax-free to that person's registered plan (RRSP or RRIF). In certain circumstances, the RRSP can be transferred to a financially dependent child or grandchild, even when there is a surviving spouse. Speak to your tax advisors about these options.

If there is no surviving spouse or common-law partner, the RRSP assets are transferred to the estate. Since 2009, any decrease in value of RRSP assets while held in the estate may be used to decrease the income reported on the deceased's final return.

Tax-Free Savings Plans. Accumulated earnings in your TFSA are not taxable, but earnings after death no longer accumulate tax-free. However the assets may be rolled over to the TFSA of a surviving spouse or common-law partner.

Life insurance policies. Death generates numerous tax consequences which can be expensive, particularly for single taxpayers. To preserve wealth, however, the acquisition of a life insurance policy can make some sense and can lead to numerous tax advantages, especially if deemed dispositions of capital assets result in a hefty tax bill.

ESSENTIAL TAX FACT | When an individual buys an insurance policy, the premium is not deductible. But, subsequent benefits or proceeds paid out to beneficiaries are tax exempt.

Income earned within whole life or universal life insurance policies will generally accumulate on a tax exempt basis provided that the policies have a limitation on the size of the investment component. These features should be discussed with your insurance advisor. The proceeds from a life insurance policy can help to pay the taxes which arise on the deemed disposition of taxable assets as at the date of death.

It makes sense to prepare early for your terminal wealth by assessing the place of life insurance in your estate plans.

Summary of Asset Transfer Rules

Asset	Other Plan	Transfers in Life to				
		Spouse	Minor Child	Adult Child	Infirm Adult Child	Charity
Life Insurance[1]	N/A	Tax-deferred transfer possible	Tax-deferred transfer possible	Tax-deferred transfer possible	Tax-deferred transfer possible	Accrued gains are taxable as ordinary income. Donation credit for FMV.
RRSPs/ RRIFs	Transfers to another registered plan are tax-free	Proceeds taxed as ordinary income.	Proceeds taxed as ordinary income.	Proceeds taxed as ordinary income.	Proceeds taxed as ordinary income.	Proceeds taxed as ordinary income. Donation credit for FMV.
RPPs	Transfers to another registered plan are tax-free	N/A	N/A	N/A	N/A	N/A
RESPs	Transfers to another RESP are tax-free (limitation apply)	N/A	N/A	N/A	N/A	N/A
RDSPs	Transfers to another RDSP are tax-free (same beneficiary)	N/A	N/A	N/A	N/A	N/A
TFSAs	Transfers to another TFSA are tax-free	No income tax consequences	No income tax consequences	No income tax consequences	No income tax consequences	No income tax consequences. Donation credit for FMV.

Summary of Asset Transfer Rules (continued)

		Transfers in Life to				
Asset	Other Plan	Spouse	Minor Child	Adult Child	Infirm Adult Child	Charity
SBCS[2]	N/A	Transfers are at ACB or FMV. A spousal loan may be required to prevent attribution of income and capital gains.	Transfers are at FMV. Accrued gains will be taxable. Kiddie tax will apply to income earned from the shares.	Transfers are at FMV. Accrued gains will be taxable.	Transfers are at FMV. Accrued gains will be taxable.	Transfers are at FMV. Accrued gains will be taxable. Donation credit for FMV.
QFP[3]	N/A	Transfers are at ACB or FMV. A spousal loan may be required to prevent attribution of income and capital gains.	Transfers may be at any value between the ACB and FMV. Taxable gains of difference between ACB and elected transfer value.	Transfers may be at any value between the ACB and FMV. Taxable gains of difference between ACB and elected transfer value.	Transfers may be at any value between the ACB and FMV. Taxable gains of difference between ACB and elected transfer value.	Transfers are at FMV. Accrued gains will be taxable. Donation credit for FMV.
Capital Assets[4]	N/A	Transfers are at ACB or FMV. A spousal loan may be required to prevent attribution of income and capital gains.	Transfers are at FMV. Accrued gains will be taxable. Income (but not capital gains) will be attributed back to the transferor.	Transfers are at FMV. Accrued gains will be taxable.	Transfers are at FMV. Accrued gains will be taxable.	Transfers are at FMV. Gains are not taxable if they are for publicly traded bonds or shares. Donation credit for FMV.
Principal Residence	N/A	Accrued gains are exempt.	Accrued gains are exempt.	Accrued gains are exempt.	Accrued gains are exempt.	Accrued gains are exempt. Donation credit for FMV of the residence.
Non-Capital Assets	N/A	No income tax consequences.	No income tax consequences.	No income tax consequences.	No income tax consequences.	No income tax consequences. Donation credit for FMV of asset donated.

			Transfers at Death to			
Asset	Estate	Spouse	Minor Child	Adult Child	Infirm Adult Child	Charity
Life Insurance[1]	N/A	Tax-deferred transfer possible	Tax-deferred transfer possible	Tax-deferred transfer possible	Tax-deferred transfer possible	Accrued gains are taxable as ordinary income. Donation credit for FMV.
RRSPs/ RRIFs	Proceeds are fully taxable	Tax-free transfer allowed to spouse's plan.	Tax-free transfer to annuity for minor child.	Proceeds are fully taxable	Tax-free transfers are allowed to disabled child's RRSP, RDSP or annuity.	Proceeds are fully taxable. Donation credit for FMV.
RPPs	N/A	N/A	N/A	N/A	N/A	N/A
RESPs	Estate can be succeeding subscriber – no tax consequences	Spouse can be succeeding sub- scriber – no tax conse- quences	N/A	Adult child can be suc- ceeding sub- scriber – no tax conse- quences	Adult child can be suc- ceeding sub- scriber – no tax conse- quences	N/A
RDSPs	N/A	N/A	N/A	N/A	N/A	N/A
TFSAs	No income tax conse- quences	No income tax conse- quences	No income tax conse- quences	No income tax conse- quences	No income tax conse- quences	No income tax conse- quences. Donation credit for FMV.
SBCS[2]	Gains will be taxable but deceased may claim $375,000 capital gains exemption. Deemed proceeds FMV at death.	Gains will be taxable but deceased may claim $375,000 capital gains exemption. Transfer at any amount between ACB and FMV.	Gains will be taxable but deceased may claim $375,000 capital gains exemption. Transfer at FMV.	Gains will be taxable but deceased may claim $375,000 capital gains exemption. Transfer at FMV.	Gains will be taxable but deceased may claim $375,000 capital gains exemption. Transfer at FMV.	Gains will be taxable but deceased may claim $375,000 capital gains exemption. Transfer at FMV. Donation credit for FMV.[6]

Asset	Estate	Spouse	Minor Child	Adult Child	Infirm Adult Child	Charity
QFP[3]	Gains will be taxable but deceased may claim $375,000 capital gains exemption. Deemed proceeds FMV at death.	Gains will be taxable but deceased may claim $375,000 capital gains exemption. Transfer at any amount between ACB and FMV.	Gains will be taxable but deceased may claim $375,000 capital gains exemption. Transfer at any amount between ACB and FMV.	Gains will be taxable but deceased may claim $375,000 capital gains exemption. Transfer at any amount between ACB and FMV.	Gains will be taxable but deceased may claim $375,000 capital gains exemption. Transfer at any amount between ACB and FMV.	Gains will be taxable but deceased may claim $375,000 capital gains exemption. Transfer at FMV. Donation credit for FMV.[6]
Capital Assets[4]	Accrued gains taxable. Deemed proceeds FMV at death.	Transfer at any amount between ACB and FMV.	Transfer at FMV.	Transfer at FMV.	Transfer at FMV.	Transfer at FMV. No gain on publicly traded bonds or shares. Donation credit for FMV.
Principal Residence	No taxable gain. Deemed proceeds FMV at death.	No taxable gain. Transfer at FMV.	No taxable gain. Transfer at FMV.	No taxable gain. Transfer at FMV.	No taxable gain. Transfer at FMV.	No taxable gain. Transfer at FMV. Donation credit for FMV.
Non-Capital Assets	No tax consequences.	No tax consequences.	No tax consequences.	No tax consequences.	No tax consequences.	No tax consequences.
Life Insurance	Life insurance proceeds are received tax-free.					Donation credit for amount of benefit

Notes

[1] Only whole or universal life policies that have a cash surrender value are considered to be capital assets that can be transferred. Rollovers, where allowed, are only tax-free if the transferor is the insured.

[2] Small business corporation shares: These shares qualify for the $750,000 ($375,000 taxable) capital gains deduction.

[3] Qualified Farm Property/Qualified Fishing Property: These properties qualify for the $750,000 ($375,000 taxable) capital gains deduction.

[4] Capital Assets include investments such as stocks, bonds and real estate.

[5] Non-Capital Assets include investments such as GICs, T-Bills, etc. which are not subject to capital gains tax.

[6] Transfers of SBCS and QFP shares to charity at death avoids the normal holding period for donations.

CONCLUDING THOUGHTS

File an audit-proof tax return

I have seen grown men tremble; mothers lose sleep and business owners pale at the thought: the tax man cometh. Hiding in the closet won't help; neither will filing the audit envelop at the bottom of the deepest kitchen drawer, or worse, File G. It will happen to all of us at some time, so a coping strategy for audit selection is always required. The best defense? File an audit-proof tax return, know your appeal rights and use them well with the right advocacy team.

File an audit proof return. Now is the right time to make sure you have all the back up documentation for every figure on the tax return you are filing. A big secret to dealing with the taxman: retrieval is everything!

> **ESSENTIAL TAX FACT** | You are required to keep your tax records (both soft and hard copy) for a minimum of six years.

It's not unusual for the CRA to request records for the current tax year and two years back. The whole process usually starts with a letter, but the auditors can also contact you in person. Ask for the letter first before you begin, so that you know exactly what they are looking for, the time frames and set up some time for them to come back. You can request an extension to their proposed time frame, but if you do, make sure you meet the deadline.

Know that there are certain provisions that are routinely audited. On the income reporting side, expect four lines to be of particular interest: Line 126, Rental income; Line 127, Taxable capital gains; Line 128, Support payments received; and Line 135 to 143, Self-employment income. There are no surprises here: tax audit frequency is higher in those areas.

For average Canadian employees and pensioners, it's the deductions from total income that are of high interest to the taxman. Expect to be asked to verify claims for RRSP deductions, particularly if there has been an excess or over-contribution to the plan.

Moving expenses, child care, employment expenses claimed by commission sales people or long distance truckers, business investment losses and the investment carrying charges claimed by investors—all are favorite targets for verification.

Investors should also be on high audit alert for the right documentation when they claim exploration and development expenses, security options deductions, losses of all kinds including capital, non-capital and limited partnership losses and of course, the capital gains deduction.

Several non-refundable tax credit claims are easy targets, as well. Common requests for verification occur for high tuition fees claimed for young adults studying in Canada and abroad. The sick, disabled, or their caregivers, should know that claims for the lucrative disability amount, medical expenses and large charitable donations, can often be checked as well.

And here's a big audit tip for hopeless hoarders: store those tax records in a high, safe and dry place; the box marked prominently with the current tax year (2010 Returns), pristinely sorted documents within. Recreating what happened years from now can be extremely time consuming and stressful, and you want to avoid a net worth assessment at all costs. (That's when the taxman tells you what he thinks your income and deductions and credits should be, leaving you to prove otherwise.)

ESSENTIAL TAX FACT | It's not unusual for a full blown audit to happen right in your home or at your business premises.

Always be nice. But if, despite your best behavior, he or she is just not seeing things your way, what's the process for challenging resulting adjustments to your return?

Know your appeal rights. Canada's tax system is based on those principles of self assessment and voluntary compliance, and to be honest, it works well.

ESSENTIAL TAX FACT | You have the rights to arrange your affairs within the framework of the law to pay the least taxes legally possible.

But, if required, know that your further appeal rights include negotiation at a local level with an appeals officer, and either an informal or a formal trip into the court system, depending on the amounts of money or principles involved.

When you're a model tax filing citizen; that is, you file your returns on time, and voluntarily tell the taxman about that unintentional overstatement of deductions or understatement of income—before he tells you—you'll avoid expensive penalties by using the Taxpayer Relief Provisions. That's an important opportunity. This year, Canadians can correct errors and omissions to returns up to ten years back (for the math challenged among us, this means you'll have until December 31, 2012 to correct or file 2002 tax returns.)

ESSENTIAL TAX FACT | The onus of proof is always on you first to show that you have "self assessed" properly.

That can be tough for some, because, let's face it, taxes are complicated. What's more, you face several moving targets: constantly changing tax law, frequent changes in your personal life, and quite possibly, the testy relationship you could find yourself in with the auditor parked in your basement.

Either way, you're wise to invest in some tax knowledge, or get some knowledge-able help, especially when under the microscope. Make your professional dollars pay off—select an advisor who is an educator and who can set you straight. If the errors on your tax return are yours, save yourself a lot of time and money and simply correct them, pay your bill and move on.

You'll need an audit expert, as well as a sharp tax technician, someone who knows the law and is a good negotiator too. Ask lots of questions of your potential audit pro, including how many taxpayers he or she has represented to CRA. Remember, there is no such thing as a stupid tax question, and you should never feel intimidated to ask what's on your mind.

A professional team you trust is especially important when you've caught the taxman's eye. You're on the defensive, you may be emotional, and an impartial third party who has gone through the audit routine many times can ease your pain. Your pro is your advocate, your voice of reason, and should know the process and the law well. Work with your team to get the results you need.

ESSENTIAL TAX FACT | All tax disputes begin with the filing of a Notice of Objection, if your requests for adjustment on an informal basis fail. Do so within the required time frames.

That puts your "taxes in dispute" and stops collection activities. It also preserves your rights to go on through the appeal system.

At the start of this book we noted that your Notice of Assessment or Reassessment is an important document. Since all timelines are based on the dates on these notices, don't misplace them.

Here's to many happy returns! I sincerely hope that you have enjoyed your read through the Essential Tax Facts that can help you accumulate, grow, preserve and transition more of your wealth within your family. This should begin with filing an accurate tax return, to your family unit's best benefit, but it ends with the resolve not to allow tax erosion—during your lifetime or at death—diminish the hard work you have put into your financial legacy.

Best wishes,
EVELYN JACKS

INDEX

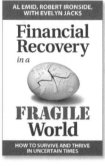

EDUCATION
OPPORTUNITIES Only From

LEARN TO BE A CERTIFIED TAX PRACTITIONER OR BOOKKEEPER

This is a great way to help the people around you, do important work and make extra money. If you liked this book, you may like to become a certified professional and make a second income, too.

For a FREE information brochure on our self-study programs contact us toll free:
1-866-953-4769

To sign up for a free subscription to Knowledge Bureau Report for all the latest tax, investment, retirement and economic news, visit:
www.knowledgebureau.com

About Knowledge Bureau

Knowledge Bureau is a national certified educational institute which provides continuing professional development to practicing professionals in tax and financial services leading to certification and designation. We are the home of the Distinguished Financial Advisor (DFA-Tax Services Specialist™) and Master Financial Advisor (MFA™) designations.